The Principal's Guide to Winning Grants

Y0-BDX-469

David G. Bauer

Jossey-Bass Publishers • San Francisco

This edition copyright © 1999 by Jossey-Bass Inc., Publishers, 350 Sansome Street, San Francisco, California 94104. Previous version copyright © 1994 by Scholastic Inc.

Substantial discounts on bulk quantities of Jossey-Bass books are available to corporations, professional associations, and other organizations. For details and discount information, contact the special sales department at Jossey-Bass.

Interior design by Bruce Lundquist.

Manufactured in the United States of America.

Library of Congress Cataloging-in-Publication Data

Bauer, David G.
   The principal's guide to winning grants / David G. Bauer.—1st ed.
      p.   cm.
   Rev. ed. of: The principal's guide to grants success. c1994.
   Includes bibliographical references.
   ISBN 0-7879-4494-7
   1. Educational fund raising—United States—Handbooks, manuals, etc.
2. Schools—United States—Finance—Handbooks, manuals, etc.   3. Education—Research grants—United States—Handbooks, manuals, etc.   4. Proposal writing in education—United States—Handbooks, manuals, etc.   5. Proposal writing for grants—United States—Handbooks, manuals, etc.   I. Bauer, David G.   Principal's guide to grants success.   II. Title.
LC243.A1B36   1999   98-44060
379.1'3 — dc21   CIP

FIRST EDITION
PB Printing   10 9 8 7 6 5 4 3 2 1

The Principal's
Guide to
Winning
Grants

Contents

Exhibits, Figures, and Tables

Introduction

THIS BOOK is intended to assist principals of public and private P–12 schools in developing and maintaining a grants system that uses grant funds to meet their schools' mission. It is the second book in a three-part series on grantseeking. Book one, *The Teacher's Guide to Winning Grants*, focuses on the teacher's role in grantseeking; book three, *Successful Grants Program Management*, is aimed at the district administrator.

The challenges in seeking and administering alternative sources of funding for public and private P–12 schools require a new and more efficient system to support and monitor the grant-proposal development process. The old system, characterized by an assistant district administrator pumping out forms requesting federal entitlement funds and formula grants, is not equipped to deal with the decentralized, site-based management concepts that are dramatically affecting our schools and communities today. The "new" concepts of local decision making, community ownership, and investment provide the principal with opportunities to encourage parents and community to buy into the responsibility of developing resources for educating their children. When parents, teachers, students, and the community come together to develop goals, objectives, and curriculum for excellence in education, they soon realize the limitations of the educational system's normal resource allocation process. However, with some creativity, they can achieve their educational goals by routing their energies toward developing more resources through public and private grants.

The grants marketplace can provide a tremendous resource for your school. In fact, it provides your teachers with access to billions of dollars' worth of opportunities to change and supplement their curriculum, purchase equipment, and develop new programs. *But they must know how to obtain the funds.*

The reaction of some school systems to this newly developed parental, teacher, and community interest may be to request that a group's grant or proposal ideas be submitted to a central office, where a hired grant writer looks at the possibility of developing a proposal for outside support. This will not produce the winning grants your school needs. Today's proposals need to include empowered and motivated volunteers who want action, and the principal should provide the crucial link to this free, inspired source of labor by doing the following:

- Helping parents and teachers develop their grant-proposal ideas into a fundable form

- Playing a pivotal role in developing the necessary coordination between the district's central office and the school's grants effort

- Increasing the school's and community's commitment to solving its problems, taking responsibility for finding solutions, and owning its successes

One advantage of using the grants marketplace to achieve educational improvement is that with a minimum of assistance, volunteers can become involved in preparing proposals. Districts provide varying degrees of support, but most grantseekers prepare proposals at their own expense and in their spare time. Forward-thinking administrators should encourage and support this investment of their staff's and volunteers' time with an efficient proposal development system.

The aim of this book is to describe the basic elements of successful grantseeking. In so doing it summarizes and sometimes repeats information contained in *The Teacher's Guide to Winning Grants*. The material is arranged so that you can evaluate the relevance of and need for each facet of the grants system based on your particular situation. The perfect system does not exist. But the more components of a model grant system that you can adapt and include in your system, the more you can expect from the grants marketplace. As an additional help, each chapter ends with a checklist to evaluate and improve your grants system.

Remember, the changes necessary to improve your grants plan may be difficult to achieve. Therefore, use restraint in developing your plan. Read this entire book and then determine what your grants system needs. Discuss with your staff the areas to be improved. Encourage their input and utilize it where appropriate. Discuss with your central administration your school's needs and how administrators can help you address them.

Effective grantseeking is not an accident and has little to do with good luck. From the principal's perspective, the two crucial ingredients for successful grantseeking are good planning and the development of an efficient support system.

Bauer Associates supplies several valuable products and services created to support your school's grantseeking efforts. For a price list of our materials, visit our website at http://www.dgbauer.com. To discuss the possibility of having David Bauer conduct a grants-training seminar for your school or district, phone 1-800-836-0732.

The Author

DAVID G. BAUER, one of the most highly sought after speakers on grantseeking, is president of David G. Bauer Associates, Inc., a consulting firm created in 1981 to provide educationally based grantseeking and fundraising seminars and materials. In addition, he has recently served as the Director of Development for the Center for Educational Accountability and Associate Professor at the University of Alabama at Burmingham School of Education. He has also been the Director for Extramural Funding and Grants Management at the University of Rochester School of Medicine, Department of Pediatrics, and Assistant to the President of the State University of New York College of Technology. Bauer, an acknowledged grants expert and lively lecturer, has taught more than 25,000 individuals successful grantseeking and fundraising techniques.

Mr. Bauer is the author of *The How To Grants Manual, The Complete Grants Sourcebook for Higher Education, Administering Grants, Contracts and Funds, Successful Grants Program Management, The Fund Raising Primer, The Educator's Internet Funding Guide,* and *The Teacher's Guide to Winning Grants.* He is also the coauthor of *The Complete Grants Sourcebook for Nursing and Health.* In addition, he is the developer of three videotape series—*Winning Grants 2, How To Teach Grantseeking to Others,* and *Strategic Fund Raising*—and two software programs—*Winning Links* and *Grant Winner.*

Chapter 1

The Principal's Role in Supporting Grantseeking

THE POSSIBILITY OF WINNING a grant gives the principal an exciting opportunity to apply concepts in successful leadership and management. As educational administrators we are challenged to work through those we manage to achieve our school's objectives. But it is difficult to develop an environment in which staff members feel sufficiently empowered to willingly invest their time and effort with little regard for up-front pay-offs. With the proper introduction, and a support system that responds to legitimate concerns, grantseeking can create this environment. Grantseeking can actually become a vehicle that enables the principal to develop an exciting and cooperative relationship with teachers, support staff, parents, and the school and community.

Encouraging the Grants Process

Agreed, your job is already hard enough with its new and daily changing responsibilities. You work seventy hours a week, and now you are being asked to get excited about expanding your activities to include aggressive grantseeking. But the grantseeking you will promote is based on helping *others* better meet the needs of your students, teachers, and community through *their* active involvement. Those who carry out and support the project will willingly take part in the research and writing if you provide them with a system that supports their efforts.

To win grants, you must know where they come from. Chapter Four provides in-depth data on the grants marketplace, but the following 1998 estimates for 1997 will give you an idea:

- Foundations will grant over $13 billion.
- Corporations will grant over $8 billion.
- The federal government will grant over $85 billion.

What percentage of these grants will go to which levels of schools? This is the subject of Chapter Four. But the amount going to preschools, elementary schools, middle schools, and high schools from all three major types of funders has been increasing. This includes increases to public, private, and charter schools.

Your school's opportunity to access this $106 billion grants market-place provides you, the school administrator, with a unique motivational tool that can be used to develop exciting goals and objectives as well as the projects and programs to achieve educational progress. To top it off, you can do this by using outside resources and without tremendous up-front expenditures. Remember, these grants are made each year, and the amount has increased almost every year since recording started in 1953.

Some elementary and middle or junior high and high schools employ grant writers to develop proposals. But this centralized approach is not how grantseeking is conducted by the majority of schools and other non-profit organizations.

For example, at colleges and universities, the grants office does very little proposal writing. It may perform a search for potential grant resources and provide budgetary, submittal, and sign-off assistance, but seldom does it write the proposal. So who is paid to write a proposal? The answer is no one. The key personnel involved in developing the proposal are paid from the grant once it is approved, and in most cases the successful project director or principal investigator is released from his or her normal duties to carry out the project. No costs for proposal preparation are reimbursed through grant funds; these are considered costs incurred before the award date, and it is unethical or illegal to claim them.

Be very careful in hiring outside grant writers. Pay them by the hour or on a fixed contract. Don't base anything on acceptance; you owe them for their work. And *never* get involved in percentage-based grantseeking. Paying a 5 or 10 percent fee to a consultant for writing your school's grant proposal is considered a cost incurred before the award date and is illegal on federal and state grants and unethical with foundations and corporations. Furthermore, grantors will wonder whether you can do the work if you can't write the proposal.

If individuals cannot receive payment for preparing proposals, why do they do it? One motivation is simply the opportunity to make a difference, to be involved in developing a solution to a problem. By using techniques that encourage your school's employees and volunteers to become involved and to make a difference, you provide them with the possibility of attracting grant funds that can be used to do the following:

- Institute a novel solution to a problem

- Expand a program to new populations

- Provide for increased educational achievement

- Develop the school's resources, such as equipment and facilities

To begin the process of improving your school through outside grant support, you must know your school's needs and where your opportunities lie. One very effective way to find out is to ask your teachers, parents, staff, and interested community residents to identify the greatest problems and opportunities facing your school. Announce an open forum or special meeting that focuses on setting goals and priorities for your school and assessing its needs. The meeting may be organized according to area of concern or grade level. But you must inspire a sense of urgency and provide hope that the needed change can take place. The following activity may help you accomplish these goals.

Bring in a stack of play money or lottery tickets. Let the focus group know that there are billions of dollars in grants available for funding the school. Organize the participants into small groups and ask each group to develop a list of areas of need. Give each group a stack of play money or lottery tickets and have them determine which area of need the proceeds should be used for. To complete the task, each group should develop a prioritized list of needs, which will provide valuable insight into your school or community's ability to identify and articulate its most pressing problems and educational needs.

This exercise can be done with community groups, teacher groups, student clubs and organizations, unions, and open sessions. You may want to ask groups to share their lists. Ultimately it is helpful if your school's advisory committee and teacher and parent groups come to an agreement on the top three or four problem areas.

The next step is to capitalize on your teachers' and volunteers' interest in these problems by having them brainstorm possible solutions. You can use the lottery tickets to promote interest; if one is a winning ticket, the group can use the proceeds to start solving the problem right away! The purpose of the brainstorming session is to identify unique, innovative, creative solutions that can be incorporated in a proposal to attract funding from a grantor who is interested in seeking educational change. For example, if improved reading is targeted, you may wish to explore how new technology and software can help. But do not select technology as the need or problem. School technology is a *means to an end, not* the subject of a good proposal. You could ask the technology group to meet with other groups to see how technology could assist in solving their problems and put the request together.

As you involve the entire school and community in taking responsibility for identifying problems and creating solutions, you may begin to see some very positive outcomes. Dr. Dennis Waitley, in his book *The Psychology of Winning,* says that individuals move in the direction of their dominant thought every moment of their lives. If their dominant thought is negative, they will move in a negative direction. For example, if your school and community believe that problems in your school are hopeless and overwhelming, they will focus on these negative perceptions and the problems will get worse.

However, by using your school's potential for grant support to develop a prioritized list of problems and solutions that will reduce or eliminate them, you can change your group's entire focus to a positive, problem-solving perspective. Groups sometimes believe so strongly in their solutions that they institute them even if they are not awarded a grant. In some cases the money is found by reallocating existing funds.

Actually, schools should be moving in positive directions anyway and deserve to have more resources to do their job. But reality is harsh, and it is easy to get sidetracked and to focus on the negative. The bottom line is that by stressing the possibility of a grant and making your teachers and volunteers aware of the amounts of grant funds available for model and innovative projects, you can help your school and community focus in a positive direction.

Individuals invest their time and effort in the grants process for many reasons besides wanting to make a difference, and your grants system should allow for and foster these. When asked why they donate their time and effort to prepare a proposal, grantseekers often say they are motivated by the following:

- The feeling that they were part of a team or group (the social aspect of grantseeking)

- Recognition for their work; they like seeing their names in school publications and the newspaper and are thrilled at being asked to make presentations at meetings to inform their peers about their project

- A sense of achievement and fulfillment that comes from using their talents and abilities

- The feeling of power from controlling materials, equipment, and their own budget

The role of the principal in encouraging the grants process begins with an understanding of how grant funds can be used to address the problems in your school. Of course, you must be honest with your staff and inform them that in the grants marketplace success is achieved only some of the time; failures will occur. However, remind potential grantseekers of the following.

1. By assessing your school's positive and negative aspects, you will be designing a plan for the future that capitalizes on the school's strengths and prioritizes its needs. School problems are also grant opportunities. (Assuming that its personnel develop positive dominant thoughts, your school will continue to move in a positive direction.)

2. Grant success depends on many factors, but motivation and a can-do, problem-solving spirit are two basic ingredients. With a good grants system, half or more of grant requests can be successful. (Elementary and junior high schools have only recently begun to expand their grantseeking, so detailed success rates are difficult to verify, but principals who have employed the concepts outlined in this book have reported a 50 percent success rate.)

3. You can't win if you don't play the game. Of course there will be some work and some failure, but sitting around the faculty room complaining is a waste of time and energy.

4. A positive, proactive effort will provide enough information to realistically assess your chances of success before you write the proposal. The first step is *not* to write a lengthy, detailed proposal; finding an interested funder comes first.

5. Grantseeking is not a last minute, three-day miracle that produces heartburn and grantseeker burnout. A chaotic, reactive grants system wastes time and money and does not meet your school's predetermined needs, goals, or objectives.

The positive and organized grants system outlined in the following chapters shows how you, the principal, can initiate and utilize the grants opportunity. The results of grantseeking can be far-reaching, but the grants atmosphere is critical to your success.

One public school administrator I know set up a grants reward system that consisted of public recognition for grantseekers, an annual award dinner, plaques, and even small cash awards. And the system was funded on a grant! Yes, a foundation realized that a small grant to reward and thank grant writers would result in far more grant funds than it could ever distribute to the school. Be creative. You can provide staff with the proper environment to stimulate grantseeking.

When you visit a business or an organization that is striving to create the best atmosphere possible, take note of the motivational techniques it employs. When visiting a hotel, notice the plaques and pictures of the employees of the month and find out what rewards employees received in addition to the public recognition.

As an administrator at a public school, I proposed using a grant to address my district's prioritized list of needs. I provide this example because no matter what your list of priorities or needs is, I believe the possibility of procuring grant funds should be explored before you use your own budget and school funds to meet these needs.

In my district, a community advisory group and the elementary school teachers and staff determined that one of their priorities was to develop a health-education curriculum at the elementary level that would form the basis for the junior high school health-education program. The teachers were concerned about risk-taking behavior and carelessness that had caused several students to be severely injured and wanted to explore how those behaviors related to health-related problems such as drug and alcohol abuse.

We formed an elementary health curriculum advisory committee and developed a proposal to submit to a government funding source. The teachers developed a model curriculum that included the scope and sequence of the objectives at each grade level. The proposal requested funds that would enable the teachers to preview and ultimately purchase the materials *they* felt comfortable using with their students. Parents were also involved. The parents' advisory committee developed a parents' education kit that included take-home sheets, suggested topics for home discussion, and follow-up activities.

The classroom leaders participating in the project met for fifty-four contact hours and were awarded graduate credit from a nearby university (they paid tuition fees) or in-service credits if they did not want or need the graduate credit.

The teachers were motivated and involved because they had control over what to purchase and how to use it. Getting a grant to buy the materials gave them additional incentive to get involved in creating the solution. This process of utilizing the grants system can be employed by other schools.

Although several aspects of the principal's role in encouraging and supporting grantseeking could be explored, this book highlights the *major* areas and provides the direction and insight that will promote grants success.

Ensuring Quality and Coordination

Another critically important aspect of the principal's role as the leader in the grants process is that of ensuring quality and coordination. Your school and the entire district will be judged by the quality of the proposal that you submit to the grantor. Foundation, corporate, or government officials will base their opinion of your entire school system and of your school in particular on the quality of your proposal, and you, the principal, are ultimately responsible for this quality. Your role in the grants process is to ensure that every proposal submitted represents your school and community's best effort, and you must be willing to be judged on each proposal.

In summary, you are crucial in promoting a positive grants atmosphere in your school. Your role in supporting the process of proposal preparation will depend on your knowledge of and interest in the process of securing grants. The following chapters provide you with information and techniques that will help you develop a dynamic grants system. Review the checklist that follows and evaluate the ways in which grants are utilized and grant winners recognized in your school. Make suggestions on how these methods can be improved. Your suggestions for change will provide the basis for your annual plan for grants success.

CHAPTER 1 CHECKLIST

Evaluation and Planning Worksheet

Complete this assessment to help develop your plan.

1. **Base Data: Grants Activity in (year)**

   # of proposals submitted _____

   # of proposals awarded _____

   # of proposals rejected _____

2. **Use of Grants Potential to Identify Problems/Opportunities:**

   a. Do you have a grants advisory committee?   _____ yes   _____ no

   b. If yes, who comprises it?

   _____ parents   _____ staff   _____ teachers

   _____ community corporate leaders   _____ content experts

   other (please list) _____

3. **Recognition for Grantseekers (Please Check):**

   _____ Press Releases for Committee Work

   External Recognition (Newspaper, Radio, TV, etc.) for:

   _____ submittal of proposal

   _____ grants success rate

   _____ award of grant

   Internal Recognition (Newsletter, Announcements, etc.) for:

   _____ submittal of proposal

   _____ grants success rate

   _____ award of grant

   Other Recognition Techniques:

   _____ cash awards   special entitlements:

   _____ plaques   _____ privileged parking

   _____ trophies   _____ day off

   _____ awards dinner   other entitlements _____

4. **Education of Faculty, Staff, and Community on the Opportunities that Grantseeking Presents:**

   _____ citing of grants to other schools

   _____ publishing of grants facts in newsletters

   other (please list) _____

   _____

Setting Up a Proactive Grants System in Your School

AS YOU LEARNED IN CHAPTER ONE, you can use the possibility of attracting outside funding to focus on your school's needs. You, the school leader, can use grantseeking as a low-investment, high-return strategy that brings the community, teachers, parents, and students together to develop positive, action-oriented solutions to your school's problems.

In order to sustain interest, build upon this involvement, and create at least a 50 percent grants success rate, you need to develop an organized, proactive grants system. This is not easy in the changing environment of educational administration. Twenty years ago, your central office was responsible for seeking grants. Current circumstances, including site-based management, school and community involvement, and local empowerment, have altered your and your district's traditional roles in the grants system. This book will help you create the right system for your school and determine how your district's rules and procedures will affect your new system. If necessary, obtain permission from your central administration and push for policies and regulations that your district office needs to enact in order to avoid unregulated grants competition, poor image with funders, and problems in grant administration.

The techniques and strategies involved in setting up a successful, proactive grants system are tried and proven. The more of these techniques you incorporate, the higher your rate of success will be and the more motivated you will become to develop a positive, can-do atmosphere in your school. But these techniques must be coordinated with the grants efforts of your district's central office. Be aware that sometimes district grants policies and procedures have not kept pace with changes in school management.

Developing a Proactive Grants System for Your School

The first step in proactive grantseeking is to develop focus groups that identify and prioritize your school's needs, problem areas, and areas of excellence or programs you want to improve. The reason more schools do not use the grants marketplace to its full potential is that they view grantseeking as a reactive activity that is driven by grantors who publicize a program and a deadline that allows the grantseeker little or no time to prepare a proposal. This, in turn, causes the grantseeker to hastily develop an idea, write up a proposal, and put all the pieces together in a mad rush. The chaos of the final seventy-two hours of reactive grantseeking can turn people off to the entire process.

To make matters worse, funding sources or grantors can spot last-minute proposals, and when they do they wonder:

- Why didn't the grantseekers start earlier?

- Where are the letters of endorsement and the statements of support from the school board, the community, and the district?

- Why didn't the grantseekers contact us to discuss the best approach?

- Are the potential grantees just looking for money? Would they propose any idea that they thought would look good to a funding source?

- How does this project relate to their school's stated mission and their predetermined goals and objectives?

No wonder teachers are not lining up to get involved in the grants process. You have to be sadomasochistic to want to be involved in a reactive grants system.

So what is the alternative? Grantseeking can be a positive process controlled by the grantseeker, which minimizes stress and last-minute herculean efforts.

The purpose of your grants system is not to get the proposal out the door but to fulfill the grantor's needs through your school's project at a price the grantor can afford. In order to develop a fundable and interesting project, your grants system needs to focus on the needs and projects your school and community feels are important. When this has been accomplished, you should search for grant sources that are interested in the same educational change and improvement. When a grantseeker takes the proactive approach of developing project ideas first, he or she appears less like a grantseeker who will do anything for money and more like one who wants funding only for projects that move the school toward its predetermined goals.

Proactivity affords grantseekers the time to research the potential funder to discover who else it has funded and for what projects, so that they are reasonably sure that the funder will be interested in their project. With advance time and knowledge, grantseekers can also establish preproposal contact. Many funding sources encourage grantseekers to talk with them before writing a formal proposal to be certain that the proposed approach will meet the grantor's requirements. The chances of grants success are dramatically increased by making this contact! By knowing the grantor's funding pattern and discussing your school's approaches to the need with the grantor, you can begin to develop a sound basis for a productive grantor-grantee relationship.

If you are starting to get the impression that grantseeking is going to take up too much of your time, relax. You may not even be the best person to contact the grantor. Your classroom leaders may not be the ideal choices either. The best person to make preproposal contact is a volunteer who:

- Is involved in the project (proposal)

- Has donated her or his time

- Is a member of a school or community advisory committee

- Has paid her or his own way to see the grantor

- Will not profit from the grant award

Many grant applications require documentation of community involvement. Grantors may want to see minutes of meetings involving the individuals or families who will be affected by the award and implementation of the proposed project. By involving the entire school and community in the grantseeking process you will have the commitment and cooperation of the volunteers.

Developing Community Advisory Groups

I have suggested in *The Teacher's Guide to Winning Grants* that teachers discuss with their principals the concept of developing focus groups or community advisory groups to address the problems facing their classrooms. This should be the first step in developing support for grantseeking. As the administrator, you have input that is critical in coordinating the development of these groups, for which the structure of your community may already provide the basis. Whether or not it does, it is important that the advisory group members who deal with grantseeking be selected very carefully. You may want to form a grants advisory group as a subcommittee of your larger focus groups. Be careful of using the word "grant" in the group name. It may be better to focus the name of the group on the problem area to be attacked. For example, calling your group the Reading Improvement Advisory Group may make it easier for you to recruit members. There is no best way to create the structure, as long as you keep in mind the skills that are needed and the types of individuals who can best carry out the tasks involved in successful grantseeking.

Exhibits 2.1 through 2.6 are sample letters and worksheets that will help you develop your grants advisory group and build a proactive, successful grants system. Naturally, the materials should be tailored to your particular school and situation. As previously stated, you could develop either several grants advisory groups or one grants advisory group and several problem-specific focus groups. The focus groups could provide the grants advisory group with suggestions for projects.

Worksheet for Planning a Grants Advisory Group

Use this worksheet (Exhibit 2.1) to develop a tentative list of the individuals you would like to have participate in your grants advisory group.

Exhibit 2.1

WORKSHEET FOR PLANNING A GRANTS ADVISORY GROUP

Review the suggested categories of individuals to include and write down names.

Whom to Invite

_____ Parents
_____ Corporate Leaders
_____ Foundation Board Members
_____ College Professors/Educators
_____ Retired Teachers
_____ Wealthy/Influential People
_____ Others (Please Add)

Review the Skills/Resources Needed list below and write the bolded skill or resource next to the possible committee members you have listed above. Avoid inviting volunteers who are overzealous about children but have no resources or contacts.

Skills/Resources Needed

- **Commitment** to children and education
- **Contacts** with people on foundation/corporate boards
- **Travel** to areas of the state/nation where there are more funders
- Willingness to share **telephone credit card** for grant-related calls
- **Marketing/sales skills**
- **Budgeting** and financial analysis skills
- Access to equipment and materials necessary to produce **audiovisual** aids depicting need
- Other

Avoid placing well-intentioned zealots on the committee. Although these outspoken individuals may be highly motivated, they can turn off the other committee members as well as potential funders if they lack the listening skills needed to truly grasp what the grantor is looking for.

Look for individuals who will make the grantseeking process less work for you. Assess the skills and resources that the committee members will bring to the group.

Grants Resources Inventory Worksheet

The Grants Resources Inventory Worksheet (Exhibit 2.2) lists some of the resource areas that will be helpful in grantseeking. The worksheet can be used in several ways. First, quickly reviewing the worksheet may trigger the names of potential members of the grants advisory group (see Exhibit 2.1). Second, once you have identified potential participants you can ask them to complete the inventory by noting their own skills and abilities and also listing any other potential members next to the corresponding resource area. For example, if Sylvia Smith is filling out the inventory, she may indicate that she can provide sales skills. She might also indicate that

---

Exhibit 2.2

GRANTS RESOURCES INVENTORY WORKSHEET

Please put a check mark next to any resource area in which you can help. Use the section at the end of the worksheet to briefly describe the resources you could provide. If you are willing to contact funding sources, please list the areas of the United States that you visit frequently.

Resource Area

_____ Evaluation of Projects
_____ Computer Programming
_____ Computer Equipment
_____ Printing
_____ Layout and Design Work
_____ Budget Skills, Accounting, Developing Cash Flow, Auditing
_____ Purchasing Assistance
_____ Audiovisual Assistance (equipment, videotaping, etc.)
_____ Travel
_____ Long Distance Telephone Calls
_____ Searching for Funding Sources
_____ Sales Skills
_____ Writing Skills/Editing Skills
_____ Other Equipment/Materials
_____ Other

Description of Resources: _____

Areas Frequently Visited: _____

an acquaintance of hers, John Doe, might be willing to provide computer programming services.

Once you have your group members selected, don't be overly concerned with rules regarding their attendance at committee meetings. If the member promises to provide the resources and skills needed, what difference does attendance make? For instance, salespeople who travel a lot may not spend much time in their offices or at home. It may be easy for them to make preproposal contact with a grantor in another part of the state or country but difficult for them to attend meetings.

A very productive sales executive on one of my grants advisory groups never attended a meeting but was instrumental in procuring several grant awards. When he was in the same city as a potential grantor, I would fax all the pertinent information to him at his hotel. This would include a description of the proposed project and information on the grantor, such as its funding history or pattern. He would then set up an appointment with the grantor to discuss the project. After his meeting with the funding source he would fax information back to me concerning the appropriate strategy to pursue in the proposal. He was highly successful at getting in to see federal and state grantors as well as foundation and corporate sources. In many cases, he was actually given preferential treatment over grant and education professionals, who were, after all, *paid* to be there. My advisory group member was donating his time; he was actually being paid to be somewhere else. In reality, the preproposal visit was costing him money. Many grantors will respond favorably to such a committed volunteer.

You need advisory group members who are free to travel and who have skills or resources in marketing, budgeting, printing, computer programming, and so on. What could be more ideal than a finished proposal, produced by a committee member donating his or her office and secretaries, and having the budget checked by his or her finance department?

Worksheet for Initiating a Grants Advisory Group

Discuss your plan to develop a grants advisory group with the faculty and staff of your school and ask them to suggest names of people they would be willing to contact and co-invite with you to take part in the group (see Exhibit 2.3). You will be amazed at how many excellent contacts they suggest. Don't be surprised if you discover that the spouse of one of your long-time volunteers or staff members is the marketing director of a local corporation and that he or she would be happy to donate to your grants effort resources from graphics to preproposal contact!

Exhibit 2.3

WORKSHEET FOR INITIATING A GRANTS ADVISORY GROUP

Potential Members	Who Will Contact Them	When	Results	Skills/Resources You Expect

Sample Letter to Potential Committee Member

You will need to tailor this invitation (Exhibit 2.4) to the individual and to the scope of the grants advisory group's work. For example, a small school may have one group to assist in all grantseeking activities, whereas a large school or one with diverse and critical areas of concern may have several grants advisory groups, each focusing on one particular problem area such as illiteracy, delinquency, school dropout, drugs, alcohol, sexually transmitted diseases, and so on. Note that I did not include lack of technology as an example. Your school probably already has a technology advisory group or committee to assess its wiring, hardware, and software needs. You may be able to find a few grantors who fund technology, but your group's potential will increase dramatically as it demonstrates the technology's *use*. Make sure all your advisory groups reflect the varied skills you will need. For example, you will need more than technology gurus to improve your school's technology resources. Don't fill the group or committee with techno-whizzes when you will need sales and marketing to sell your program to the community.

Exhibit 2.4

SAMPLE LETTER TO POTENTIAL COMMITTEE MEMBER (INVITATION TO PARTICIPATE)

Note: *You may telephone potential committee members first and then send them this letter, or send them this letter and then telephone them.*

Dear _____:

The children in [name of school/classroom] invite you to become involved in developing and implementing solutions in their education. Your past work in _____ demonstrates your commitment and concern for children, their education, and our community. We are in the process of developing a grants advisory committee, which we would like you to be part of. Your commitment and concern have prompted this invitation to join with a select group of individuals in developing solutions and resources to education-related problems and needs.

I look at the problems associated with educating children as opportunities—to become involved in developing creative solutions to the educational inadequacies that hold our children back from

_____

_____

[Add pertinent statistics. For example, "National reading scores for fourth graders are _____. In our school _____ percent of fourth graders read below this level." Include some outcomes, such as, "Students who lack reading skills _____."]

This letter is your invitation to do something about this problem. [Number] of your fellow citizens are receiving similar invitations to join our informal group. The purposes of the group include:

- Brainstorming suggestions for improving our educational programs for _____ , and
- Capitalizing on the group members' skills and contacts for getting our proposals in front of foundation, corporate, and government funding sources.

Last year corporations and foundations awarded over $20 billion in grant funds. Elementary and middle schools are receiving a growing portion of these funds as private funding sources become more concerned about our children's education. Our knowing whom you know may give us the advantage we need to share in this funding.

Please attend our meeting on [date] at [place] and learn how you can play an important role in our grants development process. A study in *Grants Magazine* indicates that there is up to a 500 percent increase in grants success if the funding source has personal contact with the proposal developer before the proposal is written. A simple phone call to set up an appointment with a prospective funder may elicit a favorable response to our proposal, and *you* could provide this essential contact.

Please set aside the date of _____ to attend our first meeting. I know you will enjoy learning how we can work together to improve our educational system.

Sincerely,

The important point to get across in this letter and in your phone conversation with a potential committee member is that you are hoping that this person will lend her or his brainpower and resources. You are not asking for money. You are not fund-raising. You are grantseeking. Grants are provided by foundations, corporations, and government agencies, and any help that your advisory committee member can give in setting up a meeting or even a telephone conversation with a possible funding source will increase your chances of success.

It is important that the potential committee know that $106 billion in grants will be given away in 1998 and that you are asking its members' help in getting some of that grant money for your school. Reassure them that they will not be involved in asking for a friend's personal donation but only for foundation and corporate funds.

Remember, you establish the requirements for committee membership. Individuals may ask how long they must serve. I suggest that you leave it up to them.

Sample Letter Inventory of Linkages and Resources

The timing of this letter (Exhibit 2.5) is very important, and the quantity and quality of the linkages derived from it will most likely correspond to the prestige of the grants advisory group member who signs it. For that reason have your *most* distinguished group member sign the letter and introduce the concept of linkages at your advisory group meeting. This will increase the likelihood that inventories and worksheets will be completed and returned.

Chapter Six underscores the advantages of preproposal contact. Because your time, travel, and access to funders are limited, uncovering *who knows whom* makes contact more likely and at the same time increases your school's credibility through involving others in education. However, even in the best of situations you may not uncover a link to a potential grantor. Be assured that grants are made to credible schools with well-organized proposals and projects even though they have no connections or endorsements. But you will maximize your grants success and minimize the time you spend grantseeking if you encourage committee members to use their contacts.

Corporate people know the value of contacts. Knowing who plays bridge, golf, or tennis with whom is exceedingly valuable, especially when you consider that most corporate proposals are funded locally. The grants value of contacts in the corporate arena is surpassed only by that in the foundation marketplace.

Exhibit 2.5

SAMPLE LETTER
INVENTORY OF LINKAGES AND RESOURCES

Dear _____:

The problems/opportunities that we have discussed at our grants advisory committee meetings have solutions, but the implementation of the solutions costs money. We will seek this money through grant funds from foundations, corporations, and possibly state and/or federal sources.

Foundations and corporate sources granted over $20 billion last year, and this figure will likely increase again this year. These funding sources make these awards every year, and every year the funds they distribute will increase. However, these grantors are limited in staff support. In fact, while there are 45,000 foundations, they employ only 3,200 individuals, and fewer than 1,000 have offices. Taking these factors into consideration, it is very important to carefully plan our approach, especially since research indicates that contacting the grantor before writing the proposal increases success by 500 percent.

That's where you come in. We are not soliciting you for money, nor do we want a list of all your wealthy friends. What we are asking is that you provide us with a list of your friends, associates, and relatives who have a relationship with grantors so that we will know who to call to help us get a foot in the door.

The attached "Foot-in-the-Door Worksheet" is aimed at gathering the information we need. This webbing and linkage information will help us to know when to ask you for your assistance in securing personal or telephone contact with a grantor. Your responses will be kept confidential, and the only person that will have access to this information is [name of individual]. While we are a neighborhood school, we can still reach out to a variety of funding sources, and the linkages you provide us will help us do so.

When our research indicates that we have developed a project that is particularly suited to a funder that you know, we will contact you to discuss the project, the funder, and your desire to assist us. We may just need a foot in the door, or you may want to accompany us on a visit to the potential funding source or even visit them yourself. In any event, we will not contact any of the sources you suggest without your prior approval.

In addition to your suggested sources, it is also very important that you let us know of any grant-related resources that you can provide or help us procure. For example, nothing makes a more powerful statement than a volunteer taking time out from a business trip or a vacation to make contact with a funder. Since the volunteer is not paid to make the visit, he or she has great credibility with the funding source. Remember, the use of resources like your travel itinerary, sales skills, and telephone credit cards for long-distance calls all demonstrate how cost-efficient our grantseeking and proposed solutions can be.

Please review and complete the attached Grants Resources Inventory Worksheet and the Foot-in-the-Door Worksheet before our next meeting on _____ so that we can work together to make a difference. If we do not receive the worksheets before this date, please expect us to call you to arrange to pick them up.

Sincerely,

Consider the following facts: there are only about three thousand employees working for forty thousand foundations, and fewer than a thousand foundations even have an office. Some of the larger foundations will talk to potential grantees on the phone, but thirty-nine thousand do not even have a phone. What each foundation does have is a board of trustees. In most cases, five to ten individuals comprise the board, and they meet a few times a year to act on the requests of nonprofit organizations.

If a member of your grants advisory group knows a foundation board member or trustee, discuss your proposed project with him or her in advance of a board meeting. (You will learn more about developing pre-proposal contact with each specific type of funder in Chapter Six.)

Foot-in-the-Door Worksheet

This worksheet (Exhibit 2.6) will help you develop your links to individuals who may be able to assist your grantseekers. These links can often provide inside information on a grantor that will help you tailor your appeal to your school's needs and the funder's priorities.

You will establish more valuable connections if you provide an opportunity for your grants advisory group to review the needs, priorities, and projects that your focus groups have developed. Ideally, selected members of the focus groups should make a presentation to the grants advisory group emphasizing the process through which their groups assessed your school's problems and opportunities. This is essential to increasing the grants advisory committee's sense of involvement and to making them feel that they too have ownership of the solutions. The grants advisory group's involvement in the solutions is imperative. A lack of input from them will result in fewer links and may also result in their approaching potential funders with weak statements such as "The school I am working with has some grant ideas they want to discuss with you" instead of an attention-grabber like "We at the _____ school have developed several solutions to our problems with _____, and we would like to discuss them informally with you." The committee members' depth of commitment and the detail with which they complete the Foot-in-the-Door Worksheet will also depend on their involvement in developing solutions and the degree to which they feel part of the solutions. Naturally, if your grants advisory group members are also members of your community focus groups they will be actively involved in brainstorming and prioritizing the areas that need to be improved. The worksheets in Chapter Three will help you establish a list of needs and develop solutions to them.

Exhibit 2.6

FOOT-IN-THE-DOOR WORKSHEET

Name and Title: _____

Home Address & Phone (Winter & Summer):

_____

_____

Business Address & Phone:

_____

_____

1. **What foundation boards are you currently a member of?**

    _____   _____

    _____   _____

2. **What foundation boards are you a past member of?**

    _____

    _____

3. **What foundation boards do members of your family serve on?**

    Name of Relative   Relationship   Name of Foundation

    _____   _____   _____   _____

    _____   _____   _____   _____

4. **What foundation boards do your friends and associates serve on?**

    Name of Friend/Associate   Name of Foundation

    _____   _____

    _____   _____

5. **What corporations do you have a relationship with?**

    Name of Corporation   Relationship to Corporation

    _____   _____

    _____   _____

6. **What corporate relationships do relatives, friends, and associates have?**

    Relative/Friend/Associate   Corporation   Relationship to Corporation

    _____   _____   _____   _____

    _____   _____   _____   _____

7. **What federal, state, city/county funding agencies do you have contacts in?**

    Name of Agency   Name & Title of Contact
    (Department/Division/Program)

    _____   _____

    _____   _____

    _____   _____

(continued)

Exhibit 2.6 (continued)

8. **What contacts do you have with federal, state, and city/county elected officials who could influence education-related appropriations? If the federal official is a senator or representative, indicate what state he or she represents.**

    Name and Title:_____

    Federal/State/City/County? _____

    Which State? _____

    Which City? County?_____

    Name and Title:_____

    Federal/State/City/County? _____

    Which State? _____

    Which City? County?_____

9. **What other clubs, groups, or organizations are you a member of or have a consulting, advisory, or other relationship with?**

    Name of Organization   Nature of Your Relationship

    _____   _____

    _____   _____

When you and your most influential grants advisory group members feel that the other group members are ready to buy into and work for school change, discuss the concept of linkages with them and mail or hand out the Inventory of Linkages and Resources Letter (Exhibit 2.5) and the Foot-in-the-Door Worksheet.

How to Use the Information You Receive

In my first experience collecting information on linkages, I researched the databases on possible funders, selected those that were close by and whose interests showed a strong match with my school's newly brain stormed projects, and then determined if we had any links to them. For instance, if the Smith Foundation appeared to be a likely prospect, I reviewed the advisory committee members' worksheets to find out if we had a contact who could get his or her foot in the door on behalf of our school.

Bauer Associates' *Winning Links* is a PC-compatible software program designed to assist in the database development of contacts and linkages. It allows the user to retrieve information necessary to access foundations, corporations, and government funding agencies. For more information, call 1-800-836-0732.

Another way to use the information collected on the Foot-in-the-Door Worksheet is to review the data and research those foundations, corporations, government agencies, and service clubs that your people have connections with. Determine what types of efforts the potential grantors fund and compare these with your list of needs and brainstormed projects.

The Foot-in-the-Door Worksheet and the data gathered from your Grants Resources Inventory will provide you, the principal, with command of communication. You will know whom to ask to call those funding sources that you do not have access to.

Corporate and community leaders know the value of the linkage process and are surprised that schools do not use it more often. Although educators may want to believe that the best proposal will win, reality tells us that a well-prepared proposal, pushed to the top of the pile by a mutual friend, will get the most attention and will likely be funded.

The concept of developing a database of linkages is so attractive to corporate leaders that you should consider submitting a proposal to a local corporation to fund the development of your system. Corporate representatives are keenly aware of the benefit-to-return ratio of their investments in nonprofit organizations. By funding you to develop and implement a linkage system, they will enable your school to attract funding from other sources, without increasing corporate taxes. That is a good investment!

When you discuss the possibility of funding your linkage system with a corporation (or a foundation), be sure to include in your grant request the cost of the following items:

- A computer
- A laser printer
- Software
- Data input expenses

When I introduced this concept to a local family foundation, my office was funded for a $15,000 linkage system that included all these items plus a modem and a subscription to a grants database. You would probably be happy with much less, and the smaller the amount you request, the greater your chances of getting it. By the way, my funding source remarked that she made the grant in honor of her father, who had become a millionaire through his amazing ability to remember who knew the people he needed to meet!

Use the checklist at the end of this chapter to begin assessing your system's access to preproposal contacts, webbing and linkages, and grants advisory committees and to help you develop a plan for improvement.

CHAPTER 2 CHECKLIST

Evaluation and Planning Worksheet

1. **Data—What percentage of the proposals submitted by your school in the past year have:**
   a. used preproposal contact?   _____%
   b. been developed at the last minute?   _____%
   c. been endorsed by a community advisory committee?   _____%

2. **Do you have a group or committee already in existence that could function as your grants advisory group?**
   _____ yes   _____ no
   If yes, what group? _____
   If no, could you initiate a grants advisory group?   _____ yes   _____ no

3. **Could your school's grants effort use a webbing and linkage system?**
   _____ yes   _____ no

4. **If you answered yes to question 3, would you attempt to develop a webbing and linkage system for your school's grants effort?**
   _____ yes   _____ no
   If yes, who would act as coordinator to introduce the concept? _____

5. **What other groups, committees, or booster clubs could produce more linkages for your school?**
   Club Name: _____   Contact: _____
   Club Name: _____   Contact: _____
   Club Name: _____   Contact: _____

6. **If you have any corporate contacts, review them and identify one or two individuals who might be interested in providing grant funds to support the development of your linkage system. Record the results of your discussions with them.**
   Linkage: _____
   Contacted on: _____
   Results: _____

   Linkage: _____
   Contacted on: _____
   Results: _____

Chapter 3

Getting Ready: Assessing Needs, Establishing Goals, and Developing Solutions

AS THE PRINCIPAL, you bring substantial credibility and status to the grantseeking process. By involving yourself in the development and support of focus groups, grants advisory committees, and brainstorming sessions, you will promote an atmosphere of cooperation and problem solving that reaches far beyond grantseeking. A grants system that generates needed funds for your school, with few up-front costs and lots of voluntary participation, can be an exciting part of your leadership role.

We know that when classroom leaders develop negative attitudes and want to be paid up front for every extra effort they make, it is difficult to get them excited about *anything,* let alone something that is not in their job description—like grant writing. However, grantseeking actually provides an opportunity to develop a positive attitude in teachers, staff, parents, and students and even provides an opportunity for teachers to earn extra money. A proposal to fund two or three miniprojects can create a spark that ignites a desire for change. A small grant of $3,000 from a local foundation dispersed in three $1,000 awards to classroom leaders could help you identify those individuals who care enough to make an extra effort to try to improve the educational system.

It is not necessary to develop enthusiasm and motivation in your entire staff or school. A few parents, students, and teachers who want to improve education can start the ball rolling, especially when you establish a grants system that provides the assistance and guidance they need.

Most, if not all, grant awards are intended to change a situation. Few awards are made to continue a program in its existing form. Even when granting funds to a school for an existing exemplary educational program, the grantor's underlying motivation is to fund the expansion of the program or to make it qualitatively better. At first glance, it may seem easy to demonstrate the need to address the educational inadequacies and problems that you face each day. But whether you seek to expand a successful program or change an inadequate one, the needs section of a proposal is frequently the most underdeveloped. One reason for the inadequate development of the statement of need and of the data to adequately substantiate the problem lies in the fact that those who live with the deficient situation day after day see it so clearly that they think it will be obvious to the grantor too or that the grantor will at least take their word for it. The adage "you can't see the forest for the trees" seems to sum up grantseekers' inability to clearly define their school's problem to others.

In addition, grantseekers are sometimes reluctant to document the need more clearly because it is depressing or upsetting to them. Your task as the principal is to develop a positive focus on those areas of need as well as of excellence that grant funds will create.

The formula in Exhibit 3.1 may help you initiate discussions that will identify your school's needs and document their importance.

Assessing Need

Most focus groups and brainstorming sessions center too soon on developing solutions and do not pay enough attention to determining how they know a problem exists. Whether because of the reasons stated previously or because of a strong desire to improve the situation, they often move too quickly from documenting the problem to the what-are-we-going-to-do-about-it stage. Insufficiently assessing need impairs the groups' ability to motivate a grantor and causes the brainstormed solutions and projects to be inspired more by personalities and group dynamics than by a clear documentation of the need.

Exhibit 3.1

FORMULA FOR SUCCESSFUL GRANTSEEKING

Needs +	Solutions +	Commitment =		Educational Advancement
of your students, classroom, community, and society	ideas and strategies to adapt change, strengthen the education system	the extra effort of you, your colleagues, and parents	∞*	new strategies, equipment, and materials to meet the challenges of education

Grantseeking provides the catalyst in this equation. Change occurs at an increased rate.

Gap Diagram

To help the group members focus on the present situation and the desired state of affairs, they should construct a gap diagram (see Figure 3.1) for each identified school or community need. Limit the number to five to determine the areas of highest priority. Each member of the focus group should then rank the needs, labeling them 1, 2, 3, and so on, according to the order in which they should be addressed. The rank orders should be combined to form a prioritized list of needs. You may want to use play money or lottery tickets (see Chapter One) to help the group identify and prioritize the needs.

It is very easy for your technology group to fall into a fatal trap at this point. If it identifies the need or gap as educational technology, it may use the equipment and technology on hand as what currently exists and what it would love to have as the other end of the gap. Even the few grantors that fund technology are bound to ask what will change if they make the grant. When need is expressed this way, all you can say is "We will have all this equipment installed and operating." And that is not what they want to hear! They want to know what will change in the education of children: What will they learn? How will they do better? Remember, technology is a means to make change.

Needs Worksheet

The Needs Worksheet (Exhibit 3.2) gives you additional help in documenting need. The first step is to determine which problem or need the group will focus on and to record it on the worksheet after "Problem Area."

Before the group brainstorms solutions, ask its members to provide information that demonstrates the current state of affairs. Many individuals will enthusiastically give their opinions, and some will provide very compelling stories and case studies that illustrate the need. Record all these examples and their sources on the worksheet. Although some grantors prefer statistics and facts, the human-interest quality of examples and stories is often effective in motivating a potential funding source.

Figure 3.1

THE GAP

What exists now. What is real.	What could be. The goal.
What the present situation is.	The desired state of affairs,
How many students are at this stage.	the level of achievement

---

Exhibit 3.2

NEEDS WORKSHEET

Completing this worksheet will help you step back from possible solutions and projects and establish that there is a gap between what is now and what should be.

Problem Area: _____

_____

_____

Documentation of the Need to Address This Problem:

What Exists Now	**Source of Data**
The Present State of Affairs	
(Studies, Facts, Surveys, Case Studies, etc.)	(Organization)
	(Journal, Newsletter, Newspaper, etc.)
	(Date of Publication)

Note: *Consider performing a survey of your classroom, school, and/or community to document that the problem exists.*

Also, record any pertinent studies and facts and their sources. In many cases, the group will not have a total command of the facts. Maybe there has never been a formal statistical documentation of the problem—the group just *knows* that it exists. Brainstorm the ways you could provide better documentation of the problem, such as attendance records, grades, and so on.

In many cases, a grant of $3,000 to $5,000 to document the extent of a problem can be acquired from a small funding source in your community. Because many small grantors have limited funds, their motivation for making an award to develop a needs assessment is to increase your chance of attracting funds from outside the community. Accurate, timely data and established mechanisms for collecting baseline data allow you to perform pre- and postproject evaluations, making your school more fundable.

Most groups want to move quickly to solutions and must be reminded of the grantors' need to document the change that will occur as a result of funding your project. Often the lack of sound preliminary and preassessment data complicates the postassessment and evaluation required by certain funds sources. By taking the time now to carefully review how you know there is a need you will bring to light the indicators of change that can be built into the evaluation.

Devoting time to developing a clear assessment of need will also give your group a sense of common interest and the motivation to do something about the problem.

Needs Worksheet Sample

In the sample worksheet (Exhibit 3.3), the group focused on parental involvement in supporting constructive informal education. At their first meeting, the group members realized that though they all believed that a

---

Exhibit 3.3

NEEDS WORKSHEET Sample

Completing this worksheet will help you step back from possible solutions and projects and establish that there is a gap between what is now and what should be.

Problem Area: Parents' lack of involvement in their children's formal education and lack of support for constructive informal educational experiences.

_____

_____

_____

Documentation of the Need to Address This Problem:

What Exists Now—
The Present State of Affairs

4 out of 5 parents reported that they regularly discuss schoolwork with their children. Yet two-thirds of the children said their parents rarely or never talked about school with them.

Two-thirds of the parents claimed to place limits on television viewing. Two-thirds of the children said they had no limits on television viewing.

The middle school group (8th graders) reported watching 21.4 hours of television per week, in comparison to spending 5.6 hours per week on homework.

50 percent of the parents reported attending school meetings, but less than one-third had ever visited their child's classroom.

66 percent had never talked to school officials concerning their child's homework.

Source of Data

Department of Education, Office of Educational Research and Improvement, Study reported in the _Wall Street Journal_ on January 3, 1992. 25,000 middle school children surveyed.

Note: _You could include findings from surveys of your classroom, school, or community; a consortium of classes; or a comparison to a classroom in Europe or another part of the world._

lack of support for school activities and unsupervised television viewing were detrimental to the behaviors elementary teachers wanted reinforced at home, they lacked facts. Therefore, each group member was asked to bring documentation of the problem to the next meeting.

In the end, this group used data and studies from the U.S. Department of Education and other state and federal agencies to document the need for parental involvement in children's education. As you can see from the sample, the measurement indicators for change were suggested through the methods used to demonstrate the problem and the gap (hours of television viewing, visits or contacts with child's classroom). The group could also have conducted an informal survey of the school's own students and parents, providing interesting comparisons to the national study and perhaps showing that the local problem was as bad or worse than the national problem. Including a local study might also have made the group a better choice for a grant because it would demonstrate the group's commitment in time and resources to documenting baseline data that could be helpful in the posttest or final evaluation. Not only would another study add more current data, it could also touch on time spent by students on the Internet and playing video games.

Establishing the Goals of Your Project

After establishing the data necessary to document need, the group's next task is to establish goals. To do this, members should ask themselves what would result if the needs outlined on the needs worksheet were addressed and the problem was solved.

Goals Worksheet

This worksheet (Exhibit 3.4) helps the group focus on the opposite end of the gap continuum: the desired state of affairs. Because of the critical and often negative outlook of our society, group members may excel at documenting the problem but falter when asked to reverse their perspective and identify positive outcomes that will result from eliminating it.

Completing the Goals Worksheet gives your group a clearer direction. It will also help the group members realize that although projects, programs, and research are meaningful ways of moving toward desired outcomes, they are *not* goals. They are techniques and strategies to close the gap between what is now and what ought to be.

Exhibit 3.4

GOALS WORKSHEET

Problem Area:_____

_____

_____

_____

_____

If the needs documented on the Needs Worksheet were fulfilled and the problem was eliminated, what would result? What is the *desired* state of affairs? The ultimate end? The answer to these questions states the goal. The Needs Worksheet documents what exists now. The Goals Worksheet documents what ought to be. The goal provides purpose, direction, and motivation for grantseeking.

Goal: _____

_____

_____

_____

_____

Record studies, quotations, and research findings that document what ought to be. Provide sources and dates.

Studies—Quotations—Research Findings   **Source—Date**

Note: *This is not the place to list solutions. Means of closing gaps are solutions; they are discussed in Chapter Five.*

Goals Worksheet Sample

In the Needs Worksheet sample (Exhibit 3.3) the problem has been identified as parents' lack of involvement in their children's education. In the sample Goals Worksheet (Exhibit 3.5), the stated goal is for parents and teachers to work together as responsible partners to maximize children's educational achievement. This goal will never be fully attained, but it will provide direction and purpose for teachers and parents to work side by side.

It is best if the group can cite experts who validate and confirm the goal as well as studies that confirm that the goal is worth pursuing and that progress toward it is likely to produce results. Note that in the sample, several studies, articles, and quotations are cited.

Exhibit 3.5

GOALS WORKSHEET Sample

Problem Area: Parents' lack of involvement in their children's formal education and lack of support for constructive informal educational experiences.

If the needs documented on the Needs Worksheet were fulfilled and the problem was eliminated, what would result? What is the *desired* state of affairs? The ultimate end? The answer to these questions states the goal. The Needs Worksheet documents what exists now. The Goals Worksheet documents what ought to be. The goal provides purpose, direction, and motivation for grantseeking.

Goal: Parents and teachers acting as responsible partners who work together to maximize children's educational achievement.

Record studies, quotations, and research findings that document what ought to be. Provide sources and dates.

Studies—Quotations—Research Findings	Source—Date
Students whose parents discussed their schoolwork recorded higher grades.	Dept. of Education Study, *Wall Street Journal* 1/3/92
Television viewing restrictions tended to boost grades.	Dept. of Education Study, *Wall Street Journal* 1/3/92
"Burden of education should not be on the teachers and schools alone." Education Department study says, "Parents have a major role to play."	Dept. of Education Study, *Wall Street Journal* 1/3/92
Home-based guidance program in Rochester schools demonstrates educational improvement in low-income students. Homeroom teacher acts as liaison between schools and parents. When teacher makes home visits, children do better in school.	Harvard University, 3-year study, Berea, OH, *Democrat & Chronicle* 11/28/91.
Preschool children from single-parent homes have better verbal skills than children from two-parent homes (more one-on-one communication).	Unpublished study 1989–90, Deidre Madden, Baldwin Wallace College, Berea, OH, *Democrat & Chronicle* 11/28/91.
Harrison, Arkansas—Students score in top 10 percent of the nation in test scores, yet Arkansas ranks 272 of 327 in education taxes. One of the lowest tax rates in the U.S. Money may not be the resource that makes the difference. Parents volunteer in their children's classrooms one hour per week. Duties include making copies, grading papers, working with students, listening to students read. Basically, the parents save teachers time. Parents and teachers meet on school councils and determine the educational goals for next year. Each school reports progress toward goals in a newspaper advertisement. School system received 10 new computers donated by civic clubs. Parents made speeches at clubs.	*USA Today* 11/18/91; study identifies good schools through "School Match" of Columbus, Ohio. "School Match" provides information to families moving to new areas.
Frank Newman, President of Education Commission, states, "They're saying parents are important and teachers are important and they should be part of running the schools."	

Developing Solutions

Worksheet for Developing Solutions and Projects to Reduce the Problem

Use this worksheet (Exhibit 3.6) when brainstorming possible solutions, projects, programs, research, interventions, and protocols that may help you reduce the problem and progress toward the stated goal.

When you are brainstorming, express all ideas for solutions without critique or in-depth analysis. Even those solutions that seem less than feasible should be stated because they may lead to other, more achievable solutions.

Exhibit 3.6

WORKSHEET FOR DEVELOPING SOLUTIONS AND PROJECTS TO REDUCE THE PROBLEM

Problem: _____

_____

_____

List any and all proposed solutions. No discussions, please. Discuss the ideas after the time allotted for brainstorming has expired. Then request each participant to rank order the proposed solutions, with 1 being the favorite.

Rank   **Proposed Solutions/Projects to Reduce the Problem**

-
-
-
-
-
-
-
-
-
-
-
-
-
-
-
-
-
-
-
-
-
-

Jot down the suggested solutions on the worksheet. Give a copy of the worksheet to each member of the group. Then set a precise time limit to discuss each proposed solution.

Worksheet for Developing the Top Two Suggested Solutions to the Problem

After the discussion, have the members rank order the solutions and place the top two on the Worksheet to Develop the Top Two Suggested Solutions to the Problem (Exhibit 3.7). The members of the group should address each of the issues on the worksheet to the best of their ability (estimate of total cost, cost per student or teacher, number of beneficiaries, drawbacks, and so on).

Exhibit 3.7

WORKSHEET FOR DEVELOPING THE TOP TWO SUGGESTED SOLUTIONS TO THE PROBLEM

Problem: _____
_____
_____
_____

Describe the top two proposed solutions briefly and give a rough estimate of the cost of each. Also provide an estimate of the cost per student or teacher. Include the number of individuals who would benefit directly from each solution and the number who could benefit indirectly through duplication of the approach at other schools. List the drawbacks of each (that is, those things that would impede its success).

Ask the following of each solution. Would you fund this idea with a grant? Will the benefits justify the money expended?

Solution #1:

Solution #2:

Sample Worksheet for Developing the Top Two Suggested Solutions to the Problem

This sample worksheet (Exhibit 3.8) shows one group's preferred solutions to the problem of lack of parental involvement in children's education.

Exhibit 3.8

WORKSHEET FOR DEVELOPING THE TOP TWO SUGGESTED SOLUTIONS TO THE PROBLEM Sample

Problem: Parents' lack of involvement in their children's K–12 in-school education and lack of support for outside-of-school education activities such as the completion of homework.

Describe the top two proposed solutions briefly and give a rough estimate of the cost of each. Also provide an estimate of the cost per student or teacher. Include the number of individuals who would benefit directly from each solution and the number who could benefit indirectly through duplication of the approach at other schools. List the drawbacks of each (that is, those things that would impede its success).

Ask the following of each solution. Would you fund this idea with a grant? What is the extent of the benefits for the money expended?

Solution #1: Develop a parent-teacher-student education contract that outlines each party's responsibility to support education. Review and renew every month on a three-part carbonless form.
Cost: $2 per student
Benefits: Students, parents, and teachers each have a copy of the expectations

Solution #2: Provide an electronic interface (Internet access or fiber-optic cable) where parents can access their children's homework assignments and homework help, and incorporate solution #1 into this solution.

CHAPTER 3 CHECKLIST

Evaluation and Planning Worksheet

1. **Does your school have a prioritized list of needs to be addressed?**

   _____ yes   _____ no

2. **If the answer to question 1 is yes, and if you have a system for developing this prioritized list of needs, could the system be improved?**

   _____ yes   _____ no

   If yes, how (techniques, changes, additions, etc.)?_____

   _____

   _____

   _____

   _____

3. **If you do not have a prioritized list of needs or a system for developing one, do you have any existing groups or committees that could develop this list?**

   _____ yes   _____ no

   If yes, please list the groups and/or committees and the names of the appropriate contact people.

Group	Contact Person
_____	_____
_____	_____
_____	_____
_____	_____
_____	_____
_____	_____

4. **List the information, resources, and materials you could provide to your school's groups to help them develop each of the following areas.**

   Problem Areas: _____

   _____

   _____

   Needs: _____

   _____

   _____

   Goals:_____

   _____

   _____

   Solutions: _____

   _____

   _____

Chapter 4

The Grants Marketplace: What a Principal Needs to Know

YOU NEED TO DEVELOP a conceptual framework based on where the grant funds are and in what amounts. Developing and encouraging effective grants strategies and decisions does not require that you abandon your other administrative duties to practice grantseeking full time. General knowledge, coupled with a theoretical decision-making strategy and links to the Internet or a computer-based grants retrieval system, will dramatically improve your school's grant program and enhance your image as a top-notch administrator.

To increase your information about the grants marketplace at minimal cost, invite a college or university professor or administrator to become a member of your grants advisory group. Individuals from higher education are usually more familiar with the competitive grants mechanism and have access to the resources of their universities' grants offices, including grants professionals and computer-based grant information retrieval systems. Your relationship with a representative of higher education will be mutually beneficial. Professors are usually eager to become involved with P–12 schools because they can provide teaching and research experience for their graduate students and also enable them to make outside money. Your cooperation will provide your school with grants resources, help in evaluation, and give you the status of having an individual with an advanced degree and a list of published articles on your side.

Grants marketplace information is available through computers, but you need a basic knowledge of the marketplace in order to help your classroom leaders develop their grants strategy.

The grants marketplace can be broken down into the following basic elements:

- Federal grant opportunities
- State grant opportunities

- Large national general-purpose foundations

- Special-purpose foundations

- Community foundations

- Family foundations

- Corporate foundations

- Large corporate (nonfoundation) giving programs

- All other corporations

The Grants Marketplace Quiz

In order to lead your school to grant success, you need to increase your "grants I.Q." and that of your faculty, staff, and grants advisory groups. The Grants Marketplace Quiz (Exhibit 4.1) will help you and your group develop a targeted, proactive, success-based grantseeking effort based on knowledge of where the grants funds really are.

Use the quiz in a nonthreatening and relaxed way by asking the members of your group to take wild guesses at the answers, assuring them that the quizzes do not have to be signed. It is a good idea for you to take the quiz also and to share your answers with the group. Then display the correct answers on an overhead screen, board, or flip chart so that the members can correct their quizzes. It is important for you to explain why the group's overall scores on the quiz are low, if indeed they are. Point out that newspapers, journals, and newsletters focus on exceptionally large grant awards, causing people to believe that all are the million-dollar variety. This is simply not the case.

Discuss how inappropriate grants strategies could evolve if the members of the group were to base their grantseeking on overinflated ideas about the grants marketplace. This is why it is so important to develop a realistic appraisal of the marketplace, which will also encourage the group members to think about the links they may have to potential funders.

The corporate representatives on your grants advisory group will particularly approve of approaching the grants area with knowledge of where the funds are and how much is granted each year. These individuals are comfortable with the idea of competition and want to know the chances of success.

You may wish to expand your discussion of the correct answers to the quiz (see Exhibit 4.2) by including the background information that follows the answer key.

Question 1—The figure of 625,000 is somewhat misleading. There are actually many more 501(c)(3) tax-exempt organizations because several

---

Exhibit 4.1

THE GRANTS MARKETPLACE QUIZ

1. How many 501(c)(3) tax-exempt charitable organizations are recognized by the Internal Revenue Service? _____

2. How many elementary schools, middle schools, and junior high schools are there in the United States? _____

3. How much money will the federal government grant through its 1,300+ granting programs this year? _____

4. What was the total amount of funds distributed to nonprofit groups through foundation grants, corporate grants, bequests, and individuals in the past year? _____

5. What percentage of total funds is granted by each of the following four sources?
   a. Foundation Grants   _____%
   b. Corporate Grants   _____%
   c. Bequests   _____%
   d. Individual Giving   _____%
   100%

Foundations

6. Approximately how many grant-making foundations are there? _____

7. The business of approximately how many foundations is carried out in offices?

   _____

8. How many grants of more than $10,000 were awarded in the past year? _____

Corporations

9. How many corporations are there in the United States? _____

10. What percentage of corporations takes a deduction for charitable contributions?

    _____

11. Which of the following forms of corporate support to nonprofit organizations has experienced the greatest increase in the past five years?
    a. products
    b. cash
    c. securities
    d. loans

---

nonprofits can operate under one number approved by the IRS. For example, a university may have a center, an institute, and a museum all operating under one number.

Question 2—It is important to focus on the competition for grant funds that exists between all nonprofit organizations, and especially on the competition from other P–12 schools. Keep in mind, however, that

---

Exhibit 4.2

THE GRANTS MARKETPLACE QUIZ Answer Key

1. How many 501(c)(3) tax-exempt charitable organizations are recognized by the Internal Revenue Service? **625,000**

2. How many elementary schools, middle schools, and junior high schools are there in the United States? **71,887**

3. How much money will the federal government grant through its 1,300+ granting programs in 1998? **$85 billion**

4. What was the total amount of funds distributed to nonprofit groups through foundation grants, corporate grants, bequests, and individuals in 1997? **$143.5 billion**

5. What percentage of total funds is granted by each of the following four sources?
   a. Foundation Grants **9.3%**
   b. Corporate Grants **5.7%**
   c. Bequests **8.8%**
   d. Individual Giving **76.2%**
   <u>100%</u>

Foundations

5. Approximately how many grantmaking foundations are there? **45,000**

6. The business of approximately how many foundations is carried out in offices? **1,000**

7. How many grants of more than $10,000 were awarded in the past year? **78,296**

Corporations

8. Approximately how many corporations are there in the United States? **5 million**

9. What percentage of corporations take a deduction for charitable contributions? **35%**

10. Which of the following forms of corporate support to nonprofit organizations has experienced the greatest increase in the past five years?
    a. products
    ✔b. cash
    c. securities
    d. loans

---

many of these schools have never applied for a grant, and others have applied for government funding only. Now is the time for your school to capitalize on the trend in the foundation and corporate grants marketplace to award grants for early intervention to preschools and elementary and middle schools.

Question 3—The federal government will grant approximately $85 billion in 1998, but far more than this will be appropriated to programs. For example, the Department of Education will not award all of its $38 billion appropriation in grants, because a large portion must be used to pay for overhead, office space, and salaries and fringes for the program officers and staff. In other words, the amount *appropriated* to a program is not the same as the amount *awarded* in the form of grants.

Your school's ability to gain access to federal grant funds is a function of how your project is defined and who it is supposed to benefit. The Department of Education is only one source of federal funds. You can also apply for federal grant money that is distributed to your state as well as for funds from federal programs that focus on drug and alcohol prevention, the humanities, science, literacy, health, and many other related areas.

Question 4—The total amount of nongovernment funding for nonprofits is calculated each summer for the previous year. The estimate for 1997 was $143.5 billion, a sum that may startle your grants advisory group members. Moreover, most individuals think that the portion of this money granted by foundations and corporations is much higher than it really is.

Once you reveal the correct percentages, some group members may express a strong desire to go after individual giving—76.2 percent or $109.35 billion. That is, until you inform them of the following:

- 47 percent of individual giving is to religious organizations

- For the remaining $57.96 billion, fund-raising techniques must be employed to access these funds, including special events, direct mail, telephone solicitation, and so on.

Seeking grants from foundations and corporations usually consists of preparing a well-targeted, two-page letter proposal. Compare this simple process with the stringent proposal requirements of government agencies, and the $21 billion plus in grants from foundations and corporations begins to look very good. Grantseeking in general is a better alternative to securing external resources than other traditional fund-raising techniques.

Grants advisory group members should be made aware that the federal government has far more financial resources than private agencies (foundations and corporations) do. Therefore, private agencies often prefer that potential grantees look to government sources first. This information will help your group understand why it is important to support federal as well as private grantseeking.

Question 5—Highlights the differences between the 1,300 plus federal programs and the 45,000 foundations. Each foundation thinks of itself and the projects it supports as invaluable and unique!

Question 6—No one knows exactly how many federal employees are involved in the grants area. If you include program officers, staff, and auditors, the number must be staggering. But because foundations often have limited funds, they feel that the more staff they have, the fewer grants they can make. If they do not have an office, they need few, if any, paid staff. For this reason fewer than a thousand foundations occupy offices.

The forty thousand foundations actually employ only slightly more than three thousand individuals. Keep in mind also that some large foundations have a hundred or more employees, and thousands of smaller foundations have none.

Armed with these facts, your grants advisory group members will clearly understand how important it is to utilize an informal webbing and linkage system in contacting foundation and corporate board members.

Question 7—This information will help your group set realistic expectations based on sound knowledge of the grants marketplace. Only seventy-eight thousand plus grants in excess of $10,000 were reported to the Foundation Center in 1997, so receiving a $100,000 foundation grant is an admirable achievement.

The positive aspect is that there are hundreds of thousands of grants for under $10,000. This is good news for classrooms and schools that can formulate interesting proposals for small requests to support programs or projects that can influence many students.

Question 8—There are several reasons why many corporations are not deeply involved in philanthropy. The root of their lack of involvement goes back to the late 1930s, when it was actually illegal for corporations to make gifts to nonprofit organizations.

Question 9—In reality, many more corporations make gifts than take deductions. Many do not report deductions for these gifts so as not to invite IRS audits. In addition, many owners and executives make contributions from their personal funds. Incorporate the following basic facts of corporate philanthropy into your school's strategy for grantseeking.

1.   Corporations do not give away money. They "invest" it and expect a return.

2.   Corporations invest where they live and where the children of their workers go to school.

3.   Corporations value involvement. Many will not make a grant unless their employees volunteer time to the nonprofit applicant.

Do not make the mistake of thinking that only large corporations make grants. The research section that follows shows that it often pays to approach smaller corporations. Especially keep in mind corporations that you have a link with—for example, smaller corporations with employees who are graduates of your school.

Question 10—The correct answer is cash, but the amount has barely exceeded the rate of inflation. Gifts in the form of products may be less costly than cash, and may reduce inventories, provide a write-off for dated products, entice future purchasers, and lead to maintenance contracts or agreements. For all these reasons, corporations like to donate products and equipment. Products and equipment may even exceed cash support but there is no way to validate this.

The Grantseekers' Matrix

Now that you have a basic idea of where the grant money is and how many billions of dollars are available, you need a systematic approach to identifying what types of organizations will be interested in funding the programs, projects, and equipment you need. The Grantseekers' Matrix (Table 4.1) provides the basis for such an approach.

Column 1 of the Grantseeker's Matrix describes the various types of projects—demonstration, research, equipment, replication, consortia, and international. Columns 2 through 9 provide the grantseeker with insight into how the various categories of grantors view the major variables that determine grants success.

Column 1: Type of Project

There are six basic categories or types of grant proposals listed on the Grantseeker's Matrix. Your task may be to help your school's grantseekers focus clearly on a need and several methods to address it, but this matrix will enable grantseekers to look at changes in approaches that would expand the number of potential funders and increase funding opportunities. You can change the nature of your project from research to demonstration to international. The secret here is to practice the golden rule of grantseeking: the funder has the gold and therefore makes the rules. You are not going to convince funding sources to change their needs or rules. Instead, you will have to adjust your approach accordingly.

Demonstration

In this category of grants the funder's interest is in developing models for change. The emphasis is on proving what works and on demonstrating change. The funder who awards demonstration grants prefers innovative approaches and ideas. For example, this type of funder would be enthused by the idea that a project could become a model for other classrooms, curricula, or schools.

Table 4.1

GRANTSEEKERS' MATRIX

Type: _____

1 Type of Project	2 Geographic Need	3 Award Size	4 School's Image	5 Credentials of Project Director	6 Preproposal Contact	7 Proposal Content	8 Review & Decision	9 Proposal Information and Administration
Demonstration A								
Research B								
Equipment C								
Replication D								
Consortium E								
International F								

Research

At first glance this category of grants may appear to be out of the question for your school. But give it a second look! By utilizing a link to a college or university you may be able to develop your school's ability to attract these funds. A demonstration or model project can become a research project if you incorporate a control group and a statistical analysis component in the project plans. The best part is that to do so your school does not need a vast computer system and experts in statistical design. These resources already exist at your local college or university.

Equipment

Sources that fund educational equipment directly are relatively rare. However, grantors want to fund projects that will make a difference. To that end they will allow the purchase of a limited amount of equipment if it plays an integral part in the project.

Even when you solicit hardware from a computer equipment manufacturer, the manufacturer will want to know the following:

- Why do you want the equipment?
- Who will use it?
- How many will benefit from it?
- What curriculum changes will occur?
- How will in-service training be used?

By the time you finish writing a proposal for equipment, you will realize that you have really developed a model project and that, in fact, your chance of success in attracting the equipment will depend on the quality of your plan or project and how it will influence change or educational advancement.

Replication

Funders of this category of grants do not want to be involved in discovering *what works* or *how and why* something works—the rather risky ventures of research and model projects. Rather, they want their grant money to be used to encourage others to use or replicate the techniques that have been proven, usually under someone else's grant funds, to have a positive effect.

Consortium

Funders of this type of grant are interested in a partnership of grantseekers, each of whom brings outstanding qualities to the proposal:

- An increased likelihood of success

- A *sharing* of expensive resources and equipment rather than a duplication

Any type of grant can be a consortium grant. For example, you can develop a demonstration, research, equipment, or replication grant that is also a consortium grant. In many cases grantors encourage consortium grants, and some even mandate or require them.

Consortium proposals have been around for many years, but are just now coming into their own as a powerful and cost-effective mechanism to achieve the outcomes suggested in proposals. Successful grantseekers will enter the year 2000 knowing how to utilize consortium arrangements to maximize cost efficiency and improve their competitive edge. The remainder of this decade will be marked by larger problems and fewer resources. Those schools that make the most of the limited resources available to them will win the funding.

International

Many grantors have links to other parts of the world. The political and social changes in Europe and the former Soviet Union, as well as the increasingly international interests of governments and corporations, all point to a marked rise in the success rates for international proposals.

Changes in trade and tariff rules and the growing number of multinational corporations may mean that a local corporation has a vested interest in another country. Including an elementary school from that country in your project plan may dramatically improve your chances for funding. For example, one of the largest United States–based manufacturers of blue jeans has just constructed a large manufacturing facility in Poland. A proposal that encourages educational change or that focuses on capitalism or any other of a number of corporate concerns, *and* that promotes an educated work force in Poland, might be considered very attractive by such manufacturers.

Finding an international partner is not difficult, especially if your grantseekers submit the proposal and initiate the contact in the United States.

Column 2: Geographic Need

In most cases, your school must demonstrate a considerable local need for the solution you propose. Some grantors are interested in projects that address that same need in other areas. For example, your solution to your school's need may have a national or international impact, and highlighting this aspect of your project in your proposal might improve your fundability. In other cases, however, the mention of a national or international focus may have little, no, or even a negative impact on your fundability if the grantor is interested only in projects that address local needs.

Column 3: Award Size

The amount of grant funds needed to implement your solution is a critical factor in determining which type of funding source to approach. It is possible to ask several different types of grantors to fund part of your project, keeping your request within each one's budget, and in so doing to obtain funds for a considerably larger project than any one grantor could support.

Column 4: School's Image

What is the image or reputation of your school? Must you be designated as an outstanding school to attract funding from certain types of grantors?

Column 5: Credentials of Project Director

Each type of funding source has different criteria for what constitutes a credible project director. Local reputation has a positive impact on some grantors; others value doctoral degrees, records of publications, and previous grant awards.

Column 6: Preproposal Contact

The value of preproposal contact (contact before the proposal is written) cannot be overemphasized. However, some types of funding sources do not allow it. The vast differences in this particular area have a lot to do with whether a funding source has a grants staff, program officers, an office, or board members who can be approached through linkages.

Column 7: Proposal Content

This column summarizes the preferred format for the proposal and the application procedures. The purpose of this column is not for your prospective grantseeker to ascertain which type of funding source has the shortest application. Just because a grantor does not require a lengthy, detailed proposal does not mean that proposal preparation will be easy. In fact, creating a two-page letter proposal to a foundation or corporation with no guidelines or required format can be much more difficult than preparing a lengthy application to a government funding source.

Column 8: Review and Decision

Who reads and reviews your school's proposal, what their biases, background, and education are, how much time they spend reviewing each proposal, and what scoring system they use are important factors for you to consider in preparing a winning proposal. Naturally, your school's proposal should be written with the reviewer in mind. The use of educational jargon may be acceptable to one type of reviewer and not to another.

Having this information before submitting your proposal will enable your grantseekers to perform a preliminary mock review of the proposal and to prepare the best possible proposal.

Column 9: Proposal Information and Administration

It is important to know what the funding source will expect after the grant is awarded. Each type of grantor has different rules, regulations, and guidelines that you must comply with. This column gives you an idea of what will be required of you as a school administrator.

The Government Grantseekers' Matrix

Review the Government Grantseekers' Matrix (Table 4.2) to determine your general strategy for approaching this $85 billion marketplace or to help you evaluate a specific project's viability for government funding.

As you can see from Column 2, often the need must exist outside of your school and geographic area. The award sizes are generally well above $10,000 per year, and awards of $50,000 to $250,000 are not uncommon. Your school's credibility should be high, and the credentials of the project director fairly well established.

If after reviewing this matrix you know that you want to pursue a federal grant opportunity, you can go directly to Chapter Five for in-depth information on searching for government grants. But I suggest that you review *all* of the matrices to familiarize yourself with the requirements of and differences between each type of funder and to acquire valuable information on which to base alternative grant strategies.

Foundation Grantseekers' Matrices

These matrices are shown in Tables 4.3 through 4.7.

Large National General-Purpose Foundations

Large national general-purpose foundations prefer demonstration and model projects (see Table 4.3). It is estimated that almost 50 percent of their grants are aimed at developing models and projects that promote changes in their particular fields of interest.

These larger foundations may look a bit like government grantors because they generally do not fund replication grants, and because they offer larger grants and prefer to fund well-credentialed project directors.

Table 4.2

GOVERNMENT GRANTSEEKERS' MATRIX

Federal grants to elementary and middle schools come from the Department of Education and other programs that have an interest in children and families. The Department of Agriculture, Health and Human Services, the National Science Foundation, and the National Endowment for Arts and Humanities can all be considered as possible grant sources. More than a thousand federal programs grant over $85 billion annually.

Type of Project	Geographic Need	Award Size*	School's Image	Credentials of Project Director	Preproposal Contact	Proposal Content	Review & Decision	Proposal Information and Administration
Model/Demonstration—Great variety of areas: Curriculum (math, science, reading, etc.) Learning-disabled, at-risk youth	Local/Regional State National	Medium to large	National/Regional	Being well-known is a plus; published or spoken at conferences, etc.	Write, phone, go see	Long, detailed forms	Peer review by experts	Must follow OMB curricular; long and elaborate forms and financial requirements
Research—Areas: Teaching Learning Vocation Fed. Dropouts Gifted	Local/National	"	National	Experts must be involved—subcontract or consortium or consortium with colleges/ universities	"	"	"	"
Equipment—For acquisition (not very common); allowed when integral part of model or research	Local	Small to medium	Regional	Not essential	"	"	"	"
Replication—Not common unless Feds want regional sites or to expand to target population	Local	"	"	Local/Regional expertise	"	"	"	"
Consortium—More common now; allows use of experts and facilities at lower cost	Local/national/ schools of consortium partners	Medium to large	National/ Regional		"	"	"	"
International—Interested in understanding U.S. language and culture, capitalistic system	Local National International	"	"		"	"	"	"

*Size of award is provided as rough guideline. Small is under $5,000, medium is $5,000–$50,000, and large is $50,000 and up.

Table 4.3

FOUNDATION GRANTSEEKERS' MATRIX: Large National General-Purpose Foundations

Examples: Ford, Rockefeller, and MacArthur Foundations

Type: Relatively small in number (fewer than 50), this group has a large percentage of the assets and makes the majority of grants. They fund both nationally and internationally on a broad area cf interests. They have paid staff and offices.

Type of Project	Geographic Need	Award Size	School's Image	Credentials of Project Director	Preproposal Contact	Proposal Content	Review & Decision	Proposal Information and Administration
Model/Demonstration Projects—Variety of interests by subject area and outcomes	Local/Regional/National	Varies, but funds large & medium $50,000+	Regional or national image helps	Expertise in school district very important	Phone, write letter, make a personal visit	Many have guidelines, specific forms and restrictions	Staff are experts in field and hire outside expertise to evaluate	Many have application instructions and forms. Some produce annual reports and newslette's. Many have program specialists and auditors who may make preaward and postaward visits. Administration follows established CPA guidelines
Research—Many prefer a systematic research approach with statistical design and evaluation; want to know what works	"	"	Good to include a university	Very important. Utilize higher education linkages to Ed.D, Ph.D, colleges/universities	Critical to proposal acceptance	Length varies but 10–20 pgs. common.	"	
Equipment—Allowable as part of the project methodology; most avoid funding equipment alone	"	"	"	"	"	May do a preliminary review of your concept before you are invited to submit	"	
Replication—Most prefer to fund a model and dissemination of the project, not replication	"	"	"	"	"		"	
Consortium—More interest today than in the past. Look at IRS 990 to assist in choosing a past grantee as a partner	"	Larger sizes	Images of both partner schools important	Need to have experience and degrees in both partners	"	"	"	
International—Growing interest in the world, but still want to help out at home; discuss a possible foreign site to provide a comparison; look at IRS 990 to locate countries or languages of interest	Local/Regional & International	Larger to accommodate travel expenses	"		May be difficult to get both partners together with funder. Use conference calls & teleconference	"	"	These grantors may have overseas staff

They generally occupy an office and have staff or paid reviewers (consultants) who are experts in the field to critically evaluate proposals.

In some cases, you may approach a local foundation or corporation for a small grant to develop preliminary data or test part of your model; then go to a larger foundation for a grant to develop your project further before you approach a federal grants source for funding the implementation of your program.

Special-Purpose Foundations

Although there are only a few hundred special-purpose foundations, they have a lot of impact on their areas of interest (see Table 4.4). They are motivated by a strong desire to effect *immediate* change in the area of special needs. Your ability to improve the problem is paramount in their minds, and the rules and requirements imposed on the special-purpose foundation's grantees are not as stringent as those of government and large foundation funding sources.

When submitting a proposal to these funding sources, it is less important to demonstrate an outstanding image and impressive credentials than it is to captivate and excite them with a novel and cost-effective approach to producing change in the needs area they value.

Community Foundations

Community foundations are excellent grant resources for schools (see Table 4.5). Not every community has one, but they are the fastest-growing sector of the foundations marketplace, and more than three hundred of them exist today. If your area is fortunate enough to have a community foundation, you have a superb source for funding those projects (such as replication and needs assessment) that the other funding sources do not support. Although the size of a community foundation grant is usually small, the impact it can have on your students and on your ability to make your school appear more fundable to other grantors is impressive.

If your area does not have a community foundation you would do well to help initiate one. A community-minded lawyer and banker on your grants advisory committee could get the ball rolling, and your school could soon have a new and unique source for grant funds. Even if your school has initiated a school foundation, a local community foundation should not be viewed as competition. It is just one more funding source.

Family Foundations

In some ways family foundations (see Table 4.6) resemble community foundations. Built into their board of directors is a strong geographic homing device that is reflected in their granting pattern. They fund what they

Table 4.4

FOUNDATION GRANTSEEKERS' MATRIX: Special-Purpose Foundations

Examples: Exxon Education Trust, Carnegie Foundation

Type: This type of foundation has a narrow, rather specific focus. There are special-purpose foundations for education and for the different levels of education, but don't overlook those that fund subject areas of interest to elementary and middle schools, such as music, art, literacy, literature, health, etc.

Type of Project	Geographic Need	Award Size	School's Image	Credentials of Project Director	Preproposal Contact	Proposal Content	Review & Decision	Proposal Information and Administration
Model/Demonstration Project—They prefer project grants that call attention to their field or cause	Special needs population in your area	Large and medium	Not as critical as your ability to make a difference in their special interest	Important but not critical	Contact by phone, write, go see	Varies, usually have a proposal format; some use a concept paper to approve you to submit full proposal	Staff may be experts in target area	Use annual reports and tax returns to learn what they like and what type of organization they prefer as a grantee
Research—Only in their special interest. Usually the larger foundations like some research. On average, 10–20% of grant money awarded for research	"	"	"	Very important	"		Use some outside reviews	"
Equipment—Some will fund equipment; others will allow it if it is necessary to carry out the project/research	"	"	"	Important but not critical	"	"	"	"
Replication—Not usually priority unless a model was very successful	"	"	"	"	"	"	"	"
Consortium—Interested if the alliance will have more impact on the special interest	Special needs population in your area and your partner's	"	"	"	"	"	"	"
International—Several are interested in international as well as national	"	"	"	"	"	"	"	"

Table 4.5

FOUNDATION GRANTSEEKERS' MATRIX: Community Foundations

This type of foundation is named after the geographic area of concern. All its grants must benefit the specific area and the boundaries used to separate the designated area—the Cleveland Foundation, the San Francisco Foundation, and so on. Even smaller cities have them (such as the Utica [New York] Foundation), and some areas have a statewide foundation (such as the North Dakota Foundation). Community foundations exist to support their particular community and are not under political or government sponsorship. They provide an excellent source of funds for elementary and middle school grants, but usually in smaller amounts.

Type of Project	Geographic Need	Award Size	School's Image	Credentials of Project Director	Preproposal Contact	Proposal Content	Review & Decision	Proposal Information and Administration
Model/Demonstration Project—This type of grantor prefers to grant money to projects that are sure to make a difference	Need in the specific geographic area of community	Small; grants up to $10,000, many in the $5,000 range	How well your organization is known in your community and specifically by the board members	The local image of the project director and key individuals involved in the project	Contact with the designated official of the foundation is recommended	Usually a short 2–8 pg proposal	Usually a process involving the board. Key factor is that the board is representative of the community	Many with annual reports; their 990 A.R. IRS tax return is very helpful. Most do not have many staff or support personnel, so follow-up is limited
Research—Not usually funded	Only concerned with local need, not field of education			"				
Equipment—May fund small purchases that show a lot of use	"	"	"	"	"	"	Greater range in socioeconomic status, more women and minorities on the board	
Replication—A good area; they have proof that it worked someplace else	"	"	"	"	"	"		
Consortium—Interested if all partners are in the same geographic area	"	"	"	"	"	"		
International—Not a good bet; maybe if there is a strong ethnic group in the community								

Table 4.6

FOUNDATION GRANTSEEKERS' MATRIX: Family Foundations

Over 30,000 of this type. Most are small, have little or no staff and no office, and meet once or twice per year. They support their families' concerns and values, with an eye to the past and the family member who created the foundation. They represent a valuable resource to elementary and middle school education because you can provide them with a lot of results for a small grant and because you have access to children and thus to the future.

Type of Project	Geographic Need	Award Size	School's Image	Credentials of Project Director	Preproposal Contact	Proposal Content	Review & Decision	Proposal Information and Administration
Model/Demonstration Project—Of interest to many family foundations. They fear long-range support, so project must show self-sufficiency or other support later	This type of funder has a very specific geographic grant-ing perspective, and the need and your project must be in their area	Small, under $10,000 or even under $5,000	The credibility of your school, the district, and any of your contact people (friends) makes the difference	Project director's image in the school or community is important	Since staff is limited, most state no contact except by letter. Your only opportunity is through "friends" who have contact with the board members	Most want a 1–2 pg letter proposal or letter of inquiry; usually no attachments are allowed. You must submit full proposal	Usually read by board members. You write to the level of expertise of the board. They are often family members and close friends or business associates	Most do not publish an annual report. Information on what they prefer to fund is in their IRS tax return. IRS return found at Foundation Center Regional Collections. Administration should follow standard business practices and establish CPA guidelines. Little or no audit, follow-up, or compliance issues
Research—Most want to invest money in what works; not a lot of interest in research	Local. Interest if family had/has a child with educational problem	Some medium-size but relatively rare	Letters of endorsement from community groups help also	Very important				
Equipment—Popular, as tangible things are preferred. Computer is better than teacher's aide	Local							
Replication—Good source for replicating a successful program	Local		Local reputation important					
Consortium—Okay, but only if both partners are in their area of concern	Local							
International—Not best funder unless there is an ethnic relationship								

like, and they like programs that enhance educational opportunities in the geographic regions they care about.

Research is not a top funding priority for them. Because they seek to have a more immediate impact, they gravitate toward replication, equipment, and targeted model projects.

Corporate Foundations

Education is the top priority of the 1,300 plus corporate foundations (see Table 4.7). Approximately 33.5 percent of their grants go to education, and P–12 schools have been the recipients of an increasing percentage of these funds. The key to procuring corporate foundation funds is your school's proximity to corporate plants or offices, the number of corporate workers who are motivated volunteers at your school, and the visible return on the corporate foundation's investment.

Corporate Grantseekers' Matrices

These matrices are shown in Tables 4.8 and 4.9.

Large Corporate Grantors

This group (see Table 4.8) is interested in schools located close to their plants, distribution centers, and stores. Despite what grantseekers are apt to think, large corporate grantors are not particularly motivated by press releases that make them appear like good corporate citizens. Some corporations do not even want their grant awards to be publicized, because that could result in more requests for grants. Instead, large corporate grantors are motivated by projects that position their products with students or teachers, help them develop and improve products, or produce a better-educated workforce.

All Other Corporations

Corporate grantmaking (see Table 4.9) was not practiced until a 1953 court case upheld the legality of a corporate grant to a university. Thus the history of corporate support is short, and the practice is not as widespread as many believe. But do not let this hold back your grantseekers. Smaller corporations are still a very valuable resource for your school. Because they are local, they may have ties and linkages to your school, and they certainly have a vested interest in your community. If you approach this group properly, the results may exceed your expectations.

Your grants advisory group members from the corporate community will be your key to corporate grants. When a corporate peer approaches a small corporation, explains the project and the direction your school is taking, and then invites the corporation to make a grant, you will get results!

Table 4.7

FOUNDATION GRANTSEEKERS' MATRIX: Corporate Foundations

Corporate granting is divided into two major categories: those companies that use a separate private foundation to make grants and corporations (see Table 4.8) that make grants directly from the corporation and have no foundation. Of the 2.5 million corporations in the United States, 1,287 corporate foundations are included in the National Directory of Corporate Giving. They make a significant portion of corporate grants, and the corporate foundation grantseeker has access to IRS Annual Reports so you can verify your approach and the amount you are seeking. In general, this group spends more time reading your proposal than the family foundation.

Type of Project	Geographic Need	Award Size	School's Image	Credentials of Project Director	Preproposal Contact	Proposal Content	Review & Decision	Proposal Information and Administration
Model/Demonstration Project—Of interest to corporate foundations, especially if it affects their products, profits, or workers	The need must fit the granting perspective. May have a national agenda or a primary focus on needs in their field of corporate interest	Medium, $10,000 to $50,000; and large, over $50,000	The more well-known your school, the better. National rankings, scores, awards, etc., help	Credentials nationally are important as is local image with corporate officials, plant managers, and sales representatives	Phone, write, go see the funder to describe the project. Many have staff	Some have guidelines and even an application form	Review may be done by some staff with knowledge of education. Decision made by the board	May have annual reports that provide information on grant interests. You can also review IRS tax returns. Administration follows established CPA guidelines; some site visits and audits
Research—Interested if it advances corporate interests								
Equipment—Some support; best chance is for equipment the company produces								
Replication—Some interest if there are proven results								
Consortium—Great approach if your partner is also in same area as corporate interest								
International—Could be a great component if corporation is owned overseas or has a plant there								

Table 4.8

CORPORATE GRANTSEEKERS' MATRIX: Large Corporate Foundations

Of the 2.5 million corporations, only 700,000 are reported to make grants to any nonprofit organization. Those grants total less than $6 billion. The large corporate grantors have such good public relations that most grantseekers think that there are billions more in corporate grants than there are. From the perspective of education, this type of grantor offers a large resource because estimates are that 40 percent of corporate grants go toward education. Although higher education has traditionally received the greatest portion, elementary and middle schools are attracting increasing interest.

Type of Project	Geographic Need	Award Size	School's Image	Credentials of Project Director	Preproposal Contact	Proposal Content	Review & Decision	Proposal Information and Administration
Model/Demonstration Project—Interest if there is a direct or indirect benefit to the company	The need for the project must be prevalent locally, but must correspond to the values of the corporation	Medium, $10,000 to $50,000; some large, $50,000 and over	Your school should have a relationship with the company, not necessarily a record of grant support. Should have company support in the form of loaned executives and employees as volunteers	Should have regional image and credentials	Contact sales people, plant managers, regional supervisors by phone and personal contact. Involve them in the project and work through them unless application has different instructions	Some have an application form. Many prefer a 2–5 page letter	Several have staff and a few employ one outside reviewer	Little or no verifiable information available. Most entries in published directories are not verified. Some site visits and very few audits
Research—If the research will contribute to the field of interest and enhance product development								
Replication—Some interest if there are proven results								
Equipment—Will grant company products, especially if the grant will put them in a position to sell more products to school, students, or parents								
Consortium and International—Depends on where the company has other plants, facilities								

Table 4.9

CORPORATE GRANTSEEKERS' MATRIX: All Other Corporations

This group includes smaller and medium-sized companies, about 600,000 of the 700,000 corporations reported to make grants to any nonprofit organization. They have great concern for the communities in which they live and work. They listen because of their concern for their workers and the education of their workers' children. Most are not planning on opening a business in another country and want quality education nearby. Get a list of local corporations from your Chamber of Commerce. Try to involve them in your advisory committee. How many of their workers' children are in your school? But remember, these companies are still concerned about their products and profits. They are not as motivated by a burning desire to do good things as you may think. They want something for their investment.

Type of Project	Geographic Need	Award Size	School's Image	Credentials of Project Director	Preproposal Contact	Proposal Content	Review & Decision	Proposal Information and Administration
Model/Demonstration Project—Some interest, but concern is for what works	Basic concern is where the company is located and how the project will affect its workers, children, and community	Most are small, up to $10,000; some medium, $10,000 to $50,000	Your record in receiving grants is not very important. Involvement and familiarity with your school is greatest asset	Being known locally is what matters. No need for regional or national image; that could even detract from what you do locally	Definitely make contact with corporate decision maker by phone and in person. Cold proposals have little success. Involve the corporation's employees on your committees and use your "friends"	Few have application forms or formats. Most instruct you to write a letter	Most have no full-time staff and few have part-time. They meet a few times per year and may not even read all the proposals—unless they are looking for yours	Little or no verifiable data available. Use "friends" to perform a credit check through Dunn and Bradstreet or another reviewer. More profitable the better. Few rules, almost never an audit. Follow CPA guidelines
Research—Little or no interest unless a product could benefit								
Equipment—May donate used equipment or the equipment they sell								
Consortium—Sharing with other schools, public and private, would look good, maximize resources								
National/International—Not interested unless they have investments other places								

Corporations know that voluntary grantmaking to local schools is better than a tax increase. After all, they get recognition and a good feeling from voluntary giving but just a canceled check from the tax collector for nonvoluntary giving (tax increases).

Service Clubs and Organizations Matrix

See Table 4.10. You will get a much better response from service clubs and organizations when you ask them to fund a specific project or proposal instead of money for general purposes. Most of these groups exist to serve the community, so they actually need projects and causes to get involved in. They sponsor fund-raising events not only to raise money but also to get their members motivated and involved and to demonstrate their community spirit. Naturally, a good public image helps them recruit new members.

Their involvement with your school provides you with the opportunity to have other citizens tell your school's story to the community. This grassroots involvement of service clubs and organizations will have dramatic effects, but these groups need your faculty and advisory groups to provide them with specific projects for smaller amounts of money that they can take on as a challenge.

Chapter Five will provide you with information on identifying service clubs and organizations and suggestions on how to approach them.

Review the end-of-chapter checklist.

CHAPTER 4 CHECKLIST

Evaluation and Planning Worksheet

1. **What existing opportunities do you have to increase the "grants I.Q." of your school/ community? (Group gatherings, faculty meetings, speeches, luncheons, Parent Teacher Association meetings, and so on)**

   _____

   _____

   _____

   _____

   _____

   _____

   _____

   _____

   _____

   _____

   _____

   _____

   _____

Table 4.10

SERVICE CLUBS AND ORGANIZATIONS GRANTSEEKERS' MATRIX

These nonprofits include service organizations, Hellenic groups, and business and professional organizations. They are ready and willing grantmakers, provide linkages to friends that you need, and in many cases raise money to grant to your school's projects, programs, and needs. Members of these organizations understand that by donating computers, for example, they increase the quality of education locally but do not increase taxes. Many schools have used them to involve the community in its schools. NOTE: Make a list of your school and community's service clubs and organizations. When and where they meet may be listed on a sign as you enter your community.

Type of Project	Geographic Need	Award Size	School's Image	Credentials of Project Director	Preproposal Contact	Proposal Content	Review & Decision	Proposal Information and Administration
Model/Demonstration—Not much interest in developing and discovering what works	Primary concern of this type of funder is local need	Most are small; up to $10,000	Local perception of your school's ability to serve the community and how the school has implemented other grants is critical	Local credibility is essential. Credibility based on caring about education and kids is more important than publishing	Essential to phone, go see individuals. For many groups the entree is to speak at their meeting to inform them of what you are doing. Remember, a volunteer from your grants advisory committee can do this	Most have a simple 3–4 page application or suggest a letter proposal	Some service clubs have a grants committee or a committee for education of youth that recommends the proposal to the main group for approval	Some organizations produce an annual report that states what activities and groups they have supported. Best source is a linkage or friend who belongs to the group. Follow-up is usually not formal. You can ask to give a result speech one year later, etc.
Research—Little or no interest in studying why something works	How will the grant change things in the community?	"	"	"	"	"	"	"
Equipment—Interested when it shows good cost-benefit ratio and is used by teachers and students	"	"	Concerned about image regarding access to programs and equipment.					
Replication—Interested in implementing what worked in another school	"	"		"	"	"	"	
Consortium—Some interest, but the larger the project the more the cost goes up	"	"	Concerned with record of theft and maintenance					
National/International—Some groups have strong international ties to other countries. German, Polish, African groups might like to sponsor a second site	"	"		"	"	"	"	"

Chapter 5

Finding the Best Funders: Matching Projects to Grantors

ESSENTIALLY, YOUR BEST GRANTOR is the one who values your project enough to fund it. The novice grantseeker may believe the best grantor is the one that offers the easiest, fastest, and shortest road to the money. But to be successful requires that your grants system include the ongoing development and sustenance of mutually beneficial relationships. These are enhanced when your search for funders is based on how you can meet their needs while meeting your school's needs. This should be the basis for identifying and selecting potential grantors. The purpose of this chapter is to provide you with information that enables you to focus on funders whose past granting patterns indicate that your project would be of interest to them. At this point you can see why many well-intended projects designed to help schools meet with failure. Unless the problem and gap are defined in a way that appeals to a grantor, and the project costs and its benefits fit the grantor, you could waste a lot of time.

For example, I have worked with several hundred P–12 schools who have defined their problem as lack of technology and have gone to the largest corporation in town with a list of equipment needs. They received little if anything. They then turned to foundations and got even less.

Only 1.2 percent of foundation grants go to technology, whereas 44 percent go to projects. Not only does this point to the importance of defining the problem correctly, it also indicates that you must word your search efforts carefully or miss your best opportunities.

This chapter describes a variety of sources you can use to search for grantors. Whether you are searching in printed material or computer databases, you generally gain access to grant opportunities by using key search words. For example, if your project is aimed at increasing the reading level of dyslexic children, your key words might include *handicapped, learning disabled, reading, literacy, disadvantaged children,* and so on. Thus the first task of the group that generates potential solutions is to describe them using as many key search words as possible.

To help, provide them with the worksheets shown in Exhibits 5.1 through 5.3.

Expanding the Universe of Grantors Worksheet

Refer to Exhibit 5.1. By increasing your list of key search words you expand your universe of potential funders. At first glance, this may seem counterproductive because you are trying to narrow your list of potential funding sources to the best five or six. But your ultimate goal is to help your staff locate the grantor who is most likely to fund your school's project. By altering your project slightly, you can do the following:

- Expand your list of key search words
- Increase your list of potential funding sources
- More greatly appeal to a particular funding source's values
- Dramatically increase your grants success rate

Exhibit 5.1

EXPANDING THE UNIVERSE OF GRANTORS WORKSHEET

1. **What is the subject area the project will impact?**

_____ Preschool Education	_____ Science Education
_____ Elementary Education	_____ Humanities Education
_____ Middle School Education	_____ Music Education
_____ Health Education	_____ Art Education
_____ Reading Education	_____ Social Studies Education
_____ Other: _____	_____ Other: _____

2. **What problem areas could your project be aimed at affecting?**

_____ Alcohol	_____ Drugs	_____ Handicapped
_____ Adult Literacy	_____ Dropouts	_____ Homeless
_____ Computer Literacy	_____ Gifted and Talented	_____ Immigrants
_____ Disadvantaged	_____ Other: _____	_____ Other: _____

3. **How does your project currently relate to the problem areas identified in question 2?**

_____

_____

_____

_____

_____

(continued)

__Exhibit 5.1 (continued)__

4. **How could the project be changed to relate to other problem areas?**

_____
_____
_____
_____
_____

5. **Type of grant:**
Equipment
Technology
Research
Model/Demonstration
Needs Assessment

6. **Geographic considerations—How could the project be altered to appeal to funders who value:**
   - Local Problems/Solutions?
   - Statewide Problems/Solutions?
   - Regional Problems/Solutions?
   - National Problems/Solutions?
   - International Problems/Solutions?

Key Words Worksheet for Government Grantseeking

This list of search words (Exhibit 5.2) has been taken from key federal grant listings. Your grantseekers should review the list and circle the key words that they could use in their search for government funding sources.

Key Words Worksheet for Foundation and Corporate Grantseeking

This worksheet (Exhibit 5.3) lists some of the key words that can be used to search for nongovernment or private funding sources. Before you begin your search, review this list and circle the words that relate to your project.

Searching for Government Grants

State Grant Funds

Many state grant funds for education come from the federal government, which has an organized, easy-to-track grants system that the states do not. You can find out about federal money to your state by using key search words to uncover related federal grant programs and then checking to see if state education agencies are eligible recipients under the federal regulations. If the funds are distributed in a block grant or according to a formula, you need to talk to your state education department to locate the

---

Exhibit 5.2

KEY WORDS WORKSHEET FOR GOVERNMENT GRANTSEEKING

The federal government uses the following subject index in describing grant opportunities in education. Review the list and indicate the key words that relate to your project. You may find it helpful to make a brief notation of any significant ways you could change your solution to make it relate to that key word.

The following descriptors relate to federal programs dealing with the whole area of education.

Adult Education	Elementary Education	Indian Education
Disadvantaged Education	Health Education	International Education
Early Childhood Education	Humanities Education	Tools for Schools

The following descriptors relate to federal programs dealing with elementary education.

Elementary Education Arts	Handicapped	Neglected and Delinquent
Elementary Education Bilingual	Homeless Children	Physical Fitness
Chapter 1	Immigrant Children	Private Schools
Chapter 2	Impact Aid	School Dropout Prevention
Computer Learning	Math/Science	Talent Search
Disadvantaged/Deprived	Migrant Education	Technology
Drug-Free Schools	Elementary Education Minorities	Upward Bound
Gifted and Talented Students		

---

individual in charge of those funds. This approach gives your grantseekers command of the federal grants process. Once they have it, they will be better received by state granting officials, who are impressed by grantseekers who can say, "A search of federal grant programs related to our school's need in the area of _____ has led us to the state, because federal regulations stipulate you as the recipient of those funds under program _____." By contrast, a novice grantseeker may lose credibility by telephoning the state and saying, "Hi. Do you have any grant funds for _____?"

Contacting state granting officials may require coordination through your school's district grants office (if you have one). It may know of additional state funding opportunities.

Information developed through your webbing and linkage system may lead you to a state contact who can help you initiate your search for state funding. The contact person may not be able grant awards, but he or she may know people in the office who do. This person may have an inside way to get the basic information you need to compete for the funds.

Federal Grant Funds

These funds come from taxes and are therefore subject to freedom of information laws. Using your key search words, you can use several easily accessed data retrieval systems to locate government grant opportunities.

Exhibit 5.3

KEY WORDS WORKSHEET FOR FOUNDATION AND CORPORATE GRANTSEEKING

The following key words are used in many electronic data retrieval systems and printed reference books. Review the list and indicate the key words that relate to your project. You may find it helpful to make a brief notation of any significant changes in your solution in order to relate to that key word.

Adult/Continuing Education Programs

Alternative Modes/Nontraditional Study

Arts Education Programs

Bicultural/Bilingual Education Programs

Biological Sciences Education Programs

Business Education Programs

Career Education Programs

Children/Youth

Cognition/Information Processing

Communications Education Programs

Computer-Assisted Instruction

Computer Science Education Programs

Computer Sciences

Conference Support

Early Childhood/Preschool Education

Educational Counseling/Guidance

Educational Reform

Educational Studies—Developing Countries

Educational Testing/Measurement

Educational Values

Elementary Education

Employment Opportunity Programs

Employment/Labor Studies

Energy Education Programs

English Education Programs

Environmental Studies Education Programs

Fine Arts Education Programs

Foreign Language Education Programs

Foreign Scholars

Gifted Children

Handicapped Education Services

Handicapped Vocational Services

Handicapped/Special Education Programs

Health Education Programs

Humanities Education Programs

Illiteracy

Information Dissemination

International Studies Education Programs

Journalism Education Programs

Learning Disorders/Dyslexia

Mathematics Education Programs

Minority Education Programs

Music Education Programs

Nutrition Education Programs

Opportunities Abroad

Parental Involvement in Education Philosophy

Philosophy of Education

Physical Education Programs

Physical Sciences Education Programs

Precollegiate Education—Arts Education Programs

Precollegiate Education—Bilingual Education Programs

Precollegiate Education—Economics Education Programs

Precollegiate Education—Humanities Education Programs

Precollegiate Education—Professional Development

Precollegiate Education—Science/Math Education Programs

Prizes/Awards

Professional Development

Professional/Faculty Development

Reading Education Programs

Remedial Education

Rural Education

Rural Services

Rural Studies

Teacher Education

Telecommunications—Education Materials

Vocational/Technical Education

Women's Education Programs—Business Management

Women's Education Programs—Science/Engineering

Women's Studies Education Programs

Youth Employment Opportunity Programs

The following list contains databases that explain where federal grants information is generated and what kinds of information are accessible. If someone working in higher education is on your grants advisory committee, ask him or her to use your worksheet for developing solutions (see Exhibits 3.6, 3.7, and 3.8) and key words worksheets to carry out a grants search through the college grants office. Most colleges and universities are users of the Internet and of the following on-line databases.

- **SPIN**—The Sponsored Programs Information Network (SPIN) is a grants database that lists most federal government programs and many foundation and corporate grant opportunities. You do not need to purchase the system if you can work through your local institution of higher education. SPIN was originally developed by the State University of New York's Research Foundation to help the approximately sixty colleges and universities in the New York state system search for grant opportunities. It has since been adapted and marketed to institutions of higher education throughout the United States.

- **IRIS**—You may have a link to someone at a college or university that uses the Illinois Research Information System (IRIS). This database started the same way as SPIN and provides similar information.

- **DIALOG**—Many school and community libraries are connected to the DIALOG database, which has hundreds of useful components. Among these is the ORYX database, which has information on federal grants.

If you have free access to one of these databases, you could begin your search immediately. But first you should know what kinds of data these retrieval systems contain and how the federal grants system operates.

Most grantseekers fear the federal grants process because they do not act proactively. They do not realize that grantseeking does not have to be last-minute, chaotic, and reactive. The best way to develop successful federal proposals and to deal effectively with the pressure of deadlines is to be knowledgeable about the federal grants process and to start early. After working with several school districts, I can assure you that elementary- and middle-school grantseekers can note several federal deadlines a year in advance and take advantage of all available resources to meet deadlines and even submit proposals early. In other words, your grantseekers can learn to develop a controlled approach to federal grantseeking that allows them to carry out their regular responsibilities and still apply for federal funds.

The federal government grants over $85 billion each year in a strictly organized yearly cycle. I refer to this cycle as the *federal grants clock* (see Figure 5.1).

Most federal grantseekers know that application packages are normally sent to prospective grantees four to eight weeks before the completed applications are due and that the grants are usually awarded four to six months after submission. The key to proactive government grantseeking is knowing what else occurs during this time and how your actions can dramatically increase your success rate and decrease the madness associated with trying to meet last-minute deadlines.

Do not wait until you receive an application package. Begin now to increase your grant opportunities and begin developing your school's proposal. *Start early!* To do so you need to have a working knowledge of how the federal grants clock works.

1. The application package is disseminated.

2. Deadline: most grantseekers do not begin their grants work until they receive the application package. This leaves only a short time to work on the proposal before the deadline occurs. The inflexible

Figure 5.1

THE $85 BILLION FEDERAL GRANTS CLOCK™

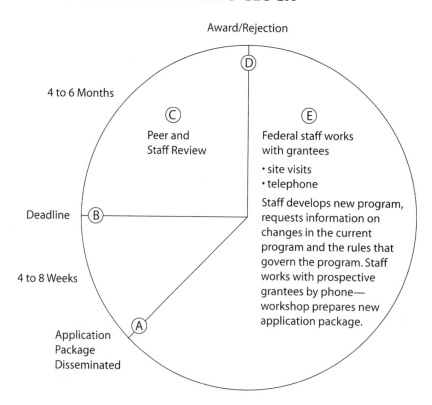

The clock operates Monday through Friday (except federal holidays) 52 weeks per year. The federal government's year begins on October 1 and ends September 30.

federal grants clock chimes on the hour proposals are due, and submitting a proposal five minutes late delays consideration of it for one year!

3. Peer and staff review: proposals are read, scored, and ranked.

4. Award or rejection notices are sent out.

5. During the final phase of the clock, the federal grants staff begins to get ready for another grants cycle and works with the current grantees.

If you understand the predictable and programmed nature of the federal grants clock, you will be able to initiate your school's grantseeking long before the application packages are mailed. To start early, you also need to have a working knowledge of the basic federal grant information publications—the *Catalog of Federal Domestic Assistance* (CFDA) and the *Federal Register.*

The Catalog of Federal Domestic Assistance

Produced in the fall of each year, the CFDA lists the 1,300+ programs that disseminate approximately $85 billion in grants annually and provides the grantseeker with all sorts of valuable information, including deadlines.

You may purchase the CFDA from the Superintendent of Documents, U.S. Government Printing Office (telephone 202-212-1800) for under $100. However, the CFDA is also provided free to at least two libraries in each congressional district. Your congressperson should know which libraries have been designated as Federal Depository Libraries. In addition to these designated libraries, most public libraries have a copy, as do college and university libraries and grants offices. The CFDA is also available on the Internet. All 1,400 plus programs can be accessed on-line. In fact, the Department of Education has a search tool on its website that includes the CFDA. Go to www.ed.gov and click on the Programs and Services icon. You will find a link there to the CFDA that is updated fairly often.

There are many reasons to use the CFDA, the first and foremost being that it gives you access to $85 billion in grant funds. But even if you are planning to pursue only foundation or corporate grants, you should be knowledgeable about existing federal programs in your project area. So armed, you are better able to explain to a prospective private grantor why you are approaching it instead of a federal agency. For instance, if you know for certain that there are no federal funds designated for your project area or that federal funding is limited to three projects in your field across the entire country, it will be easier for you to demonstrate why private grant support is so necessary.

The most efficient way to locate the granting agencies that are your best opportunities is to compare the key search words you circled on your Key Words Worksheets with the indexes in the CFDA. The CFDA has five indexes.

- Deadline Index: this is not very useful when you are searching for education-related grants, because the Department of Education does not publish many program deadlines early in the federal year.

- Applicant Eligibility Index: this allows you to determine which granting programs are restricted to state applicants and which are designated for local education agencies, such as your school district. If your project falls under a granting program restricted to state recipients, check with your state education department to determine how the previous year's funds were allocated.

- Agency Program Index: this lists all programs in numerical order by five-digit codes. There are 164 Department of Education programs listed in this index.

- Functional Index: there are 20 basic functional categories of federal support and 176 subgroupings. Under education there are 23 subgroupings. Elementary and secondary education have two references.

- Subject Index: this is the most useful index for locating both Department of Education grant opportunities and those in other departments with an interest in education.

For example, assume that your school has a project idea related to the use of parent-teacher-student involvement through electronic interface. When searching for federal grant opportunities for this project, your grantseekers could use "educational technology," "elementary education," and "telecommunications" as their key search words and look in the CFDA's indexes for program matches. By looking in the Functional and Subject indexes they could match your school's interests with federal programs—for example, the CFDA 84.303 Technology Challenge Grants.

Exhibit 5.4 is a reproduction of CFDA 84.303 from the catalogue. The information contained in the CFDA is crucial to a proactive grantseeking system and in enabling you to start the grantseeking process early. It will also help you make preproposal contact with the appropriate funding agency.

Exhibit 5.4

(1) **84.303 TECHNOLOGY CHALLENGE GRANTS**

(2) **FEDERAL AGENCY: ASSISTANT SECRETARY FOR EDUCATION RESEARCH, STATISTICS, AND IMPROVEMENT, DEPARTMENT OF EDUCATION**

(3) **AUTHORIZATION:** Elementary and Secondary Education Act of 1965, Title III, Part A, Section 3136, as amended, 20 U.S.C. 6846.

(4) **OBJECTIVES:** The grants under this program support the development, interconnection, implementation, improvement, and maintenance of an effective educational technology infrastructure, including activities to provide equipment, training for teachers, school library and media personnel, and technical support. The primary goals of the program are to promote the use of technology to support school reform, support network and telecommunication connections to improve student learning, and support professional development in the integration of high-quality technology into the school curriculum.

(5) **TYPES OF ASSISTANCE:** Project Grants (Discretionary).

(6) **USES AND USE RESTRICTIONS:** Priority is given to applications that (1) serve areas with a high percentage of disadvantaged students or with the greatest need for educational technology and directly benefit students; (2) ensure ongoing, sustained, professional development to further the use of technology in schools; (3) ensure effective and sustainable use of the technologies acquired; and (4) contribute substantial financial and other resources to achieve the goals of the project.

(7) **ELIGIBILITY REQUIREMENTS:**
Applicant Eligibility: Consortia may apply. Consortia must include at least one local educational agency (LEA) with a high percentage or number of children living below the poverty line and may include other LEAs, state educational agencies, institutions of higher education, businesses, academic content experts, software designers, museums, libraries, or other entities.
Beneficiary Eligibility: Elementary and secondary education students and teachers benefit.
Credentials/Documentation: None.

(8) **APPLICATION AND AWARD PROCESS:**
Preapplication Coordination: This program is eligible for coverage under E.O. 12372, "Intergovernmental Review of Federal Programs." An applicant should consult the office or official designated as the single point of contact in his or her state for more information on the process the state requires to be followed in applying for assistance, if the state has selected the program for review.
Application Procedure: Application forms and instructions are available from the program office. Application deadlines and other information for applicants are published in the *Federal Register*. Contact the program office for information.
Award Procedure: Awards are competitively selected following review by nonfederal experts and by program staff. The Assistant Secretary for the Office of Educational Research and Improvement approves the selection. Information on the award process is available from the program office.
Deadlines: Applicant deadlines and other information for applicants are published as a notice in the *Federal Register*. The deadline notice is included in the application package.
Range of Approval/Disapproval Time: The estimated time is 120 days.
Appeals: Not applicable.
Renewals: As required by the Education Department General Administrative Regulations (EDGAR) for direct grant programs (see 34 CFR 75.253). Generally, for multiple-year awards, continuation awards after the first budget period are made if: sufficient funds have been appropriated; the recipient has either made substantial progress in meeting the goals of the project or obtained approval for changes in the project; the recipient has submitted all required reports; and continuation is in the best interest of the government.

(continued)

Exhibit 5.4 (continued)

⑨ **ASSISTANCE CONSIDERATIONS:**

Formula and Matching Requirements: None.

Length and Time Phasing of Assistance: After an initial 12-month competitively selected award, four additional years may be awarded. The maximum length of time an award may last is five years. Awards are subject to the availability of funds.

⑩ **POST ASSISTANCE REQUIREMENTS:**

Reports: As required by the Education Department General Administrative Regulations (EDGAR) for direct programs (34 CFR 75). Generally, annual performance and financial reports are required. Reporting will be included in the grant award document.

Audits: See 34 CFR 74.26. Institutions of higher education and nonprofit organizations are subject to the audit requirements of OMB Circular No. A-133. State and local governments are subject to the requirements in the Single Audit Act and the Department of Education regulations implementing OMB Circular No. A-128.

Records: As required by EDGAR, for direct grant programs (34 CFR 75). Generally, records related to grant funds, compliance, and performance must be maintained for a period of five years after completion. As required by EDGAR, to maintain appropriate records and related grant funds.

⑪ **FINANCIAL INFORMATION:**

Account Identification: 18-1100-0-1-503.

Obligations: (Grants) FY 96 $38,000,000; FY 97 est $56,965,000; and FY 98 est $75,000,000.

Range and Average of Financial Assistance: $500,000 to $2,000,000 per year (average $1,000,000 per year) for five years.

⑫ **PROGRAM ACCOMPLISHMENTS:** Almost 600 applications were received and 24 grants were made in fiscal year 1996. 19 additional grants were continued. Approximately 300 districts participated in the program in fiscal year 1996.

⑬ **REGULATIONS, GUIDELINES, AND LITERATURE:** Education Department General Administrative Regulations (EDGAR), 34 CFR 74, 75, 77, 78, 79, 80, 81, 82, 85, and 86. Information on regulations are included in the application package and are available from the program office.

⑭ **INFORMATION CONTACTS:**

Regional or Local Office: Not applicable.

Headquarters Office: Challenge Grants for Technology in Education, Office of Educational Research and Improvement, 555 New Jersey Avenue, NW, Washington, DC 2028-5544. Contact: Thomas Carroll, Director, Challenge Grants Program, Telephone: (202) 208-3882.

⑮ **RELATED PROGRAMS:** None.

⑯ **EXAMPLES OF FUNDED PROJECTS:** A project in Towanda, PA uses interactive video-conferencing to provide services to 23 small rural school districts serving 45,000 students in PA, NY, and NJ. A project in Waukegan is promoting improved learning in math and science for 7,000 students in grades 4 through 12 by the use of multimedia computers in classrooms and Internet connections. In addition, the project is establishing technology learning community centers for students and adults to access job opportunities.

⑰ **CRITERIA FOR SELECTING PROPOSALS:** Applications are reviewed on the basis of their significance and feasibility. Detailed selection criteria are included in the application package.

CFDA 84.303 Technology Challenge Grants

Let's consider each part of the Technology Challenge Grants entry in more depth. Numbers have been inserted in Exhibit 5.4 to match the following comments.

1. *Program Title:* Technology Challenge Grants

2. *Federal Agency:* This informs you which arm of the government handles the program. Like this one, many grant programs are sponsored by the Department of Education, but you may also apply to the National Science Foundation, the National Endowment for the Arts, and so on.

3. *Authorization:* This tells you the source of the funding.

4. *Objectives:* This section provides you with the first indication of the appropriateness of your idea in relationship to the funding program.

5. *Types of Assistance:* You must know what types of assistance are provided to determine if the federal program is interested in funding projects or research or if they fund on a formula basis that allocates the funds to eligible recipients through predetermined criteria.

6. *User and Use Restrictions:* These help you to further determine if the program is an appropriate source of funds for your project.

7. *Eligibility Requirements:*

    - Applicant Eligibility—This section tells you if your school is an eligible recipient. You are designated as a Local Educational Agency (LEA). If your school is not eligible for funding under this program, this section will provide you with the information you need to determine whom you should develop a relationship with so that you can submit your proposal through their organization.

    - Beneficiary Eligibility—This section tells you the type of individual or organization that is intended to benefit from the project.

    - Credentials/Documentation—The Office of Management and Budget (OMB) publishes several management booklets that outline the rules for requesting, spending, and documenting expenditures under a federal grant.

8. *Application and Award Process:*

- Preapplication Coordination—This section outlines the OMB requirements related to your state's review and knowledge of your proposal. If you have a district grants office, it will know who to contact in your state office concerning this matter.

- Application Procedure—This describes the rules for submitting applications.

- Award Procedure—This section informs you who will review and approve your proposal. Proposals submitted to this particular program will be read by program staff and nonfederal experts.

- Deadlines—Deadlines are published in the *Federal Register* (described in the section following this CFDA example).

- Range of Approval/Disapproval Time—Period between submittal and notification of approval or disapproval. In this example, the estimated time is 120 days.

- Appeals—In this case there is no procedure for appealing the grantor's decision. Some federal programs have a specific appeal procedure.

- Renewals—This information is important when you are planning a project that may take several years.

9. *Assistance Considerations:*

- Formula and Matching Requirements—This section outlines what portion of the project's costs will be borne by your school district. If applicable, it is vital that you have a plan for the match and your school district's endorsement that it will commit this share. In this example, there are no formula or matching requirements.

- Length and Time Phasing of Assistance—The length of the project period. In this case, after an initial year, four additional years may be awarded.

10. *Post Assistance Requirements:* Your district will be required to make reports and maintain records and may be subject to audits. Don't let this section scare you. Your business office will handle it.

11. *Financial Information:*

- Account Identification—Account identification number

- Obligations—By reviewing this section you can determine if the program is slated to increase or decrease its funding level.

Note: It is estimated that the 1998 budget for this program will be $75 million, but this figure could be changed dramatically by Congress. In this example, program funds went up.

- Range and Average of Financial Assistance—In 1996, the range was $500,000 to $2 million for five years, with an average of $1 million per year. This should tell you that this program is not your best choice if your project request is $25,000 per year.

12. *Program Accomplishments:* This section provides you with important information on previously selected grantees and on the number of awards made in the past. In this case, twenty-four grants were made in fiscal 1996. This section will also inform you if the program is being phased out. For example, it may say "no new awards."

13. *Regulations, Guidelines, and Literature:* This section tells you where the rules and guidelines can be found and what administrative regulation they will follow. Most of the rules pertain to your district personnel and business office. Compliance should be discussed with your district grants office or administration.

14. *Information Contacts:*
- Regional or Local Office—Most regional offices were closed during the federal cutbacks of the early 1980s.
- Headquarters Office—This section provides the contact name, address, and phone number you will need if you select this funder as a possible source.

15. *Related Programs:* This section lists the CFDA names and codes of other sources of funds that have similar target populations and objectives. In this case none are listed.

16. *Examples of Funded Projects:* This section provides a sample of the solutions that the grantor valued highly enough to fund.

17. *Criteria for Selecting Proposals:* This section tells you where the criteria that the agency will follow in its evaluation procedure can be found. Each agency has its own criteria, and criteria may differ between programs. In this case, selection criteria are included in the application package.

The Federal Register

The *Federal Register* can be described as the federal government's daily newspaper. A free copy can be found in your congressionally designated federal depository library. If you think that reading this publication will cause you a severe case of cognitive overload, you are correct. But wait: you should not be reading this publication daily, nor should your teachers. You only need to know the purpose of the *Register* as it relates to federal grantseeking and how to use this publication to increase your knowledge of the grants cycle.

The *Register* provides the government with a mechanism to announce new opportunities for federal funding and to invite comments on what the rules should be. If Congress and the president establish new grant programs for elementary and junior high schools, the first announcement will be in this publication to invite comments on the rules that will govern the programs.

In addition, the *Register* is used to announce deadlines and to solicit feedback on the grant rules that governed the previous year's grant solicitation and award process. It is not unusual for a federal agency to print last year's rules for granting funds in the *Register* six months before the next deadline to solicit the public's opinions on the way the grants were awarded the previous year.

The public is usually given thirty days to comment on the rules. The agency reviews the comments and based on them may make changes in the rules. The public is then allowed another thirty days to comment on the changes before the final rules are printed. As these rules will govern the program's priorities and the scoring or review system, they provide valuable insight into exactly what the agency is looking for. The important point is that the proactive grantseeker needs to have advance knowledge of the information that the *Federal Register* provides.

Now that you are aware of this process, you can give your grantseekers a strong advantage over the competition. You now know that there is no need for them to wait until they receive a formal application package. They can take the initiative and telephone a federal program officer to ask when information on the rules and the deadline was printed in the *Federal Register*. This will provide them enough data to decide on the appropriateness of that grant program opportunity for their project ideas. If they decide it is appropriate, they can begin to position themselves to receive a grant.

With information from the CFDA and the *Federal Register,* the principal is placed in the grants information loop. Before you or your grantseekers begin to write or telephone federal grant program officers listed in the CFDA and *Register,* read Chapter Six, which contains information on making preproposal contact. The point here is that there is no reason to wait until four weeks before the deadline to get started. Of greater importance to you, the principal, is that your decision on which grantors to approach and how to approach them will have a dramatic effect on your role in your grants system. If *your* name is placed on federal mailing lists, you must accept responsibility for the prompt and efficient forwarding of grant information to your staff. Finish reading this book to ensure that you select and incorporate into your grants plan the functions that best fit your administrative role and style.

You and your classroom leaders can use your new knowledge concerning the two most basic federal grants publications to look like grants pros. For example, assume that your grantseekers have used their key search words and the CFDA indexes to determine that CFDA 84.303 Technology Challenge Grants looks like a likely funding source for your school's project. Your grantseeker or project director could contact Thomas Carroll, the information contact listed in the CFDA, to ask if the deadline has been announced yet and, if it hasn't, when he thinks it will appear in the *Federal Register.* They could also ask if any relevant notices have been published in the *Register,* such as comments on the rules and so on.

For example, suppose one of your teachers contacted Mr. Carroll in December and was told that the notice to invite applicants was to be printed in January and that the application deadline was expected to be March. Clearly, you would gain both an advantage over your competitors and significant insight by consulting the January *Federal Register.* Review the sample entry from the *Register* in Exhibit 5.5. Using the guide numbers on the left in the exhibit, consider the explanations of each section in the sample entry that follow.

1. *CFDA Number:* You now know that all 1,400 plus federal programs are referred to by a CFDA number.

2. *Program Title and Purpose of the Notice:* This section states the title of the program and whether the purpose of the notice is to invite applications, solicit comments, publish final rules, and so on.

3. *Purpose of the Program:* This section gives a brief description of the aim of the program.

4. *Eligible Applicants:* This section tells you of any changes that may have occurred since the comments on the rules were made. For example, if funding community organizations has proven disastrous in the past, the rules regarding eligibility may have changed, and in this granting cycle only local educational agencies may be eligible.

5. *Deadline for Receipt of Applications:* This is the last date on which the current year's applications will be accepted.

Exhibit 5.5

SAMPLE FEDERAL REGISTER ENTRY

Department of Education

(1) **[CFDA No. 84.303A]**

(2) **Technology Innovation Challenge Grants; Notice Inviting Applications For New Awards for Fiscal Year (FY) 1998**

(3) **Purpose of Program:** The Technology Innovation Challenge Grant Program provides grants to consortia that are working to improve and expand new applications of technology to strengthen school reform efforts, improve student achievement, and provide for sustained professional development of teachers, administrators, and school library media personnel. In FY 1998, the Technology Innovation Challenge Grant Program will focus on professional development by providing support to consortia that have developed programs or are adapting or expanding existing programs, for technology training for teachers and other educators to improve instruction.

(4) **Eligible Applicants:** Only consortia may receive grants under this program. A consortium must include at least one local educational agency (LEA) with a high percentage or number of children living below the poverty line. A consortium may also include other LEAs, private schools, state educational agencies, institutions of higher education, businesses, academic content experts, software designers, museums, libraries, and other appropriate entities. *Note:* In each consortium a participating LEA shall submit the application on behalf of the consortium and serve as the fiscal agent for the grant.

(5) *Deadline For Receipt of Applications:* May 29, 1998.

(6) *Deadline For Intergovernmental Review:* July 29, 1998.

(7) *Applications Available:* March 31, 1998.

(8) *Estimated Available Funds:* $30,000,000.

(9) *Estimated Range of Awards:* $1,000,000 to $2,000,000 per year.

(10) *Estimated Average Size of Awards:* $1,500,000 per year.

(11) *Estimated Number of Awards:* 20.

(12) *Project Period:* 5 years. Please note that all applicants for multi-year awards are required to provide detailed budget information for the total grant period requested. The Department will negotiate at the time of the initial award the funding levels for each year of the grant award.
Note: The Department of Education is not bound by any estimates in this notice.

(13) *Maximum Award:* The Secretary will not consider an application that proposes a budget exceeding $2,000,000 for one or more 12-month budget periods.

(14) *Applicable Regulations:* (a) the Education Department General Administrative Regulations (EDGAR) in 34 CFR Parts 74, 75 (except 34 CFR 75.102(b), 75.200(b)(3), 75.210, and 75.217), 77, 79, 80, 81, 82, 85, and 86, and (b) 34 CFR Part 299.

(15) *Priorities:* The absolute and invitational priorities in the notice of final priority and selection criteria for this program, as published elsewhere in this issue of the *Federal Register,* apply to this competition.

(16) **Selection Criteria:** The selection criteria in the notice of final priority and selection criteria for this program, as published elsewhere in this issue of the *Federal Register,* apply to this competition.

(17) **Other Requirements:** The procedures for evaluation and selection of applications in the notice of final selection criteria, selection procedures, and application procedures for Technology Innovation Challenge Grants, published in the *Federal Register* on May 12, 1997 (62 FR 26175), apply to this competition.

(18) **supplementary information:** The Technology Innovation Challenge Grant Program is authorized under Title III, section 3136, of the Elementary and Secondary Education Act of 1965, as amended (20 U.S.C. 6846). The statute authorizes the use of funds for activities similar to the following activities:

Exhibit 5.5 (continued)

(a) Developing, adapting, or expanding existing and new applications of technology to support the school reform effort.

(h) Providing ongoing professional development in the integration of quality educational technologies into school curriculum and long-term planning for implementing educational technologies.

(c) Funding projects of sufficient size and scope to improve student learning and, as appropriate, support professional development, and provide administrative support.

(d) Acquiring connectivity linkages, resources, and services, including the acquisition of hardware and software, for use by teachers, students, and school library media personnel in the classroom or in school library media centers, in order to improve student learning by supporting the instructional program offered and to ensure that students in schools will have meaningful access on a regular basis to such linkages, resources, and services.

(e) Acquiring connectivity with wide area networks for purposes of accessing information and educational programming sources, particularly with institutions of higher education and public libraries.

(f) Providing educational services for adults and families.

Note: Section 14503 of the Elementary and Secondary Education Act of 1965, as amended (20 U.S.C. 8893), is applicable to the Technology Innovation Challenge Grant Program. Section 14503 requires that an LEA, SEA, or educational service agency receiving financial assistance under this program must provide private school children and teachers, on an equitable basis, special educational services or other program benefits under this program. The section further requires SEAs, LEAs, and educational service agencies to consult with private school officials during the design and development of the Technology Innovation Challenge Grant projects. Each application must describe the ways in which the proposed project will address the needs of private school children and teachers.

⑲ **Application Deadline:** In order to ensure timely receipt and process of applicants, an application must be received on or before the deadline date announced in this application notice. The Secretary will not consider an application for funding if it is not received by the deadline date unless the applicant can show proof that the application was: (1) sent by registered or certified mail not later than five days before the deadline date, or (2) sent by commercial carrier not later than two days before the deadline date. An applicant must show proof of mailing in accordance with 34 CFR 75.102(d) and (e). Applications delivered by hand must be received by 4:30 p.m. (Eastern Time) on the deadline date. For the purposes of this program competition, the Secretary does not apply 34 CFR 75.102(a) and (b)(1) which require an application to be mailed, rather than received, by the deadline date.

Note: All applications must be received on or before the deadline date unless one of the mailing conditions noted in the previous paragraph applies. This requirement takes exception to EDGAR, 34 CFR 75.102(a) and (b)(1). In accordance with the Administrative Procedure Act (5 U.S.C. 553), it is the practice of the Secretary to offer interested parties the opportunity to comment on proposed regulations. However, this amendment makes procedural changes only and does not establish new substantive policy. Therefore, under 5 U.S.C. 553(b)(A), proposed rulemaking is not required.

⑳ **for applications or information contact:** For applications, telephone 1-800-USA-LEARN (1-800-872-5327) or fax requests to Sharon Morgan at (202) 208-4042.

The application package is also available from the Technology Innovation Challenge Grant web site at: http://www.ed.gov/Technology/chalgrnt.html. For information contact Technology Innovation Challenge Grants, U.S. Department of Education, Washington, D.C. 20208-5544. Telephone (202) 208-3882.

Individuals who use a telecommunications device for the deaf (TDD) may call the Federal Information Relay Service (FIRS) at 1-800-877-8339 between 8 a.m. and 8 p.m. Eastern time, Monday through Friday.

Individuals with disabilities may obtain this document in an alternate format (e.g., Braille, large print, audiotape, or computer diskette) on request to the contact person identified in this notice.

(continued)

Exhibit 5.5 (continued)

Individuals with disabilities may obtain a copy of the application package in an alternate format, also, by contacting that person. However, the Department is not able to reproduce in an alternate format the standard forms included in the application package.

㉑ **Electronic Access to This Document:** Anyone may view this document, as well as all other Department of Education documents published in the **Federal Register**, in text or portable document format (PDF) on the World Wide Web at either of the following sites:

http.//gcs.ed.gov/fedreg.html
http://www.ed.gov/news.html

To use the PDF you must have the Adobe Acrobat Reader Program with Search, which is available free at either of the previous sites. If you have questions about using the PDF, call the U.S. Government Printing Office toll free at 1-888-293-6498.

Anyone may also view these documents in text copy only on an electronic bulletin board of the Department. Telephone: (202) 219-1511 or, toll free, 1-800-222-4922. The documents are located under Option G-Files/Announcements, Bulletins and Press Releases.

Note: The official version of a document is the document published in the Federal Register.

(Catalog of Federal Domestic Assistance Number 84.303A, Technology Innovation Challenge Grants)

Program Authority: 20 U.S.C. 6846.
Dated: February 28, 1998.
Ricky T. Takai,
Acting Assistant Secretary for Educational Research and Improvement.
[FR Doc. 98-5735 Filed 3-4-98; 8:45 a.m.]
BILLING CODE 4000-01-P

---

6. *Deadline for Intergovernmental Review:* After your school submits its application to the federal government, a copy of it must be sent to your state's "single point of contact" with a request that he or she send the necessary comments to the federal agency by the deadline for intergovernmental review.

7. *Applications Available:* This is the date when the application package will be available. You are already ahead of the game at this point, and the following chapters will have more suggestions for getting even further ahead.

8. *Estimated Available Funds:* This is not a final figure, but it will give you a good estimate of the total amount of funding available. If the figure is significantly different from the one in the CFDA, you will know that the program is either in favor or falling out of favor. You can adjust your grants strategy accordingly.

9. *Estimated Range of Awards:* These high and low figures will help you select which of your solutions best matches the size of the expected award.

10. *Estimated Average Size of Awards:* This information gives you more focus on the average size of awards. If you envision securing $25,000 for your project and the program's estimated average size of awards is $500,000, you need to discuss the appropriateness of your project with the program officer.

11. *Estimated Number of Awards:* This figure gives you insight into how intense the competition for funding might be. In the sample entry, twenty awards throughout the entire United States is not very many, but you will discover that some other programs expect to make even fewer awards.

12. *Project Period:* This is the time allotted for support. In this case, the project period is five years. Therefore, you would have to project your objectives and measurement indicators for a five-year period.

13. *Maximum Award:* This provides you with the largest award size that will be considered within the budget periods.

14. *Applicable Regulations:* This refers to the Department of Education's grant policies that must be followed. This information is usually repeated in the application package, but by having access to it early you can control your time and use the federal grants clock efficiently.

15. *Priorities:* This section tells you where you can find the final priority and selection criteria for this program. Reviewing these will help you select the solution that will obtain the highest ranking.

16. *Selection Criteria:* Again, this section tells you where you can find the selection criteria that applies to this competition.

17. *Other Requirements:* This section states where the procedures for evaluation and the criteria for the selection of applications can be found. Once you find these items review them carefully. Make sure you are aware of how the points and weights are designated in evaluating the applications for funds and review the information to determine whether extra points will be given for special priorities.

18. *Supplementary Information:* This provides you with information on what types of activities the statute authorizes for the use of funds.

19. *Application Deadline:* This provides the rules concerning deadlines.

20. *For Applications or Information Contact:* This provides information on how to obtain application packages and how individuals with disabilities can obtain these documents.

21. *Electronic Access to This Document:* This provides information on how this document can be accessed via computer.

Searching for Foundation Grantors

The U.S. Justice Department investigated foundations in the late 1960s and raised many questions concerning some foundations' policy of keeping information on their granting patterns secret from the public. One result of these investigations was a renewed effort on the part of foundations to provide timely and accurate data on their granting programs. In fact, foundation grants were used to initiate and support a network of library collections of foundation information. The Foundation Center's National Collections now offer the best available selection of information on foundation and corporate grants. The national collections are located in New York City and Washington, D.C. To assist nonprofit organizations that are not able to gain access to the national collections, field offices are located in San Francisco, Cleveland, and Atlanta and cooperating collections have been established in libraries, community foundations, and even some nonprofit agencies throughout the United States. The organizations that house the cooperating collections do not get paid to do so, although they do receive the publications for free. Use the list in Exhibit 5.6 to locate the collection closest to you.

The Foundation Center publishes several popular reference materials on foundations, including the *Foundation Directory*. Available at your Foundation Center Regional Library, the *Foundation Directory*, published each year, is the most important single reference work available on grant-making foundations in the United States. To be included in the *Directory*, a foundation must either have assets of at least $2 million or make grants in excess of $200,000 annually. Over 8,600 of the existing foundations have met one of these criteria and are included in the *Directory*. Although fewer than one-fifth of all foundations are in this book, those that are hold over $246 billion in assets.

The Foundation Directory, Part 2: A Guide to Grant Programs $50,000 to $200,000 is another very important publication. It lists over 4,900 foundations.

Both parts of the *Directory* are indexed according to foundation name, subject area, geographic region, type of support, and key officials:

- *Foundation Name:* If you know the name of a foundation that may be interested in elementary or middle-school education, you can locate it in the directories using this index. The index entry itself will provide you with one crucial piece of information—the state in which the foundation is registered. You need to know this to locate the foundation in the directories, as the entries are in alphabetical order by state.

Exhibit 5.6

FOUNDATION CENTER COOPERATING COLLECTIONS

The Foundation Center is an independent national service organization established by foundations to provide an authoritative source of information on foundation and corporate giving. The New York, Washington, D.C., Atlanta, Cleveland, and San Francisco reference collections operated by the Foundation Center offer a wide variety of services and comprehensive collections of information on foundations and grants. Cooperating Collections are libraries, community foundations, and other nonprofit agencies that provide a core collection of Foundation Center publications and a variety of supplementary materials and services in areas useful to grantseekers. The core collection consists of:

THE FOUNDATION DIRECTORY 1 AND 2, AND
    SUPPLEMENT
THE FOUNDATION 1000
FOUNDATION FUNDAMENTALS
FOUNDATION GIVING
THE FOUNDATION GRANTS INDEX

THE FOUNDATION GRANTS INDEX
    QUARTERLY
FOUNDATION GRANTS TO INDIVIDUALS
GUIDE TO U.S. FOUNDATIONS, THEIR TRUSTEES,
    OFFICERS, AND DONORS
THE FOUNDATION CENTER'S GUIDE TO
    PROPOSAL WRITING

NATIONAL DIRECTORY OF CORPORATE
    GIVING
NATIONAL DIRECTORY OF GRANTMAKING
    PUBLIC CHARITIES
NATIONAL GUIDE TO FUNDING IN … (SERIES)
USER-FRIENDLY GUIDE

All five Center libraries have FC Search The Foundation Center's Database on CD-ROM available for patron use, and most Cooperating Collections have it as well, as noted by the symbol (+). Also, many of the network members make available for public use sets of private foundation information returns (IRS Form 99-PF) for their state and/or neighboring states noted by the symbol (*). A complete set of U.S. foundation returns can be found at the New York and Washington D.C., offices of the Foundation Center. The Atlanta, Cleveland, and San Francisco offices contain IRS Form 990-PF returns for the southeastern, midwestern, and western states respectively. Because the collections vary in their hours, materials, and services, it's recommended that you call the collection in advance. To check on new locations or current holdings, call toll-free 1-800-424-9836, or visit our Web site at http://fdncenter.org/library/library.html.

Participants in the Foundation Center's Cooperating Collections network are libraries or nonprofit information centers that provide fundraising information and other funding-related technical assistance in their communities. Cooperating Collections agree to provide free public access to a basic collection of Foundation Center publications during a regular schedule of hours, offering free funding research guidance to all visitors. Many also provide a variety of services for local nonprofit organizations, using staff or volunteers to prepare special materials, organize workshops, or conduct orientations.

The Foundation Center welcomes inquiries from libraries or information centers in the U.S. interested in providing this type of public information service. If you are interested in establishing a funding information library for the use of nonprofit organizations in your area or in learning more about the program, please write to: Rich Romeo, Coordinator of Cooperating Collections, The Foundation Center, 79 Fifth Avenue, New York, NY 10003-3076.

REFERENCE COLLECTIONS OPERATED BY THE FOUNDATION CENTER

THE FOUNDATION CENTER
8th Floor
79 Fifth Ave.
New York, NY 10003
(212) 620-4230

THE FOUNDATION CENTER
312 Sutter St., Rm. 312
San Francisco, CA 94108
(415) 397-0902

THE FOUNDATION CENTER
1001 Connecticut Ave., NW
Washington, DC 20036
(202) 331-1400

THE FOUNDATION CENTER
Kent H. Smith Library
1422 Euclid, Suite 1356
Cleveland, OH 44115
(216) 861-1933

THE FOUNDATION CENTER
Suite 150, Grand Lobby
Hurt Bldg., 50 Hurt Plaza
Atlanta, GA 30303
(404) 880-0094

ALABAMA

BIRMINGHAM PUBLIC LIBRARY*+
Government Documents
2100 Park Place
Birmingham 35203
(205) 226-3600

HUNTSVILLE PUBLIC LIBRARY+
915 Monroe St.
Huntsville 35801
(205) 532-5940

UNIVERSITY OF SOUTH ALABAMA*
Library Building
Mobile 36688
(205) 460-7025

AUBURN UNIVERSITY AT
MONTGOMERY LIBRARY*+
7300 University Dr.
Montgomery 36117-3596
(205) 244-3653

ALASKA

UNIVERSITY OF ALASKA AT
ANCHORAGE*+
Library
3211 Providence Dr.
Anchorage 99508
(907) 786-1848

JUNEAU PUBLIC LIBRARY+
Reference
292 Marine Way
Juneau 99801
(907) 586-5267

ARIZONA

PHOENIX PUBLIC LIBRARY*+
Information Services Department
1221 N. Central
Phoenix 85004
(602) 262-4636

TUCSON PIMA LIBRARY*+
101 N. Stone Ave.
Tucson 87501
(520) 791-4010

ARKANSAS

WESTARK COMMUNITY COLLEGE-
BORHAM LIBRARY*+
5210 Grand Ave.
Ft. Smith 72913
(501) 788-7200

CENTRAL ARKANSAS
LIBRARY SYSTEM*+
700 Louisiana
Little Rock 72201
(501) 370-5952

PINE BLUFF-JEFFERSON COUNTY
LIBRARY SYSTEM
200 E Eighth
Pine Bluff 71601
(501) 534-2159

CALIFORNIA

HUMBOLDT AREA FOUNDATION*+
P.O. Box 99
Bayside 95524
(707) 442-2993

VENTURA COUNTY COMMUNITY
FOUNDATION*+
Funding and Information Resource
Center
1355 Del Norte Rd.,
Suite 150
Camarillo 93030
(805) 988-0196

FRESNO REGIONAL FOUNDATION+
Nonprofit Advancement Ctr
1999 Tuolumne St., Suite 650
Fresno 93721
(209) 498-3929

CALIFORNIA COMMUNITY
FOUNDATION*+
Funding Information Center
606 S. Olive St., Suite 2400
Los Angeles 90014-1526
(213) 413-4042

EAST BAY RESOURCE CENTER FOR
NONPROFIT SUPPORT+
1203 Preservation Pkwy., Suite 100
Oakland 94612
(510) 834-1010

GRANT & RESOURCE CENTER OF
NORTHERN CALIFORNIA*+
Building C, Suite A
2280 Benton Dr.
Redding 96003
(916) 244-1219

LOS ANGELES PUBLIC LIBRARY
West Valley Regional Banch Library
19036 Van Owen St.
Reseda 91335
(818) 345-4393

RIVERSIDE PUBLIC LIBRARY
3581 Mission Inn Ave.
Riverside 92501
(909) 782-5202

(continued)

Exhibit 5.6 (continued)

NONPROFIT RESOURCE CENTER+
Sacramento Public Library
828 I St., 2nd Floor
Sacramento 95814
(916) 264-2772

SAN DIEGO FOUNDATION*+
Funding Information Center
1420 Kettner Blvd., Suite 500
San Diego 92101
(619) 239-8815

NONPROFIT DEVELOPMENT
CENTER+
1922 The Alameda, Suite 212
San Jose 95126
(408) 248-9505

PENINSULA COMMUNITY
FOUNDATION*+
Peninsula Nonprofit Center
1700 S. El Camino Real, R201
San Mateo 94402-3049
(650) 358-9392

LOS ANGELES PUBLIC LIBRARY+
San Pedro Regional Branch
9131 S. Gaffey St.
San Pedro 90731
(310) 548-7779

VOLUNTEER CENTER OF GREATER
ORANGE COUNTY+
Nonprofit Management Assistance
Center
1901 E. 4th St., Ste. 100
Santa Ana 92705
(714) 953-1655

SANTA BARBARA PUBLIC LIBRARY+
40 E. Anapamu St.
Santa Barbara 93101
(805) 962-7653

SANTA MONICA PUBLIC LIBRARY+
1343 Sixth St.
Santa Monica 90401-1603
(310) 458-8600

SONOMA COUNTY LIBRARY+
3rd & E Sts.
Santa Rosa 95404
(707) 545-0831

SEASIDE BRANCH LIBRARY+
550 Harcourt St.
Seaside 93955
(408) 899-8131

COLORADO

EL POMAR NONPROFIT RESOURCE
CENTER+
1661 Mesa Ave.
Colorado Springs 80906
(800) 554-7711

DENVER PUBLIC LIBRARY*+
General Reference
10 West 14th Ave. Pkwy.
Denver 80204
(303) 640-6200

CONNECTICUT

DANBURY PUBLIC LIBRARY+
170 Main St.
Danbury 06810
(203) 797-4527

GREENWICH LIBRARY*+
101 Putnam Ave.
Greenwich 06830
(203) 622-7910

HARTFORD PUBLIC LIBRARY*+
500 Main St.
Hartford 06103
(860) 543-8656

NEW HAVEN FREE PUBLIC
LIBRARY+
Reference Dept.
133 Elm St.
New Haven 06510-2057
(203) 946-8130

DELAWARE

UNIVERSITY OF DELAWARE *+
Hugh Morris Library
Newark 19717-5267
(302) 831-2432

FLORIDA

VOLUSIA COUNTY LIBRARY
CENTER+
City Island
Daytona Beach 32014-4484
(904) 257-6036

NOVA SOUTHEASTERN
UNIVERSITY*+
Einstein Library
3301 College Ave.
Fort Lauderdale 33314
(954) 262-4601

INDIAN RIVER COMMUNITY
COLLEGE+
Charles S. Miley Learning Resource
Center
3209 Virginia Ave.
Fort Pierce 34981-5599
(561) 462-4757

JACKSONVILLE PUBLIC
LIBRARIES*+
Grants Resource Center
122 N. Ocean St.
Jacksonville 32202
(904) 630-2665

MIAMI-DADE PUBLIC LIBRARY*+
Humanities/Social Science
101 W. Flagler St.
Miami 33130
(305) 375-5575

ORLANDO PUBLIC LIBRARY*
Social Sciences Department
101 E. Central Blvd.
Orlando 32801
(407) 425-4694

SELBY PUBLIC LIBRARY
Reference
1001 Blvd. of the Arts
Sarasota 34236
(941) 316-1183

TAMPA-HILLSBOROUGH COUNTY
PUBLIC LIBRARY*+
900 N. Ashley Drive
Tampa 33602
(813) 273-3628

COMMUNITY FDN. OF PALM
BEACH & MARTIN COUNTIES*
324 Datura St., Suite 340
West Palm Beach 33401
(407) 659-6800

GEORGIA

ATLANTA-FULTON PUBLIC
LIBRARY*+
Foundation Collection—
Ivan Allen Department
1 Margaret Mitchell Square
Atlanta 30303-1089
(404) 730-1900

UNITED WAY OF CENTRAL
GEORGIA*+
Community Resource Center
301 Mulberry Street, Suite 301
Macon 31201
(912) 745-4732

SAVANNAH STATE UNIVERSITY
LIBRARY+
Savannah 31404
(912) 356-2693

THOMAS COUNTY PUBLIC
LIBRARY*+
201 N. Madison St.
Thomasville 31792
(912) 225-5252

HAWAII

UNIVERSITY OF HAWAII*+
Hamilton Library
2550 The Mall
Honolulu 96822
(808) 956-7214

HAWAII COMMUNITY
FOUNDATION RESOURCE
LIBRARY+
900 Fort St., Suite 1300
Honolulu 96813
(808) 537-6333

IDAHO

BOISE PUBLIC LIBRARY*+
715 S. Capitol Blvd.
Boise 83702
(208) 384-4024

CALDWELL PUBLIC LIBRARY*+
1010 Dearborn St.
Caldwell 83605
(208) 459-3242

ILLINOIS

DONORS FORUM OF CHICAGO*+
New Address:
208 South LaSalle, Suite 740
Chicago 60604
(312) 431-0265

EVANSTON PUBLIC LIBRARY*+
1703 Orrington Ave.
Evanston 60201
(847) 866-0305

ROCK ISLAND PUBLIC LIBRARY+
401 - 19th St.
Rock Island 61201
(309) 788-7627

UNIVERSITY OF ILLINOIS AT
SPRINGFIELD*+
Brookens Library
Shepherd Road
Springfield 62794-9243
(217) 786-6633

INDIANA

EVANSVILLE-VANDERBURGH
COUNTY PUBLIC LIBRARY+
22 Southeast Fifth St.
Evansville 47708
(812) 428-8200

ALLEN COUNTY PUBLIC LIBRARY*+
900 Webster St.
Ft. Wayne 46802
(219) 424-0544

INDIANA UNIVERSITY NORTHWEST
LIBRARY+
3400 Broadway
Gary 46408
(219) 980-6582

INDIANAPOLIS-MARION COUNTY
PUBLIC LIBRARY*+
Social Sciences
40 E. St. Clair
Indianapolis 46206
(317) 269-1733

VIGO COUNTY PUBLIC LIBRARY+
1 Library Square
Terre Haute 47807
(812) 232-1113

IOWA

CEDAR RAPIDS PUBLIC LIBRARY*
Foundation Center Collection
500 First St., SE
Cedar Rapids 52401
(319) 398-5123

SOUTHWESTERN COMMUNITY
COLLEGE*+
Learning Resource Center
1501 W. Townline Rd.
Creston 50801
(515) 782-7081

PUBLIC LIBRARY OF DES
MOINES*+
100 Locust St.
Des Moines 50309-1791
(515) 283-4152

Exhibit 5.6 (continued)

SIOUX CITY PUBLIC LIBRARY*+
529 Pierce St.
Sioux City 51101-1202
(712) 252-5669

KANSAS

DODGE CITY PUBLIC LIBRARY*+
1001 2nd Ave.
Dodge City 67801
(316) 225-0248

TOPEKA AND SHAWNEE COUNTY
PUBLIC LIBRARY*+
1515 SW 10th Ave.
Topeka 66604-1374
(913) 233-2040

WICHITA PUBLIC LIBRARY*+
223 S. Main St.
Wichita 67202
(316) 262-0611

KENTUCKY

WESTERN KENTUCKY UNIVERSITY+
Helm-Cravens Library
Bowling Green 42101-3576
(502) 745-6125

LEXINGTON PUBLIC LIBRARY*
140 East Main Street
Lexington 40507-1376
(606) 231-5520

LOUISVILLE FREE PUBLIC
LIBRARY*+
301 York Street
Louisville 40203
(502) 574-1611

LOUISIANA

EAST BATON ROUGE PARISH
LIBRARY*+
Centroplex Branch Grants
Collection
120 St. Louis
Baton Rouge 70802
(504) 389-4960

BEAUREGARD PARISH LIBRARY*+
205 S. Washington Ave.
De Ridder 70634
(318) 463-6217

NEW ORLEANS PUBLIC LIBRARY*+
Business & Science Division
219 Loyola Ave.
New Orleans 70140
(504) 596-2580

SHREVE MEMORIAL LIBRARY*
424 Texas St.
Shreveport 71120-1523
(318) 226-5894

MAINE

MAINE GRANTS INFORMATION
CENTER*+
University of Southern Maine
Library
314 Forrest Ave.
Portland 04104-9301
(207) 780-5029

MARYLAND

ENOCH PRATT FREE LIBRARY*+
Social Science & History
400 Cathedral St.
Baltimore 21201
(410) 396-5430

MASSACHUSETTS

ASSOCIATED GRANTMAKERS OF
MASSACHUSETTS*+
294 Washington St., Suite 840
Boston 02108
(617) 426-2606

BOSTON PUBLIC LIBRARY*+
Soc. Sci. Reference
700 Boylston St., R1069
Boston 02117
(617) 536-5400

WESTERN MASSACHUSETTS
FUNDING RESOURCE CENTER+
65 Elliot St.
Springfield 01101-1730
(413) 732-3175

WORCESTER PUBLIC LIBRARY*+
Grants Resource Center
Salem Square
Worcester 01608
(508) 799-1655

MICHIGAN

ALPENA COUNTY LIBRARY*+
211 N. First St.
Alpena 49707
(517) 356-6188

UNIVERSITY OF MICHIGAN-ANN
ARBOR*+
Graduate Library
Reference & Research Services
Department
Ann Arbor 48109-1205
(313) 764-9373

WILLARD PUBLIC LIBRARY*+
7 West Van Buren St.
Battle Creek 49017
(616) 968-8166

HENRY FORD CENTENNIAL
LIBRARY*+
Adult Services
16301 Michigan Ave.
Dearborn 48126
(313) 943-2330

WAYNE STATE UNIVERSITY*+
Purdy/Kresge Library
5265 Cass Avenue
Detroit 48202
(313) 577-6424

MICHIGAN STATE UNIVERSITY
LIBRARIES*+
Social Sciences/Humanities
Main Library
East Lansing 48824-1048
(517) 353-8818

FARMINGTON COMMUNITY
LIBRARY*+
32737 West 12 Mile Rd.
Farmington Hills 48018
(810) 553-0300

UNIVERSITY OF MICHIGAN-FLINT*
Library
Flint 48502-2186
(810) 762-3408

GRAND RAPIDS PUBLIC LIBRARY*+
Business Dept., 3rd Floor
60 Library Plaza NE
Grand Rapids 49503-3093
(616) 456-3600

MICHIGAN TECHNOLOGICAL
UNIVERSITY+
Van Pelt Library
1400 Townsend Dr.
Houghton 49931
(906) 487-2507

MAUD PRESTON PALENSKE
MEMORIAL LIBRARY+
500 Market St.
St. Joseph 49085
(616) 983-7167

NORTHWESTERN MICHIGAN
COLLEGE*+
Mark & Helen Osterin Library
1701 E. Front St.
Traverse City 49684
(616) 922-1060

MINNESOTA

DULUTH PUBLIC LIBRARY*+
520 W. Superior St.
Duluth 55802
(218) 723-3802

SOUTHWEST STATE UNIVERSITY*+
University Library
Marshall 56258
(507) 537-6176

MINNEAPOLIS PUBLIC LIBRARY*+
Sociology Department
300 Nicollet Mall
Minneapolis 55401
(612) 630-6300

ROCHESTER PUBLIC LIBRARY
11 First St. SE
Rochester 55904-3777
(507) 285-8002

ST. PAUL PUBLIC LIBRARY+
90 W. Fourth St.
St. Paul 55102
(612) 266-7000

MISSISSIPPI

JACKSON/HINDS LIBRARY
SYSTEM*+
300 N. State St.
Jackson 39201
(601) 968-5803

MISSOURI

CLEARINGHOUSE FOR MIDCONTI-
NENT FOUNDATIONS*+
University of Missouri-Kansas City
5110 Cherry, Suite 310
Kansas City 64110
(816) 235-1176

KANSAS CITY PUBLIC LIBRARY*+
311 E. 12th St.
Kansas City 64106-2454
(816) 221-9650

METROPOLITAN ASSOCIATION FOR
PHILANTHROPY, INC.*+
1 Metropolitan Square, Suite 1295
St. Louis 63102
(314) 621-6220

SPRINGFIELD-GREENE COUNTY
LIBRARY*+
397 E. Central
Springfield 65802
(417) 837-5000

MONTANA

MONTANA STATE UNIVERSITY-
BILLINGS*+
Library-Special Collections
1500 North 30th St.
Billings 59101-0298
(406) 657-2046

BOZEMAN PUBLIC LIBRARY*+
220 E. Lamme
Bozeman 59715
(406) 586-4787

MONTANA STATE LIBRARY*+
Library Services
1515 E. 6th Ave.
Helena 59620
(406) 444-3004

UNIVERSITY OF MONTANA*+
Maureen & Mike Mansfield Library
Missoula 59812-1195
(406) 243-6800

NEBRASKA

UNIVERSITY OF NEBRASKA-
LINCOLN*+
Love Library
14th & R Sts.
Lincoln 68588-0410
(402) 472-2848

W. DALE CLARK LIBRARY*+
Social Sciences Department
215 S. 15th St.
Omaha 68102
(402) 444-4826

NEVADA

LAS VEGAS-CLARK COUNTY
LIBRARY DISTRICT*+
1401 E. Flamingo
Las Vegas 89119
(702) 733-3642

WASHOE COUNTY LIBRARY*+
301 S. Center St.
Reno 89501
(702) 785-4010

NEW HAMPSHIRE

PLYMOUTH STATE COLLEGE*+
Herbert H. Lamson Library
Plymouth 03264
(603) 535-2258

CONCORD COUNTY LIBRARY
45 Green St.
Concord 03301
(603) 225-8670   *(continued)*

Exhibit 5.6 (continued)

NEW JERSEY

CUMBERLAND COUNTY LIBRARY+
New Jersey Room
800 E. Commerce St.
Bridgeton 08302
(609) 453-2210

FREE PUBLIC LIBRARY OF
ELIZABETH*+
11 S. Broad St.
Elizabeth 07202
(908) 354-6060

COUNTY COLLEGE OF MORRIS*+
Learning Resource Center
214 Center Grove Rd.
Randolph 07869
(201) 328-5296

NEW JERSEY STATE LIBRARY*+
Governmental Reference Services
185 West State St.
Trenton 08625-0520
(609) 292-6220

NEW MEXICO

ALBUQUERQUE COMMUNITY
FOUNDATION*
3301 Menual NE, Ste. 30
Albuquerque 87176-6960
(505) 883-6240

NEW MEXICO STATE LIBRARY*+
Information Services
1209 Camino Carlos Rey
Santa Fe 87505
(505) 476-9714

NEW YORK

NEW YORK STATE LIBRARY*+
Humanities Reference
Cultural Education Center
Empire State Plaza
Albany 12230
(518) 474-5355

SUFFOLK COOPERATIVE LIBRARY
SYSTEM+
627 N. Sunrise Service Rd.
Bellport 11713
(516) 286-1600

BRONX REFERENCE CENTER
New York Public Library
2556 Bainbridge Ave.
Bronx 10458
(718) 579-4257

THE NONPROFIT CONNECTION+
One Hanson Place, Room 1601
Brooklyn 11243
(718) 230-3200

BROOKLYN PUBLIC LIBRARY+
Social Sciences Division
Grand Army Plaza
Brooklyn 11238
(718) 780-7700

BUFFALO & ERIE COUNTY PUBLIC
LIBRARY*+
Business & Labor Dept.
Lafayette Square
Buffalo 14203
(716) 858-7097

HUNTINGTON PUBLIC LIBRARY+
338 Main St.
Huntington 11743
(516) 427-5165

QUEENS BOROUGH PUBLIC
LIBRARY+
Social Sciences Division
89-11 Merrick Blvd.
Jamaica 11432
(718) 990-0761

LEVITTOWN PUBLIC LIBRARY*+
1 Bluegrass Lane
Levittown 11756
(516) 731-5728

FOUNDATION CENTER OFFICE AND
LIBRARY+
79 Fifth Avenue, 8th Floor
New York 10003-3076
(212) 620-4230

NEW YORK PUBLIC LIBRARY+
Countee Cullen Branch Library
104 W. 136th St.
New York 10030
(212) 491-2070

ADRIANCE MEMORIAL LIBRARY+
Special Services Department
93 Market St.
Poughkeepsie 12601
(914) 485-3445

ROCHESTER PUBLIC LIBRARY*+
Social Sciences and Job
Information Center
115 South Avenue
Rochester 14604
(716) 428-8120

ONONDAGA COUNTY PUBLIC
LIBRARY+
447 S. Salina St.
Syracuse 13202-2494
(315) 435-1900

UTICA PUBLIC LIBRARY
303 Genesee St.
Utica 13501
(315) 735-2279

WHITE PLAINS PUBLIC LIBRARY+
100 Martine Ave.
White Plains 10601
(914) 422-1480

NORTH CAROLINA

COMMUNITY FDN. OF WESTERN
NORTH CAROLINA*+
Learning Resources Center
16 Biltmore Avenue, Suite 201
Asheville 28802
(704) 254-4960

THE DUKE ENDOWMENT*+
100 N. Tryon St., Suite 3500
Charlotte 28202
(704) 376-0291

DURHAM COUNTY PUBLIC
LIBRARY+
301 North Roxboro
Durham 27702
(919) 560-0110

STATE LIBRARY OF NORTH
CAROLINA*+
Government and Business Services
Archives Bldg., 109 E. Jones St.
Raleigh 27601
(919) 733-3270

FORSYTH COUNTY PUBLIC
LIBRARY*+
660 W. 5th St.
Winston-Salem 27101
(336) 727-2680

NORTH DAKOTA

BISMARCK PUBLIC LIBRARY
515 N. Fifth St.
Bismarck 58501
(701) 222-6410

FARGO PUBLIC LIBRARY*+
102 N. 3rd St.
Fargo 58102
(701) 241-1491

OHIO

STARK COUNTY DISTRICT
LIBRARY+
Humanities
715 Market Ave. N.
Canton 44702
(330) 452-0665

FOUNDATION CENTER OFFICE AND
LIBRARY
Kent H. Smith Library Hanna
Building, Suite 1356
1422 Euclid Avenue
Cleveland, OH 44115
(216) 861-1934

PUBLIC LIBRARY OF CINCINNATI &
HAMILTON COUNTY*+
Grants Resource Center
800 Vine St., Library Square
Cincinnati 45202-2071
(513) 369-6940

COLUMBUS METROPOLITAN
LIBRARY+
Business and Technology Dept.
96 S. Grant Ave.
Columbus 43215
(614) 645-2590

DAYTON & MONTGOMERY COUN-
TY PUBLIC LIBRARY*+
Grants Resource Center
215 E. Third St.
Dayton 45402
(937) 227-9500 x211

MANSFIELD/RICHLAND COUNTY
PUBLIC LIBRARY*+
42 West Third Street
Mansfield 44902
(419) 521-3110

TOLEDO-LUCAS COUNTY PUBLIC
LIBRARY*+
Social Sciences Department
325 Michigan St.
Toledo 43624-1614
(419) 259-5245

YOUNGSTOWN & MAHONING
COUNTY PUBLIC LIBRARY*+
305 Wick Ave.
Youngstown 44503
(330) 744-8636

MUSKINGUM COUNTY LIBRARY+
220 N. 5th St.
Zanesville 43701
(614) 453-0391

OKLAHOMA

OKLAHOMA CITY UNIVERSITY*+
Dulaney Browne Library
2501 N. Blackwelder
Oklahoma City 73106
(405) 521-5822

TULSA CITY-COUNTY LIBRARY*+
400 Civic Center
Tulsa 74103
(918) 596-7944

OREGON

OREGON INSTITUTE OF
TECHNOLOGY+
Library
3201 Campus Dr.
Klamath Falls 97601-8801
(503) 885-1773

PACIFIC NON-PROFIT NETWORK*+
Grantsmanship Resource Library
33 N. Central, Suite 211
Medford 97501
(541) 779-6044

MULTNOMAH COUNTY LIBRARY+
Government Documents
801 SW Tenth Ave.
Portland 97205
(503) 248-5123

OREGON STATE LIBRARY*+
State Library Building
Salem 97310
(503) 378-4277

PENNSYLVANIA

NORTHAMPTON COMMUNITY
COLLEGE+
Learning Resources Center
3835 Green Pond Rd.
Bethlehem 18017
(215) 861-5360

ERIE COUNTY LIBRARY+
Reference Department
160 East Front St.
Erie 16507-1554
(814) 451-6927

DAUPHIN COUNTY LIBRARY
SYSTEM+
Central Library
101 Walnut St.
Harrisburg 17101
(717) 234-4976

LANCASTER COUNTY PUBLIC
LIBRARY+
125 N. Duke St.
Lancaster 17602
(717) 394-2651

FREE LIBRARY OF PHILADELPHIA*+
Regional Foundation Center
Logan Square, 1901 Vine St.
Philadelphia 19103
(215) 686-5423

Exhibit 5.6 (continued)

CARNEGIE LIBRARY OF
PITTSBURGH*+
Foundation Collection
4400 Forbes Ave.
Pittsburgh 15213-4080
(412) 622-1917

POCONO NORTHEAST DEVELOP-
MENT FUND+
James Pettinger Memorial Library
1151 Oak St.
Pittston 18640-3755
(717) 655-5581

READING PUBLIC LIBRARY+
100 South Fifth St.
Reading 19602
(610) 655-6355

MARTIN LIBRARY*+
159 Market St.
York 17401
(717) 846-5300

RHODE ISLAND
PROVIDENCE PUBLIC LIBRARY*+
225 Washington St.
Providence 02906
(401) 455-8088

SOUTH CAROLINA
ANDERSON COUNTY LIBRARY*+
202 East Greenville St.
Anderson 29621
(864) 260-4500

CHARLESTON COUNTY LIBRARY*+
404 King St.
Charleston 29403
(803) 723-1645

SOUTH CAROLINA STATE
LIBRARY*+
1500 Senate St.
Columbia 29211
(803) 734-8666

SOUTH DAKOTA
SOUTH DAKOTA STATE LIBRARY*+
800 Governors Dr.
Pierre 57501-2294
(605) 773-5070
(800) 592-1841 (SD residents)

NONPROFIT MANAGEMENT
INSTITUTE+
132 S. Dakota Rd.
Sioux Falls 57102
(605) 367-5380

SIOUXLAND LIBRARIES*+
201 N. Main Ave.
Sioux Falls 57102-1132
(605) 367-7081

TENNESSEE
KNOX COUNTY PUBLIC LIBRARY*+
500 W. Church Ave.
Knoxville 37902
(423) 544-5700

MEMPHIS & SHELBY COUNTY
PUBLIC LIBRARY*+
1850 Peabody Ave.
Memphis 38104
(901) 725-8877

NASHVILLE PUBLIC LIBRARY*+
Business Information Division
225 Polk Ave.
Nashville 37203
(615) 862-5843

TEXAS
NONPROFIT RESOURCE CENTER+
Funding Information Library
500 N. Chestnut, Suite 1511
Abilene 79604
(915) 677-8166

AMARILLO AREA FOUNDATION*+
700 First National Place
801 S. Fillmore
Amarillo 79101
(806) 376-4521

HOGG FOUNDATION FOR MENTAL
HEALTH*+
3001 Lake Austin Blvd.
Austin 78703
(512) 471-5041

FUNDING INFORMATION CENTER+
Beaumont Public Library
801 Pearl Street
Beaumont 77704
(409) 838-6606

CORPUS CHRISTI PUBLIC
LIBRARY*+
805 Comanche Street
Corpus Christi 78401
(512) 880-7000

DALLAS PUBLIC LIBRARY*+
Urban Information
1515 Young St.
Dallas 75201
(214) 670-1487

CENTER FOR VOLUNTEERISM &
NONPROFIT MANAGEMENT+
1918 Texas Avenue
El Paso 79901
(915) 532-5377

SOUTHWEST BORDER NONPROFIT
RESOURCE CENTER+
2412 South Closner
Edinburg 78539
(956) 316-2610

FUNDING INFORMATION
CENTER*+
329 S. Henderson
Fort Worth 76104
(817) 334-0228

HOUSTON PUBLIC LIBRARY*+
Bibliographic Information Center
500 McKinney
Houston 77002
(713) 236-1313

LONGVIEW PUBLIC LIBRARY*
222 W. Cotton St.
Longview 75601
(903) 237-1352

LUBBOCK AREA FOUNDATION,
INC.*+
1655 Main St.
Suite 209
Lubbock 79401
(806) 762-8061

NONPROFIT RESOURCE CENTER OF
TEXAS*+
111 Soledad, Suite 200
San Antonio 78205
(210) 227-4333

WACO-McLENNAN COUNTY
LIBRARY*+
1717 Austin Ave.
Waco 76701
(254) 750-5975

NORTH TEXAS CENTER FOR
NONPROFIT MANAGEMENT*+
624 Indiana, Suite 307
Wichita Falls 76301
(817) 322-4961

UTAH
SALT LAKE CITY PUBLIC LIBRARY*
209 East 500 South
Salt Lake City 84111
(801) 524-8200

VERMONT
VERMONT DEPT. OF LIBRARIES*+
Reference & Law Info. Services
109 State St.
Montpelier 05609
(802) 828-3268

VIRGINIA
HAMPTON PUBLIC LIBRARY+
4207 Victoria Blvd.
Hampton 23669
(757) 727-1312

RICHMOND PUBLIC LIBRARY*+
Business, Science & Technology
101 East Franklin St.
Richmond 23219
(804) 780-8223

ROANOKE CITY PUBLIC LIBRARY
SYSTEM*
706 S. Jefferson
Roanoke 24016
(540) 853-2477

WASHINGTON
MID-COLUMBIA LIBRARY*
405 South Dayton
Kennewick 99336
(509) 586-3156

SEATTLE PUBLIC LIBRARY*+
Science, Social Science
1000 Fourth Ave.
Seattle 98104
(206) 386-4620

SPOKANE PUBLIC LIBRARY*
Funding Information Center
West 906 Main Ave.
Spokane 99201
(509) 626-5347

UNITED WAY OF PIERCE
COUNTY*+
Center for Nonprofit Development
1501 Pacific Ave., Suite 400
P.O. Box 2215
Tacoma 98401
(206) 272-4263

GREATER WENATCHEE
COMMUNITY FOUNDATION AT THE
WENATCHEE PUBLIC
LIBRARY
310 Douglas St.
Wenatchee 98807
(509) 662-5021

WEST VIRGINIA
KANAWHA COUNTY PUBLIC
LIBRARY*+
123 Capitol St.
Charleston 25301
(304) 343-4646

WISCONSIN
UNIVERSITY OF WISCONSIN-
MADISON*+
Memorial Library
728 State St.
Madison 53706
(608) 262-3242

MARQUETTE UNIVERSITY
MEMORIAL LIBRARY*+
Funding Information Center
1415 W. Wisconsin Ave.
Milwaukee 53233
(414) 288-1515

UNIVERSITY OF WISCONSIN-
STEVENS POINT*+
Library-Foundation Collection
99 Reserve St.
Stevens Point 54481-3897
(715) 346-4204

WYOMING
NATRONA COUNTY PUBLIC
LIBRARY*+
307 E. 2nd St.
Casper 82601-2598
(307) 237-4935

LARAMIE COUNTY COMMUNITY
COLLEGE*+
Instructional Resource Center
1400 E. College Dr.
Cheyenne 82007-3299
(307) 778-1206

CAMPBELL COUNTY PUBLIC
LIBRARY*+
2101 4 J Road
Gillette 82716
(307) 682-3223

TETON COUNTY LIBRARY*+
125 Virginian Lane
Jackson 83001
(307) 733-2164

ROCK SPRINGS LIBRARY+
400 C St.
Rock Springs 82901
(307) 362-6212

PUERTO RICO
UNIVERSIDAD DEL SAGRADO
CORAZON+
M.M.T. Guevara Library
Santurce 00914
(809) 728-1515 x 4357

- *Subject Area:* Your Key Words Worksheet (Exhibit 5.3) will provide you with the words you need to use this index and find the foundations interested in your particular area. Remember that elementary education is becoming an increasingly popular target of funding.

- *Geographic Region:* This index will help you find foundations in your area that share your interests.

- *Type of Support:* Many foundations have severe restrictions on the types of funding they will provide. This index allows you to quickly discover this important information.

- *Donor, Trustees, and Officers (Key Officials):* This index provides you with information that may be useful in developing linkages with foundations.

All of the indexes refer to the foundations by a four-digit number that appears above each foundation's name. As mentioned, the foundations are arranged in alphabetical order according to the state they are incorporated in.

Exhibit 5.7 shows a fictitious sample set up like a real entry in the *Foundation Directory.*

To find a funder for our example project in involving parents, teachers, and students in responsible education, we turn to our key words and the subject index in the *Foundation Directory.* Determining that the (fictitious) Sebastian Jessica Foundation has an expressed interest in elementary education and educational technology, we further ascertain from the entry that our request will fall within the foundation's average grant size of $10,000 to $50,000. However, we are still not ready to write a proposal or even to telephone the foundation.

We need to learn more about the Sebastian Jessica Foundation. For example, what does it *really* value? What types of projects did it fund in 1997? What types of organizations did it make awards to? Because the *Foundation Directory* entry does not state that the foundation limits its giving to any one geographic area, we are also interested in knowing where it has awarded grants in the past.

Another popular Foundation Center publication, the *Foundation Grants Index,* can provide us with much of this information. This volume, published annually, lists approximately 73,000 grants made by over 1,000 of the largest independent corporate and community foundations. It is divided into six sections:

I. *Grants Listing:* This is an alphabetical listing by state of the foundations included in the publication. Each grant of $10,000 or more awarded by the foundation is listed under the foundation's name.

Exhibit 5.7

THE FOUNDATION DIRECTORY Sample Entry

2762

The Sebastian Jessica Foundation

2604 Northstar

Chicago 60604   (312) 896-8360

Incorporated in 1926 in IL.

Donor(s): Vastell Jessica, Mrs. Sebastian Jessica

Foundation type: Independent

Financial data (yr. ended 6/30/97): Assets, $150,444,176 (M); expenditures, $6,488,200; qualifying distributions, $6,400,200 including $4,488,200 for 126 grants (high: $300,000; low: $200; average: $10,000–$50,000). $85,200 for 65 employee matching gifts and $1,200,200 for 7 foundation administered programs.

Purpose and activities: Dedicated to enhancing the humane dimensions of life through activities that emphasize the theme of improving the quality of teaching and learning. Serves precollegiate education through grantmaking and program activities in elementary and secondary public education.

Fields of interest: Elementary and secondary public education, teaching, educational technology.

Types of support: Consulting services, technical assistance, special projects.

Limitations: No support for colleges and universities (except for projects in elementary and secondary education). No grants to individuals, or for building or endowment funds, or operating budgets; no loans.

Publications: Annual report, informational brochure (including application guidelines), financial statement, grants list.

Application information: Grant proposals for higher education not accepted; fellowship applications available only through participating universities.

Application form not required.

    Initial approach: letter

    Copies of proposal: 1

    Deadline(s): None

    Board meeting date(s): May and Nov., and as required

    Final notification: 4 weeks

    Write: Dr. Stefan Ross, Pres.

Officers: Vastell Jessica, Chair; Ann Jessica, Vice-Chair and Secy.; Stefan Ross, Pres.; Winifred L. Boser, V.P.; Franz Kirschbauer, Treas.; Bilal Ali, Prog. Dir.

Trustees: John R. Bige, Alice S. Romano, Donald C. Crowne, Jr., Charles Power, George Gaylin, P. John Passitty.

Number of staff: 4 full-time professionals; 1 part-time professional; 4 full-time support.

Employer Identification Number: 679014579

Each grant has a grant identification number. In our example, to locate a listing of the grants awarded by the Sebastian Jessica Foundation, we go to Section I, locate Illinois (the state of incorporation), and follow alphabetical order until we reach Jessica.

II.   *Grant Recipients:* This is an index of grant recipients (grantees) presented in alphabetical order by recipient name. The recipient name, state, and grant identification number are provided in each entry. This information allows you to trace the entry to the grantor by locating the grant identification number in Section I.

III. *Subject Index:* This index lists subject areas (key words) in alphabetical order. Under each subject area is a list of grant identification numbers. These numbers identify the grants that were awarded in that particular subject area. Again, the grants in Section I can be located by using their identification numbers.

IV. *Type of Support/Geographic Area:* This section is an alphabetical index by type of support (annual campaigns, building, equipment, and so on) and subject categories (education, science and social science, youth development, and so on). The grants in each subject area are listed by state and identification number. This enables analysis of geographic granting patterns as related to types of support and subject areas.

V. *Recipient Category Index:* This index provides an alphabetical listing by type of recipient organization (schools, youth development organizations, and so on). Each recipient category is further broken down by type of support awarded and the state where the recipient organization is located.

VI. *Foundations:* This is an alphabetical listing of the foundations included in the publication. It includes each foundation's address and any geographic restrictions of their giving program. By using this index, you can determine what state a particular foundation is in and can easily find its description in Section I of the publication.

Exhibit 5.8 shows a fictitious entry for the Jessica Foundation as it might appear in Section I of the *Foundation Grants Index.*

From this list we can see that the Sebastian Jessica Foundation appears to exhibit values compatible with those of our example project. It appears that a grant of $25,000 would be the Foundation's upper limit and that a proposal for $10,000 to $15,000 might stand a better chance of being funded.

Besides having many excellent books on foundation funding, your Foundation Center Regional Library has three other references you should be familiar with—Internal Revenue Service Foundation Tax Returns, Grant Guides, and FC Search.

- *The 990 Internal Revenue Service Foundation Tax Returns:* The IRS requires private foundations to file income tax returns each year. The 990–PF returns provide fiscal details on receipts and expenditures, compensation of officers, capital gains or losses, and other financial matters. Form 990–AR provides information on founda-

---

Exhibit 5.8

THE FOUNDATION GRANTS INDEX Sample Entry

Education, Elementary and Secondary

The Sebastian Jessica Foundation

No support for colleges and universities (except for projects in elementary and secondary education). No grants to individuals or for building or endowment funds or operating budgets; no loans.

2713. Association of Indiana School Administrators, South Bend, IN. $25,000, 1997. For Reorganization of Schools Project through electronic interface. 9/14/97.

2714. Association of Michigan School Administrators, Detroit, MI. $14,000, 1997. For Consortium for Schools of the Future. 10/21/97.

2715. Hazelnut School District, Hazelnut, MO. $12,500, 1997. For Internet Homework Hotline Program. 7/9/97.

2716. Kids in Between, Kansas City, MO. $10,000, 1997. For educational technology program for teachers working with children and their parents. 10/15/97.

2717. Platterton School District, Agnes Middle School, Alexandria, VA. $13,000, 1997. For staff development activities related to improving student performance through technology. 7/15/97.

---

tion managers, assets, and grants paid or committed for future payment. The Foundation Center's National Collections and field offices in New York City, San Francisco, Washington, D.C., Atlanta, and Cleveland have the past three years' tax returns of all private foundations on microfiche. Each of the Cooperating Collections has returns of private foundations located in its state and sometimes in surrounding states.

- *Grant Guides:* Published by the Foundation Center, these computer-produced, customized guides to foundation giving provide descriptions of hundreds of foundation grants of $10,000 or more recently awarded in specific subject areas. There are currently thirty-one guides available in subject areas ranging from aging to women and girls, including guides in the subject areas of children and youth, elementary and secondary education, and health programs for children and youth.

- *FC Search:* This is the Foundation Center's database of forty-five thousand foundations and corporate givers on CD-ROM.

State foundation books, which many states have, are also useful research tools. They describe the granting patterns of foundations located in a particular state. These books derive their data from the annual reports of foundations and from IRS tax returns. They are usually available at Foundation Center Cooperating Collections.

Searching for Corporate Grantors

If the corporation has a foundation, you will be able to locate its 990–AR IRS tax return. However, many corporations that have foundations also make grants directly through the corporation. Because grants made through a corporate foundation are subject to public scrutiny (the 990–AR), many corporations make grants that they do not wish to be made public through their corporate giving program.

The current IRS rules allow a corporation to take up to 120 percent of its gross profits as a tax deduction when this amount is given as grants to nonprofit organizations (501[c][3]s). However, not many corporations give this much. The national average is less than 2 percent of gross profits.

Corporate stockholders have strong opinions concerning who should and should not receive their hard-earned grant dollars. This is another reason why many corporations make grants through both a corporate foundation and a corporate giving program. When grants are made through the latter, the data are confidential, because not even a stockholder can get a copy of the corporation's tax return. In addition, when a corporation perceives that a potential project will bring it commercial benefit (for example, enhance marketplace positioning or product testing) it often makes the grant through its marketing department and usually does not take a write-off against taxable profits. Again, this type of grant will not show up on any grant list or in any research tools unless the company voluntarily supplies the information. The inability to verify corporate support accounts for the inaccuracy and lack of specificity that characterize the corporate grants marketplace.

What motivates corporations to make grants? What benefits can they receive by funding your school? By reviewing the values of corporate funders, we can see that their motivation comes from a concern for the following:

- Their workers and the children of their workers
- Product development
- Product positioning

In the example project to increase responsible educational behavior in parents, students, and teachers, the method or solution calls for the possible use of videotaping to provide a link between parent and teacher and the student's level of performance and responsible educational practices. Companies in the area with employees whose children attend the local school may be interested in the project; companies that make, sell, or distribute video recorders, players, and tapes may be interested even if they are outside the area. If the model project were to result in an educational change, these companies would benefit. In addition to the benefits related directly to education, a company producing video equipment would also come out ahead by being able to position its products with parents and students—future consumers.

So there are many reasons for companies to support grant projects. But remember, they are not simply interested in doing nice things for education and your school. They want and expect a return.

How can your grantseekers locate the companies that will be most interested in your school's project and its potential benefits? Your public library or local college library should have several helpful resources available. In addition, if you are near a Foundation Center National Collection or a Regional Cooperating Collection you and your grantseekers will have access to many resources, including two of the Foundation Center's primary corporate research tools.

One is the *National Directory of Corporate Giving,* which provides information on 1,905 corporate foundations as well as 990 direct corporate giving programs. It also has an extensive bibliography and six indexes to help you target funding prospects.

The other is *Corporate Foundation Profiles,* which contains detailed analyses of 195 of the largest corporate foundations—grantmakers who give at least $1.2 million annually. An appendix lists financial data on hundreds of additional corporate foundations that hold assets of $1 million or give at least $100,000 in grants annually.

Because companies define themselves in terms of markets and products, it would be helpful for your grantseekers to look at those funding prospects that might value your school's project because of its potential impact in their marketplace. The *Standard Industrial Classification Code Book* is an excellent tool to find out who makes what products. It is available at your public library. Once you have determined the companies that manufacture the product your school is interested in, you or your grantseekers can telephone the local sales representative or phone or write the company's corporate offices to ascertain their level of interest in your school's project.

One crucial fact to remember is that corporate grants decrease as profits go down. A look at *Dun and Bradstreet's Million Dollar Directory* will tell you how 160,000 of the largest U.S. businesses stand financially. A company that is financially weak is not a prime target for a grant request.

Corporations in your area are another good bet for grant support. Find out what these companies are and if your school serves the children of their workers. If it does, you are more likely to receive a positive response, for some of the company's future workers may come from your school.

Although corporations give where they live, they still expect a professional approach from their potential grantees. Just as companies are judged by the quality of their sales representatives, your school will be judged by the quality of the individual who approaches the company. Your grantseekers should always check with you and possibly a district administrator before approaching a company for grant support. Because many elementary and middle schools do not have a formal grants system, many classroom leaders have taken their proposals to corporations themselves and have been quite successful. Indeed, corporate support for elementary and middle schools is increasing.

Chambers of Commerce usually produce an annual listing of all the companies in their area. The listing ranks the companies by number of employees and payroll and often gives product information. This listing is an excellent research tool. You should have several members from the corporate world on your grants advisory group. One of them should be able to procure this invaluable list for your school.

Because most corporations make grants out of their profits, knowing which local companies are profitable will be a big help. If there is a stockbroker on your grants advisory committee, he or she can find out which companies in your area are paying increasing stock dividends because of increased profits. Another advantage to including business leaders in your grants advisory group is that corporations are always concerned with their customers' credit ratings. How companies pay their bills is a reflection of their fiscal situation and profitability. Hence, companies subscribe to several services that keep close tabs on their customers. Request information on what services the corporate members of your grants advisory group subscribe to and ask them to provide you with a report on the companies your school is planning to approach. The more you know about these companies, the more respect they will have for you.

Make sure your grantseekers do not overlook smaller companies and independently owned businesses in your area. These may not be able to fund a grant idea on their own, but several could band together to fund one project. Many small companies in the same type of business, whether they are auto dealers or funeral directors, belong to associations or groups that might sponsor your project. Just because a company or business does not employ hundreds does not mean it is not concerned about quality education. But small or large, for-profit companies will expect to see a sound business plan as part of your school's proposal (more on this in a later chapter).

Obtaining Grants from Service Clubs and Organizations

The service clubs and organizations that are closest to you are the most likely to make a grant to your school, but rarely of cash for general use. These groups need a proposal and a project that they can see themselves sponsoring.

As an example, one of my seminar participants from a nonprofit organization in Alaska raised over $2,000 from service clubs and organizations to sponsor her attendance at a grants workshop of mine held in Washington, D.C. She reported that she actually had fun seeking funds for the seminar and that contact with her local service clubs and organizations allowed her to develop lasting relationships with them. The clubs and organizations that sponsored her saw the benefits of sending her to a grants workshop. They realized that once she developed expertise in grantseeking, her organization's clientele would begin to benefit from improved and expanded programs made possible through her acquisition of external resources.

Following the step-by-step system outlined on the next few pages and completing the accompanying worksheets will help you match your school's projects to the "best" service club or organization in your community. A service club or organization's funding interests can be determined from the areas of support and espoused values they describe in their statement of purpose and from the projects and groups they have supported in the past.

The Foot-in-the-Door Worksheet in Chapter Two (Exhibit 2.6) requests information on links with service clubs and organizations. This webbing and linkage information will be of great help to you when you are soliciting support from these groups. Most service clubs and organizations have a contact person or corresponding secretary. Make direct contact or use any links you may have to these individuals.

In general, service clubs and organizations prefer to support projects that require smaller amounts of grant funds. In addition, they are motivated by a tight focus on the target population. A grant for equipment that will be used by many students and be made accessible to parents or other members of the community is a good example. Whether they are financing after-school programs or computer equipment, service clubs and organizations want to feel that they are making a difference in the community.

The pragmatic nature of these organizations and the fact that many of the members are businesspeople lead them to an analysis that usually includes information about the number of students or beneficiaries that will be affected, what they will be able to do, and at what price or cost per student beneficiary. Have your grantseekers complete the Target Population Worksheet in Exhibit 5.9. This will help them focus on the types of data your local service groups will respond to.

As you and your grantseekers intensify your search for these potential grantors, remember that they will make grants and adopt and support projects based on their perception of and past experiences with the grantee. In your case, the grantee is your school. It is important to realize that the members of the clubs and organizations may have a totally different view of education than you. I was once rebuffed by a local service club dedicated to supporting projects related to literacy and at-risk students, even though I was asking for a grant to support library resources. Why? Because the individuals I met with from the club never used the research section of our public school library. Indeed, one member of the service club's education committee had never used the library at all because he had been thrown out of it as an eighth grader. Changing our grant to support funding for a conversational library and including reference books and manuals on everything from herb gardening to snowmobile and motorcycle repair resulted in our project being met with much greater enthusiasm and financial support.

Exhibit 5.9

TARGET POPULATION WORKSHEET

What school/youth population do you currently serve?
- Target Age Group(s)
- Number of Youth Currently Served, by Age, Grade Level, Special Needs Population, and so on
- Geographical Area Served (School Boundaries, Open Enrollment, Population, Daily Attendance)
- Number of Programs Currently Provided by Your School (You may choose to focus your response on the target population)

From your Needs Worksheet (Exhibit 3.2), list those studies, examples, and articles that document the local need for this project and the target population that will benefit from it.

_____

_____

_____

Select an affordable ($1,000 to $10,000) solution from the Solutions Worksheet (Exhibit 3.6) and describe how it would change the local situation. (Remember your Service Clubs and Organizations Matrix [Table 4.10] here. These funding sources are not usually interested in research. They want to fund what works.)

_____

_____

_____

Service Clubs and Organizations Worksheet

Review the Service Clubs and Organizations Worksheet (Exhibit 5.10) and identify those groups that are in your area. Your public library may have a list of local service clubs and organizations, and the telephone book can be of great help. There may even be a sign as you enter your city, town, or village that lists the service organizations and the places and times of their meetings.

The Service Clubs and Organizations Worksheet is not intended to be a complete list. Feel free to add more groups to it. For example, there are many Hellenic, fraternal, and social groups and societies that will help your school.

Exhibit 5.10

SERVICE CLUBS AND ORGANIZATIONS WORKSHEET

Place a checkmark next to those service clubs and organizations that may be interested in sponsoring your project. Record contact's name and phone number and the club's/organization's areas of interest and values. Add to the list of clubs and organizations.

Check	Club/Organization	Contact/Phone	Areas of Interest/Values
_____	Rotary Club	_____	_____
_____	Junior League	_____	_____
_____	Kiwanis Club	_____	_____
_____	Zonta Club	_____	_____
_____	Jaycees	_____	_____
	Hellenic Groups:		
_____	_____	_____	_____
_____	_____	_____	_____
_____	_____	_____	_____
	Fraternal Groups:		
_____	_____	_____	_____
_____	_____	_____	_____
_____	_____	_____	_____
_____	Masons	_____	_____
_____	Knights of Columbus	_____	_____
	Church Groups:		
_____	_____	_____	_____
_____	_____	_____	_____
_____	_____	_____	_____
	Other:		
_____	_____	_____	_____
_____	_____	_____	_____

Approaching Potential Service Clubs and Organizations

Exhibits 5.11 through 5.14 provide sample letters and checklists to help you tailor your approach to service clubs and organizations. Types of contact include letters to introduce your school and its need, telephone calls, and personal visits.

The standard approach is to write, telephone, and make personal contact, but any combination may be appropriate. However, the most effective approach is personal contact. A study published in *Grants* magazine in 1989 substantiates the importance of personal contact in appealing to foundations, corporations, and government agencies by citing a 500 percent increase in success if the funding source is contacted before the proposal is written. I cannot cite a more recent study, but I am certain that if anything the importance of preproposal contact has only grown over the last nine years. This same positive effect results from personal contact with a service club or organization that you want to sponsor your project.

Exhibit 5.11

OUTLINE FOR CONSTRUCTING A LETTER TO SERVICE CLUBS OR ORGANIZATIONS

Tailor Your Letter

1. What information do you have on the service club or organization's purpose and values and the programs it has supported in the past? (Focus on this in the letter.)

    _____

    _____

    _____

    _____

2. What contacts or friends do you have in the service club or organization? Mention these in the letter so that the club or organization can confirm your legitimacy through them.

    _____

    _____

    _____

    _____

3. List any past positive experiences that your school or educational programs have had that the service club or organization may have knowledge of (awards, commendations, and so on). Consider reminding them of these; also, thank them for past support, if any.

    _____

    _____

    _____

    _____

Personal contact works because it enables your grantseekers to gather valuable information about the service club or organization face to face, information that allows them to tailor their approach to the funding source's values as well as to the size of its pocketbook. If personal contact cannot be made, then you must find information about prospective funding sources through other means before writing to them.

Other Research Tools

This chapter provides information on grantseeking materials. Many of these materials are inexpensive or free. In addition to the resources already mentioned, you may be interested in newsletters in the education and grants field. There are many, including these: *Education Grants Alert, Education Daily, Foundation and Corporate Grants Alert,* and *Federal Grants and Contracts Weekly.* All are published by Capitol Publications, Inc., 1101 King Street, P.O. Box 1453, Alexandria, Virginia 22313-2053, 800-655-5597. Contact the publisher for free samples and subscription information. The bibliography notes other resources.

Exhibit 5.12

SAMPLE LETTER TO SERVICE CLUBS OR ORGANIZATIONS

Dear _____ :

The work of the [name of club or organization] and your concern for _____ lead me to contact you with an important project. Your support of [an organization, program, or project they have funded in the past] indicates your care and concern for _____ .

The [school, school district, etc.] shares your concern and is dedicated to [statement of your purpose; be brief]. The need for our program here in [geographic area] is demonstrated by [cite studies, statistics, case studies, etc.].

Just as your club [or organization] is faced with many requests for assistance, we too face the reality of continuing a program for _____ , as well as relentlessly seeking funds to add more programs to serve _____ .

I am asking you, as business and community leaders, to consider this request of $_____ to _____ .

I have enclosed detailed information on our project and our budgeted costs. [Number] groups and organizations have already contributed to this project including _____ . [If your project has partial support from your school district, or other grant funds, mention them here.] I will be happy to report back to your club [or organization] on the benefits of the project.

I will telephone you to discuss this opportunity to maximize your club's [or organization's] investment in our school, our children, and our community.

Sincerely,

Exhibit 5.13

TELEPHONE CHECKLIST

Most communities have a directory of service clubs and organizations. Telephone the individuals listed as contact people in your community's directory.

1.   If you have written to their organization, ask if they received your letter. Tell them you know of the good work they do and why you selected them to contact.

2.   Ask if they are interested in having you or one of your grants advisory committee members speak or present your request at a meeting.

3.   Ask for their thoughts regarding your request.

4.   Inform them of the time frame under which you are operating.

5.   If appropriate, ask for an appointment to meet with them or their committee to discuss the project.

6.   Ask them what other information you could provide to help the organization make a decision.

Keep an accurate log of your phone calls to the organization and their responses.

Organization	Contact Person	Phone #	Response	Follow-Up
_____	_____	_____	_____	_____
_____	_____	_____	_____	_____
_____	_____	_____	_____	_____
_____	_____	_____	_____	_____

Exhibit 5.14

PERSONAL CONTACT/VISIT CHECKLIST

1.   Dress in the same style as the group or individual you will be meeting with.

2.   Never bring more than two people to represent your school. A grants advisory committee member or other volunteer is better than a paid staff person.

3.   Start the conversation with a comment about the service club/organization, not with your school's need. For example, you could begin by commenting on community projects the club/organization has sponsored in the past. This will break the ice and also show that you have done some research on the club/organization.

4.   Be brief and to the point.

5.   Use photographs or examples (such as case studies) of your students and programs to educate them about the need.

6.   Record your personal contacts. Keep a record of thank-you letters sent, follow-ups, and results.

Date	Individual Contacted	Results/Follow-Ups	Thank You
_____	_____	_____	_____
_____	_____	_____	_____
_____	_____	_____	_____
_____	_____	_____	_____

CHAPTER 5 CHECKLIST

Evaluation and Planning Worksheet

1. **Have you contacted your district's central office for a list of available grant research services, materials, and so on?**

   _____ yes _____no

2. **The following resources will be helpful to your grantseekers. List where they can be found and the volume number and/or date of publication, when applicable.**

   Key Search Word Worksheets _____
   _____

   Computer-Based Searches _____
   _____

   Catalog of Federal Domestic Assistance _____
   _____

   Federal Register _____
   _____

   _Foundation Directory_____
   _____

   Foundation Grants Index _____
   _____

   State Foundation Directory _____
   _____

   Foundation Center Regional Collection _____
   _____

   List of Corporations in District _____
   _____

   In addition to these basic resources, provide your grantseekers with a list of your local service clubs and organizations and the names of any school-related individuals affiliated with these groups.

   _____
   _____

3. **List any linkages you or your grants advisory group members have with college or university grants offices that could provide access to grants research. Include their names and a brief description of their relationship with the college/university grants office.**

   _____
   _____
   _____
   _____
   _____
   _____
   _____
   _____

Chapter 6

Strategies for Contacting Prospective Grantors

ONE KEY TO GRANTS SUCCESS is knowing how to use the valuable research tools outlined in Chapter Five to develop a plan for making pre-proposal contact with the grantor most likely to be interested in your project and in the benefits it will extend to your school, students, and community.

Developing District Endorsement for Your Preproposal Contact Program

Follow your district's guidelines for coordinating contact with prospective grantors. If the district requires notification or permission to seek outside funds, submit a letter to the appropriate office stating why your school should approach a particular grantor. Use your research to show how your project matches the funder's values.

If your district has no rules governing contact with funders, you may want to prevent possible trouble by submitting a letter to the central office advising them that you or your grantseekers intend to contact grant sources (list them in the letter) unless you are instructed otherwise.

If it does have rules or guidelines, they are intended to protect the image of your school system. When a grantor receives twenty-five proposals from your district and intends to fund only one, it would like to know the priority or importance your school system places on each. In other words, the grantor needs assurance that the proposal it chooses to fund will move the school and district toward its predetermined goals, objectives, and mission.

A district grants procedure also helps preserve the image of the school system by ensuring that communication with a grantor, be it preproposal contact or a completed application, is of the highest quality possible. When a principal contacts the district office before preproposal contact to get the endorsement of the school system, the grants office knows the principal understands successful grantseeking and that the school's approach to it is credible.

Assure the grants office that you simply want to confirm the grantor's potential interest in your school's project and to discuss strategy and the possibility of developing a proposal. Most grantors will require district signatures and in some cases school board endorsement, so let your district office know that you intend to provide a final proposal for early sign-off, and that it will have already passed a mock review to ensure it is of the highest quality.

No matter what your district grants system, you will find that sign-off on your proposal goes more quickly if you have employed a preproposal or early-warning system. This team approach will also help in cases where the grantor requires a matching or in-kind commitment.

By promptly alerting your central administration to a fiscal commitment, you will have a much better chance of procuring final signatures. As many grants call for a decrease in grantor support over several years, you will have time to discuss with your district your plans for increased school commitment through budget reallocation, support from the community, or a grant from a local source.

Your school's grantseekers must notify *you* that they are interested in contacting a potential grantor for the same reasons that you must notify your district's central office. Despite your best efforts to keep up with what is going on in your school, it is quite possible that an overzealous grantseeker will forget to inform you of her or his plans to contact a funder.

Develop a grantseekers' sign-on system that includes the requirement that no one initiate contact with a funding source without prior permission in writing from either you or your designated representative. For example, you may decide that the chairperson of your grants advisory committee should review all ideas proposed by your grantseekers and have the sole responsibility of signing the necessary forms or that the chairperson should review the proposed ideas and then take the requests to the entire grants advisory committee for final approval.

In any event, you must have a system in place that assures that any contact with grantors follows sound grantseeking principles and has school and district approval. Having a standard procedure and form will make your grantseekers aware of your school's guidelines on the following:

- How to contact different types of grantors
- Who should contact them
- What individuals should bring to preproposal meetings
- How they should dress
- What information they should obtain to develop a quality proposal

Your system should include giving each potential proposal a tracking number. This will help you periodically evaluate your grants system to determine how many of the proposed ideas actually result in a submitted proposal, an awarded grant, a rejection, and so on.

When and how the rules are publicized will vary according to what you and your grants advisory committee require, but they could be included in your teacher handbook or presented at orientation meetings, teacher workshops, in-service sessions, and so on.

Review Exhibit 6.1, the School Grantseekers' Preproposal Endorsement Worksheet, for possible inclusion in your grants system.

Preproposal Contact: The Principal's Role

How can a busy principal integrate preproposal contact into an already packed schedule? The key is the proper use of your grants advisory group, volunteers, and teachers. You need not be the one who makes the contact. In fact, the best person to make contact may be a volunteer. If you mobilized your grants effort through a grants advisory group, you may already have a volunteer with a sales and marketing background who would be happy to meet with a potential funding source.

Why is preproposal contact so important? Contact with grantors in advance of writing a proposal allows grantseekers to do the following:

- Confirm their research
- Learn about changes, additions, and new grantor interests
- Avail themselves of valuable information that will help them prepare their proposals (whether in the form of copies of successful grants, newsletters, or priority statements, this can be incorporated into the project and proposal)
- Understand the proposal review process and how they can become a reviewer

Exhibit 6.1

SCHOOL GRANTSEEKERS' PREPROPOSAL ENDORSEMENT WORKSHEET

To ensure that you receive maximum benefit from your school and central office's grant development services, please submit this form to your school principal when you begin to consider seeking grant funds from nondistrict resources.

1. **Grantseeker's Name:** _____

    Phone: _____

2. **Area to be addressed through grants:**

    _____

    _____

3. **How the need to address this area was identified:**

    _____

    _____

    _____

4. **Brief documentation of the need:**

    _____

    _____

    _____

5. **If potential solutions have been developed, please provide a summary of each.**

    _____

    _____

    _____

    _____

6. **Please suggest key personnel to be involved in:**
    - The development of the proposal _____
    - Implementing the project if funded (include % of time) _____

7. **List the resources that may be required to implement and maintain the project if the school and district support it.**
    - School space requirements (sq. footage, special needs) _____
    - Equipment _____
    - Supplies, materials_____

8. **Will any matching or in-kind contributions be required of the school or school district?**
    _____ yes   _____ no

If you have already conducted a search for potential grantors, please attach your list of proposals to this worksheet. By reviewing your list of potential funding sources, we will be able to determine whether any of these grantors are currently being contacted to support other school or district projects. This will minimize the chances of a potential conflict.

Permission to continue your search for funding will be evaluated. If granted, you will be required to follow the school's grants system to ensure a quality product.

I ask many grantseekers why they avoid preproposal contact. Their answers vary, but there is one consistent theme: most people would rather write a proposal and place it in the mail than risk having their ideas rejected in a face-to-face meeting with a prospective grantor.

Whatever their reasons for avoiding preproposal contact, you must help your grantseekers put them aside. Point out that such contact will be less intimidating if they do their homework and know enough about the prospective grantor to ask intelligent questions that reflect their knowledge rather than expose their ignorance.

First, encourage your grantseekers to review the appropriate Grantseekers' Matrix (Tables 4.2 through 4.10) to refresh themselves on the values and interests of the type of funder they have decided to approach. Second, have them review the research collected on each specific grantor. Naturally, any procedural information gathered on a particular funding source should be followed. In general, however, the following suggestions will be helpful.

How to Contact Government Grantors

Contact government agencies by letter, phone, and in person, when possible. The first step is to send the agency a letter requesting program information and to be put on the agency's mailing list. When appropriate, use the Sample Letter to a Federal Agency Requesting Information and Guidelines (Exhibit 6.2).

Next, call the agency. The *Catalog of Federal Domestic Assistance* (CFDA) may give the program officer's name and the agency's phone number or e-mail address. Keep in mind, however, the possibility that no one in the agency has ever heard of the individual.

Tell the person who answers the phone that you are calling for information concerning a grant program and identify the program by CFDA reference number and name.

It usually takes one or two referrals to get the correct person and program. Introduce yourself and ask to speak to the program officer or to someone who can answer a few questions.

Through research, you should have collected a considerable amount of information about the potential grantee and should use this opportunity to validate it. For example, the deadline dates and appropriations printed in the CFDA can be checked for accuracy.

Tell your new contact what you want! Remember, there are more support staff involved in the government grants process than in the foundation or corporate process, and the rules governing freedom of information must

---

Exhibit 6.2

SAMPLE LETTER TO A FEDERAL AGENCY REQUESTING INFORMATION AND GUIDELINES

Date

Name
Title
Address

Dear [Contact Person]:

I am interested in the grant opportunities under [CFDA #], [Program Title]. Please add my name to your mailing list to receive information on this program. I am particularly interested in receiving application forms, program guidelines, and any existing priorities statements.

Please also send any other information that could help me prepare a quality application, such as a list of last year's successful grant recipients and reviewers. I am enclosing a self-addressed envelope for your convenience in sending these lists.

I will be contacting you when it is appropriate to discuss my proposal ideas. Thank you for your assistance.

Sincerely,
Name/Title
Phone Number

---

be adhered to in tax-supported grantmaking. Staff members are generally willing to provide information.

Your objective is to discuss your school's approaches to solving the problem. Ask if you could fax the grantor a one-page concept paper and call after it has been reviewed. Also, ask to be put on the grantor's mailing list to receive guidelines, application information, newsletters, and so on.

Review Figure 6.1, the Proactive Grantseeker's $85 Billion Federal Grants Clock, and then ask where the agency is in the grants cycle.

Ask if the agency published information about its rules in the *Federal Register*. If so, request the date of publication and page number.

Request a list of last year's grantees. This list of grant winners will help you determine whether your school even stands a chance as an applicant or whether you would be better off developing a consortium with other districts, joining with your intermediate district, or becoming part of a college or university's grant. The list of grantees will also tell you who got how much grant money.

Ask the agency official for information on the agency's peer review system. Although the *Federal Register* may have information on the points the reviewers award for each section of a proposal, you need to know who reads the grant applications. Knowing the types of reviewers and their background will help you decide what writing style to use and how to

Figure 6.1

THE PROACTIVE GRANTSEEKER'S $85 BILLION FEDERAL GRANTS CLOCK

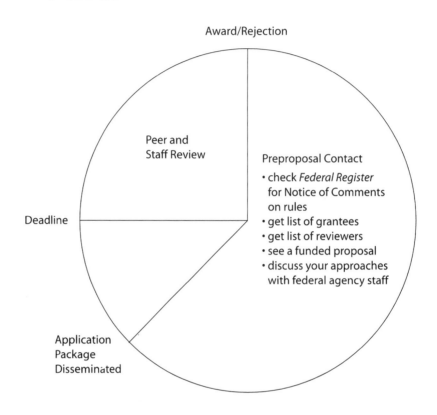

construct your proposal. In addition, you should ask the program officer how you could become a reviewer.

After the information-gathering phone call is over, the best strategy is for you, the principal, to visit the federal agency in Washington. In two or three days you can contact possible funders for several different projects.

Some federal programs actually require a preproposal meeting. These agencies want potential grantees to submit the best proposals even if they are unable to fund them. Good proposals and frequent requests for funds prove that their program is needed.

You could also invite the funding official to visit your school to observe the problem firsthand. She may come if you ask her to present an informative session on the agency's grants to other schools and districts.

You may also ask the program officer if she plans to attend an education conference or professional meeting being held in your area in the near future. If she is, you, one of your teachers, or one of your grants advisory committee members may be able to meet with her there.

If you cannot meet her yourself, who should represent you? A volunteer or advocate from your grants advisory group is best. Ideally, you and your advocate will go to the meeting together. Two is the magic number when it comes to representation.

Whoever goes, be aware that dress is important. Federal program officers generally dress quite conservatively. However, those at the National Endowment for the Humanities usually dress more casually than those in the Department of Education. Generally, the older the bureaucrat, the more conservative the dress.

Dress for Success by John T. Malloy has a section on how to dress for meeting with government bureaucrats. Although many individuals in the world of education are offended by the notion that people are judged by how they are dressed, it is worthwhile to look at this book. Malloy's work was originally funded by an education grant. The purpose of the grant was to determine whether classroom leaders' style of dress had an impact on students' learning and retention; research indicated that indeed it did. Very few educators ever read the research findings and fewer still improved their dress habits because of them, but the important point is that your representatives will be judged by what they wear, so they should dress accordingly.

What should you or your representative bring to the meeting? Bring materials that help demonstrate the need. These may include photographs and short audiovisual aids (three to five minutes long), such as filmstrips, videotapes, and slide presentations.

In addition, information on your community, school district, school, and specific classrooms may be helpful. Any of this can be left with program officers. But *never* leave a proposal.

Your representatives may also want to bring, or better yet commit to memory, a list of questions to ask the program officer.

Be sure to keep copies of all the information gathered on a prospective government funding source and to record all contacts and correspondence on the Federal Research Worksheet (Exhibit 6.3). In addition, record all information collected on agency personnel on the Federal Funding Staff History Worksheet (Exhibit 6.4).

Contacting Foundation Funding Sources

Send for information and guidelines from foundations. Many will mail you general information, grant application guidelines, annual reports, and newsletters on request. The Sample Letter to a Foundation Requesting Information and Guidelines (Exhibit 6.5) can be used with national general-purpose, special-purpose, community, and family foundations, but not with *all* foundations in these categories. Use the letter to contact

Exhibit 6.3

FEDERAL RESEARCH WORKSHEET

CFDA No. _____ **Deadline Date(s):** _____

Program Title: _____ **Gov't. Agency:** _____

Create a file for each program you are researching and place all the information you gather on this program in the file. Use this Federal Research Worksheet to:

- Keep a record of the information you have gathered
- Maintain a log of all telephone and face-to-face contacts made with the government agency
- Log all correspondence sent to and received from the agency

Agency Address: _____ **Agency Director:** _____

Telephone Number: _____ **Program Director:** _____

Fax Number: _____ **Name/Title of Contact Person:** _____

Place a check mark (✔) next to the information you have gathered and placed in the file for the foundation.

_____ Program description from CFDA

_____ Letter requesting to be put on mailing list

     _____ Sent for _____ Received

_____ List of last year's grantees

     _____ Sent for _____ Received

_____ List of last year's reviewers

     _____ Sent for _____ Received

_____ Application package—expected availability date

     _____ Sent for _____ Received

_____ Comments on rules/final rules from *Federal Register*

_____ Notice of rules for evaluation from *Federal Register*

_____ Grant scoring system—point allocation for each section. Source:

_____

_____ Sample funded proposal

_____ Federal Funding Staff History Worksheet

_____ Written summary of each contact made

_____ Grantor Strategy Worksheet

Record of Face-to-Face and Telephone Contact:

Date Contacted	Contacted by	Foundation Contact	Results	Action

Record of All Correspondence Sent and Received:

Date of Correspondence	Purpose of Correspondence	Results/Action

Exhibit 6.4

FEDERAL FUNDING STAFF HISTORY WORKSHEET

CFDA No. _____

Program Title: _____   _____

Gov't. Agency: _____

1. Name: _____

2. Title: _____
      (Agency Director, Program Director, Program Officer, etc.)

3. Business address: _____

4. Business telephone: _____

5. Birthdate: _____   Birthplace: _____

6. Marital status: _____   Children: _____

7. College/university _____

8. Degree(s): _____

9. Military service: _____

10. Clubs/affiliations: _____

11. Interests/hobbies: _____

12. Board memberships: _____

13. Other philanthropic activities: _____

14. Awards/honors: _____

15. Other: _____

Notes:

only those foundations that have application guidelines published in a resource such as the *Foundation Directory,* because only they are likely to have directors and staffs.

Note that this is an inquiry letter for information only. It is not a proposal to the foundation. If there is no response to it, a telephone call to the foundation is justified.

Of course, as fewer than a thousand of the forty thousand foundations have offices, telephone contact is very often impossible. In addition, many of the entries in foundation resource directories do not give telephone

---

Exhibit 6.5

SAMPLE LETTER TO A FOUNDATION REQUESTING INFORMATION AND GUIDELINES

Date

Name
Title
Address

Dear [Contact Person]:

My research on your foundation indicates that you provide application guidelines to prospective grantees. My organization is preparing a proposal in the area of [topic] and I would appreciate receiving these guidelines at your earliest convenience.

I would also appreciate any other information you may have that could help us prepare a quality proposal. Please add us to your mailing list for annual reports, newsletters, priority statements, program statements, and so on.

Since both of our organizations are committed to [subject area] I believe you will find our proposal idea of interest.

Sincerely,
Name/Title
Phone Number

---

numbers. Even if a phone number is listed in an entry or on an IRS tax return, do not call the foundation if the description of the foundation clearly states that there should be no contact except by letter.

If you have not gotten a response to your letter, and you are not aware of any instructions prohibiting telephone contact, by all means call and try to arrange a personal visit. If a face-to-face meeting is not possible, use the call to ask the same kinds of questions you would have asked at a meeting.

Ask the foundation official if you can fax a one-page summary of your ideas to him. Also ask if you can call him back to discuss the ideas. Arrange a mutually convenient time to call.

Steps for Contacting Foundation Grantors

If permissible, call the contact person. The principal's dilemma is deciding who should establish a relationship with the funder, an administrator or a grantseeker. Because many educators are reluctant to make preproposal contact, you may want to just get your grantseekers started and then step back. The caller may find it helpful to review the needs data first as a reminder that she is calling on behalf of your school, students, field of education, and so on, rather than for any private motive. This may help alleviate nervousness.

The caller should introduce herself and state the purpose of the call. (If a secretary or administrative assistant is reached, ask to talk to the foundation director or to a staff person best able to answer questions.) As with government grantors, one purpose of the call is to validate the information already gathered on the foundation. The caller's questions should reflect knowledge of the foundation's granting pattern and priorities. Then ask questions that will help ascertain the foundation's interest in your approaches to the problem or in increasing educational opportunities for elementary and middle school children.

It is important to demonstrate that you are different from other grantseekers. Show them that their foundation has been purposefully selected by asking questions that reflect your research. For example, "I am contacting the Sebastian Jessica Foundation because it has demonstrated its desire to see expanded parental involvement in elementary and middle schools. My research shows that 40 percent of your funds in recent years were committed to this area."

As with government grantors, tell the foundation funding source what you want. For example: "I would appreciate five minutes of your time to ascertain which of the two or three approaches I have developed for the XYZ School would elicit your foundation's greatest support and appeal to your board." You may use the fax approach here to maintain their interest.

Remember, you are presenting the funder with an opportunity to meet *their* needs. You are not begging. They are looking for good programs to support and you have one!

Ideally, you or your representative will meet face-to-face with the funder to discuss your grant approaches. You can either go to his location, or he can come to visit you at your school. By visiting your school he can observe your students and see the needs population or problem firsthand. The funder will expect to pay his way to visit you, or you to pay your way to visit him.

If a visit is made to the foundation, who should be your representative? Whether you visit the foundation or the other way around, your team should be small—usually no more than two. Select an active and concerned volunteer from your grants advisory group who is *donating* his or her time. The other person may be yourself or your classroom leader-grantseeker.

The team's style of dress should be similar to that of the foundation official. Again, your research will come in handy here, as well as the book *Dress for Success*. It is important to remember that your goal is to project the appropriate image to the prospective funding source. This is not the time to register your objections or state your values. But don't go overboard. Your team should dress in clothes they are comfortable in. The most important outcome of the visit is that the grantor hear your ideas.

What you bring to the meeting is extremely important. Focus on your objective. What do you expect to accomplish in a person-to-person visit with the potential grantor? You want the following:

- Agreement on the need or problem to be addressed

- To induce the prospective funder to discuss its interest in your solution

- Information on the grants selection process so that you can tailor your approach

- To validate your research and, in particular, ascertain the appropriateness of the size or amount of your potential grant request

To avoid the common mistake of jumping directly to the money issue, concentrate on bringing material that solidifies agreement on the need or the problem. In many cases, the grantor has difficulty seeing the problem through the eyes of a student or an educator. Your materials should be aimed at educating, rather than convincing, the grantor.

A short (three-to-five-minute) videotape or slide show, especially one produced by students as a class or school project, can demonstrate the problem very effectively. Whether it is about alcohol abuse or zoology, it tells a compelling story because it enables the funder to *see* what the need is.

A picture book that documents the need may provide the starting point for a discussion of the problem. Again, the objective of meeting with the grantor is to first establish agreement on the need for your project and then to ascertain the funding source's interests and to discuss several approaches or solutions.

Recording Foundation Research and Preproposal Contact

The purpose of preproposal contact is to validate your research on the funding source and to add to that knowledge so that you develop a grant-winning strategy. You want your grantseekers to be organized and to take advantage of every possible time-saving technique. Therefore, they should keep a file on each grantor they are researching and thinking about approaching. Keep these files together in alphabetical order. This will be a great start toward achieving an organized grants effort.

Fill out the Foundation Research Worksheet (Exhibit 6.6) for each foundation that is a possible source of funds. The worksheet helps you keep an up-to-date record of the information and materials you have gathered. It also serves as a log of all contact with each potential funding source.

Exhibit 6.6

FOUNDATION RESEARCH WORKSHEET

Foundation: _____   **Deadline Date(s):** _____

Create a file for each foundation you are researching and place all the information you gather on this foundation in the file. Use the Foundation Research Worksheet to:

- Keep a record of the information you have gathered
- Maintain a log of all telephone and face-to-face contact with the foundation
- Log all correspondence sent to and received from the foundation

Foundation Address: _____   Name of Contact Person: _____

Telephone Number:_____   Title of Contact Person:_____

Fax Number: _____

Place a check mark (✔) next to the information you have gathered and put in the file for the foundation.

_____ Foundation description from *Foundation Directory* or other source such as DIALOG, SPIN, etc.

      Note source: _____

_____ List of grants from IRS Form 990 or *Foundation Grants Index*

      Note source: _____

_____ Application information/guidelines

      _____ Sent for   _____ Received

_____ Foundation's annual report

      _____ Sent for   _____ Received

_____ Foundation's newsletter/other reports

      _____ Sent for   _____ Received

_____ Foundation funding staff history

_____ Written summary of each contact made

_____ Grantor Strategy Worksheet

Record of Face-to-Face and Telephone Contact:

Date Contacted	Contacted by	Foundation Contact	Results	Action

Record of All Correspondence Sent and Received:

Date of Correspondence	Purpose of Correspondence	Results/Action

In addition to information on a particular foundation, it is also important to collect as much information as possible on foundation officers, board members, and trustees. This information can help you and your grantseekers figure out strategies to deal with any preferences and biases you may encounter in your contact with a foundation. It will also help you pinpoint links between the foundation, your school, a volunteer on your grants advisory group, and so on.

Use the Foundation Funding Staff History Worksheet (Exhibit 6.7) to record the information you collect. Keep the worksheet in the appropriate file.

How to Contact Corporate Grantors

If your research reveals a corporate contact for grants information, you may decide to begin the grants process by writing to that person for information and application guidelines. The Sample Letter to a Corporation Requesting Information and Guidelines (Exhibit 6.8) can be sent to those corporations that actually have a grants staff and a preferred proposed format or application form.

Calling the corporate grantor is next, but before you do, review the reasons why you think the company would value your project and how your project relates to its products. If you do not know who the corporate contact is, ask whomever answers the phone who would best be able to answer your questions about the corporation's grants process. The person you are referred to may be a local plant manager or a salesperson.

As with foundation and government granting sources, state the reason for your call; for instance, "I am calling to discuss the opportunity of working together on a grant that has mutual benefits to both the XYZ School and the ABC Corporation." Request five minutes to answer your questions and suggest that you fax or mail background information. The purpose of sending background information is to solicit comments from them so that you can tailor your proposal to their needs. Be sure to let them know that you are not presenting your proposal to them at this point.

Summarize the research that has led you to contact this particular company. Let the corporate contact know that you are not approaching a hundred corporations but only a select group.

Corporations may actually spend more time reviewing grants than foundations do. One possible reason is that they have employees and offices, even though employees who act as corporate grants contacts may have several other responsibilities. This makes it possible for you to meet with the corporate grantor in person.

Exhibit 6.7

FOUNDATION FUNDING STAFF HISTORY WORKSHEET

Foundation: _____

1. Name of director/board member: _____

2. Title: _____

3. Residence address: _____   Phone: _____

4. Business address: _____   Phone: _____

5. Linkages/contacts (mutual friends/associates who can contact director/board member for you):

   _____
   _____
   _____
   _____

   List any data you have uncovered that might help you:

   - Determine ways to deal with any of contact's preferences and biases
   - Locate other possible linkages between this individual and you/your school's volunteer on your Grants Advisory Group, etc.

6. Birthdate: _____   Birthplace: _____

7. Marital status: _____   Children: _____

8. Employer: _____   Job title: _____

9. College/university: _____   Degree(s): _____

10. Military service: _____

11. Clubs/affiliations: _____

12. Interests/hobbies: _____

13. Other board memberships: _____

14. Other philanthropic activities: _____

15. Awards/honors: _____

16. Other: _____

Notes:

Exhibit 6.8

SAMPLE LETTER TO A CORPORATION REQUESTING INFORMATION AND GUIDELINES

                                                    Date

Name
Title
Address

Dear [Contact Person]:

My research on your company's grant support indicates that we share a concern for children and the importance of positive educational experiences.

[At this stage, mention your linkage if one exists.] [John Smith], your sales representative, suggested I write to request your company's proposal guidelines and requirements for funding a project I believe you will find very interesting.

In an effort to promote the most efficient investment of both our organization's time, I would appreciate any information relative to your company's funding priorities.

                                        Sincerely,
                                        Name/Title
                                        Phone Number

You may even want to invite the corporate person to visit your school to see the problem firsthand and to discuss the corporation's interest in the approaches you have developed to reduce the problem.

You may think that you, the principal, would be the best representative to meet with a corporate contact, but a volunteer might be better. You are paid by your district to represent it and your school; a volunteer is donating his or her time and may even be losing income to represent your school. Corporations will be impressed by the quality, commitment, and number of volunteers that your school can mobilize.

But don't overwhelm the corporate funder with a massive team. Two well-chosen and carefully instructed representatives will be most effective.

Although clothes do not make the person, remember that first impressions count. Dress as much as possible like the people you will be meeting with and strive to project a serious, businesslike look.

Bring information on the need for the project. As with other funding sources, you are advised to include one of the following:

- A short videotape that documents the need; include facts and, if possible, a testimony or case study for human interest

- A slide-audiotape presentation on the problem or need

- Pictures, charts, statistics, and so on

As corporations have their own style and vocabulary, it might be a good idea to ask a member of your grants advisory group from the corporate sector to make a short, corporate-style presentation to the funding source. This presentation might include colored charts and transparencies.

Recording Corporate Research and Preproposal Contact

As with foundations, you should create a file for each corporate prospect. The corporate files should be kept together in alphabetical order. Again, this will help organize your grants effort.

Fill out the Corporate Research Worksheet (Exhibit 6.9) for each of your most likely prospects for funding. The worksheet will help you keep an up-to-date record of the information you have gathered. Update the worksheet as additional information and materials are obtained. The worksheet will also be a record of all contact your grantseekers have had with the corporation.

Just as it is important to gather personal data on foundation officers, board members, and trustees, it is also important to gather personal data on corporate executives and contributions officers. You can uncover some information on corporate executives by examining various corporate resource materials such as *Standard and Poor's Register of Corporations, Directors and Executives.*

The more information you collect, the better your chances of developing an approach that will appeal to the funding source. In addition, your chances of identifying more linkages to the corporation will increase. However, please note that you should not rule out a particular corporation as a funding prospect simply because you are unable to gather personal data on the corporation's funding officials.

The Corporate Funding Staff History Worksheet (Exhibit 6.10) should be used to record the information collected. The worksheet should be stored in the appropriate corporation's file.

The Grantor Strategy Worksheet

Complete the Grantor Strategy Worksheet (Exhibit 6.11) for each funding source your grantseekers are planning to submit a proposal to. This worksheet will help you tailor both your approach to each funding source and your school's proposal to each funder's viewpoint.

Every attempt should be made to analyze the funding source's granting history. Even if preproposal contact is not possible, you must at least make sure that the amount you are requesting fits the funding source's granting pattern.

Exhibit 6.9

CORPORATE RESEARCH WORKSHEET

Corporation: _____   **Deadline Date(s):** _____

Create a file for each corporation you are researching and place all the information you gather on this foundation in the file. Use the Corporation Research Worksheet to:

- Keep a record of the information you have gathered
- Maintain a log of all telephone and face-to-face contact with the foundation
- Log all correspondence sent to and received from the foundation

Corporation Address: _____   Name of Contact Person: _____

Telephone Number: _____   Title of Contact Person: _____

Fax Number: _____

Place a check mark (✔) next to the information you have gathered and put in the file for the corporation.

_____ Description of corporate giving program from *National Directory of Corporate Giving, Corporate Foundation Profiles,* or other source.

Note source: _____

_____ Required proposal format, grant application/guidelines

_____ Corporate foundation's 990 IRS tax return

_____ List of corporate officers, sales representatives

Note source: _____

_____ Corporate product information (the Standard Industrial Classification Code)

_____ Profits/dividends information—financial status of corporation from *Dun and Bradstreet's Million Dollar Directory,* credit rating service, or other source.

Note source: _____

_____ Corporate funding staff history

_____ Information obtained from Chamber of Commerce (number of employees, payroll, etc.)

_____ Written summary of each contact made

_____ Grantor Strategy Worksheet

Record of Face-to-Face and Telephone Contact:

Date Contacted	Contacted by	Foundation Contact	Results	Action

Record of All Correspondence Sent and Received:

Date of Correspondence	Purpose of Correspondence	Results/Action

Exhibit 6.10

CORPORATE FUNDING STAFF HISTORY WORKSHEET

Corporation: _____

1. Name of funding executive: _____

2. Title: _____

3. Residence address: _____ Phone: _____

4. Business address: _____ Phone: _____

5. Linkages/contacts (mutual friends/associates who can contact funding executive/corporation for you):

   _____

   _____

   _____

   _____

   List any data you have uncovered that might help you:

   • Determine ways to deal with any of contact's preferences and biases
   • Locate other possible linkages between this individual and you/your school's volunteer on your Grants Advisory Group, etc.

6. Birthdate: _____ Birthplace: _____

7. Marital status: _____ Children: _____

8. College/university: _____ Degree(s): _____

9. Military service: _____

10. Clubs/affiliations: _____

11. Interests/hobbies: _____

12. Other board memberships: _____

13. Other philanthropic activities: _____

14. Awards/honors: _____

15. Other: _____

Notes:

Exhibit 6.11

GRANTOR STRATEGY WORKSHEET

Potential Grantor: _____   **Priority #:** _____

Deadline: _____

A. **Strategy Derived from Granting Pattern**

　　1.　$_____ Largest grant to organization most similar to ours

　　2.　$_____ Smallest grant to organization most similar to ours

　　3.　$_____ Average grant size to organizations similar to ours

　　4.　$_____ Average grant size in our area of interest

　　5.　$_____ Our estimated grant request

　　6.　Financial trend in our area of interest over past three years

　　　　_____ Up　　_____ Down　　_____ Stable

　　7.　If your proposal is a multiyear proposal, how popular have these been with the funding source in the past three years?

　　　　_____ Many multiyear proposals funded

　　　　_____ Some multiyear proposals funded

　　　　_____ Few multiyear proposals funded

　　　　_____ No multiyear funding

　　　　_____ Not applicable

　　8.　Financial data on funding source: obligation levels for last three years for grants

　　　　19_____ $_____　　　19_____ $_____　　　19_____ $_____

B. **Based on preproposal contact, which solution strategies are the most appropriate for this funding source?**

C. **Proposal Review System**

　　1.　Who evaluates submitted proposals? _____

　　　　_____

　　2.　What is the background and training of the evaluators? _____

　　　　_____

　　　　_____

　　3.　What point system will be followed?_____

　　　　_____

　　　　_____

　　4.　How much time will be spent reviewing each proposal? _____

　　　　_____

D. **Use this space to note anything special that will affect proposal outcome.**

_____

_____

_____

_____

_____

Think about who might collaborate with you on your proposal and what other groups might submit proposals that better fit the funder's requirements.

If at all possible, find out who will read and evaluate your school's proposal. For example, will your proposal be read by staff members? Board members? Program personnel? Outside experts or reviewers? Besides helping you write the proposal, this information will be vital to performing a mock review.

The prospective funding sources should be ranked by prospect potential. At this point, do not spend much time writing the proposal. Instead, your grantseekers should be investing their time analyzing their best prospects for funding.

Although some pieces of vital information will probably be missing, devise the best strategy you can based on what you know.

CHAPTER 6 CHECKLIST

Evaluation and Planning Worksheet

1. **Does your district have guidelines on contacting potential grantors?**

    _____ yes   _____ no

    If yes, do you have a copy of the guidelines?

    _____ yes   _____ no

2. **Are there unwritten rules regarding contact with grantors?**

    _____ yes   _____ no

    If yes, what are they? _____

    _____

    _____

3. **Do you have a standard form or letter that you use to apprise your central office of the funding sources you intend to approach for a grant?**

    _____ yes   _____ no

4. **Have you developed a guide for your grantseekers outlining your school's preproposal contact system and your role in assisting with preproposal contact?**

    _____ yes   _____ no

    If yes, please check (✔) those items/services you provide:

    _____ preproposal endorsement worksheet

    _____ list of services available

    _____ worksheets to help the grantseeker focus on the key components of proposal development

    _____ rules on how to contact the various types of funding sources

    _____ assistance in becoming a reviewer

    _____ a grants strategy that pulls all the data together

Chapter 7

Putting the Proposal Together: Developing a Strategy, Plan, and Budget

THE SUCCESS OF A GRANTS STRATEGY relies on selecting a grantor who is interested in the project and values its outcomes, choosing a strategy or solution that the grantor wants to support, and proving that your school is a credible partner worthy of grant funds and the affiliation and endorsement that accompanies those funds.

Your school's proposals must stand out over the competition and command the respect of prospective grantors. You will establish your school's image as a source of exemplary proposals by submitting only those that reflect a comprehensive, organized approach to grantseeking. An interested grantor wants to believe that your school has a plan to support the proposed solution and reduce the gap between what exists and what could be for the target population. Overzealous grantseekers may get caught up in the excitement of implementing the proposed project and lose sight of the need for a complete, detailed plan. Even a grantor who rejects a proposal should believe that its quality is guaranteed by your signature on your school's application.

A quality proposal is based on an easily understandable plan that provides the rationale for the proposed activities and expenditures. Some grantors require that this plan be described in a budget narrative form. Others prefer it to be visually displayed on a spreadsheet. Even when not required, a spreadsheet that provides the detail necessary to prepare and negotiate a budget should be prepared. When you suggest this level of plan detail to your grantseekers, they probably won't like it. They may tell you that developing a spreadsheet takes too much time, and ask why it should be done if the grantor doesn't require it. The answer is simple: a spreadsheet helps them create a well-developed plan, provides the detail necessary to prepare and negotiate a budget, and acts as the basis for job descriptions and evaluation of project personnel.

Not only are you, the principal, instrumental in developing and submitting proposals, but you are also responsible for putting the proposed plans in place and measuring the results. Indeed, your credibility and the reputation of your school rely on your successful completion of the grant-funded project; this is why you should be a moving force in developing a detailed plan for every grant proposal submitted for funding. Nor does the work stop when funding is obtained. The moment of euphoria when notice of the award arrives is quickly replaced by the feeling of responsibility for implementing an error-free plan.

You, the principal, may be closely involved in only a few grants, but you will initiate, enable, and facilitate many others. The greater your remove from a grant-funded program, the more nervous you will be about spending the funds and meeting the expectations of the grantor. This is why you need a project management system that allows you to track each project's progress, locate the equipment purchased under each grant, and maintain your school's credibility inside and outside your school district. Many principals complain of their inability to control and spend grant funds that were accepted by the district but never made available to the school and the project director who wrote the proposal. This can be avoided with an effective project management system.

By this point, your grantseekers should have documented a problem, come up with several possible ways to address it, and decided which will most appeal to the potential grantor. Their research on the funding source and preproposal contact should have helped them choose the solution or approach that most likely offers the prospective grantor what it wants. Now the real work of proposal development begins.

Research on the prospective funder may have included procuring a copy of proposals the grantor has funded in the past. These give you an idea of the types of objectives, methods, and format the funder prefers.

Research should have at least uncovered the funder's range of grant awards. If your school's proposal requires more funds than a grantor is likely or able to invest, you need a project plan that identifies several grantors and the amounts needed from each. The plan should also clearly delineate which parts of the project each grantor will fund.

As your grantseekers become more and more involved in developing proposals, you must remind them to view proposals through the eyes of the potential funding source and to make every effort to tailor each proposal to each prospective grantor. This reinforces the values-based approach to grantseeking. Remember, the funder may not see the methods, budget, or grant request the way you and your grantseekers do. Indeed, each type of grantor will view these differently. For example, government grantors prefer longer, well-organized proposals that allow them to easily identify matching or in-kind contributions and may require a written description linking each budget expenditure to a method. In contrast, most corporate and foundation funders prefer a short letter of proposal and use a business approach that relies on cost analysis of each step in your plan.

Whatever their type, all grantors require that you have a clearly defined plan. Just as you require teachers to have well-developed lesson plans, funding sources require grantees to have well-developed project plans before they give funds. The Project Planner (Exhibit 7.1) should help your grantseekers format grants plans.

The Project Planner

Think of the Project Planner (Exhibit 7.1) as a lesson plan or spreadsheet. The proposed plan becomes the final plan when its developers determine the solution or approach preferred by the prospective grantor. It must show the percentage of time and effort that key staff spends on the project, the use of consortium arrangements, and any matching or in-kind contributions your school will provide.

The Project Planner helps your proposal developers come up with a clear proposal methodology, plan, and budget. Once completed, it allows them to define and refine several aspects of the project:

1. An adequate staffing pattern that describes who is needed to do what tasks when (helping ensure that your job descriptions match the tasks that must be accomplished)

2. An easily scanned overview of the prescribed activities and how they relate to costs and the attainment of the objectives

3. A logical framework on which to evaluate the tasks performed by consultants

4. A detailed analysis of the materials, supplies, and equipment related to each objective

5. A defensible budget and cash forecast

6. An efficient way to keep track of in-kind or matching donations

7. A basis for dividing costs among multiple funders

8. A working document that helps you assess the involvement of multiple organizations and the responsibilities of consortium participants and subcontractors

Exhibit 7.1

PROJECT PLANNER

PROJECT PLANNER

PROJECT TITLE: _____

Proposal Developed for: _____

Project Director: _____

Proposed Start Date _____

Proposal Year _____

A. List project objectives or outcomes A. B.		MONTH		TIME	PROJECT PERSONNEL	PERSONNEL COSTS			CONSULTANTS CONTRACT SERVICES				NON-PERSONNEL RESOURCES NEEDED SUPPLIES - EQUIPMENT - MATERIALS				SUB-TOTAL ACTIVITY COST	MILESTONES PROGRESS INDICATORS		
B. List methods to accomplish each objective as A-1, A-2, ... B-1, B-2		Begin	End			Salaries & Wages	Fringe Benefits	Total	Time	Cost/Week	Total	Item	Cost/Item	Quantity	Tot cost	Total I.L.P	Item	Date	
		C/D		E	F	G	H	I	J	K	L	M	N	O	P	Q	R	S	

Total Direct Costs or Costs Requested From Funder

Matching Funds, In-Kind Contributions, or Donated Costs

Total Costs

100%   % of Total

©David G. Bauer Associates, Inc.
(800) 836-0732

Project Planners appeal most to funding sources that are familiar with and use spreadsheets themselves (corporations, for example). Such planners have only recently become an addition to government proposals. Federal program officers and their grant and contract officers are now trying to pinpoint inflated budget items, and will push grantees to agree to carry out proposals for less money than originally requested. They are simply trying to negotiate, a process that requires give-and-take. But most grantseekers just take what the federal grantor says it wants to give.

Standard federal budget forms use broad budget categories. These make it difficult to demonstrate that a project will be compromised if less money is granted than requested. But a Project Planner shows how a reduction in funds will impede methods or activities and negatively affect a proposal's objectives. This link between cause and effect is crucial to negotiating the final award because the achievement of a proposal's objectives is shown to be directly related to bringing about the change desired by both the grantee and the funder. The Project Planner allows grantseekers to present a clear picture of the relationship between project personnel, consultants, equipment and supplies, and the accomplishment of your school's proposal.

If you and your grantseekers are not familiar with spreadsheets, the Project Planner might seem a bit overwhelming. But there are many ways to complete it, and the only real mistakes one can make on a spreadsheet are mathematical (incorrect addition, multiplication, and the like).

Look at the Project Planner as a tool that helps your grantseekers identify the costs of carrying out the methods and activities in the proposed plan and how those costs will be divided among each partner in the agreement. They decide how detailed the planner's breakdown of activities needs to be. The more detailed the breakdown of the steps involved, the easier it is to document the costs assigned to each activity and to defend them in budget negotiations.

The basic purpose of the Project Planner is to provide a clear plan that results in the educational change described in the project objectives. Therefore, we must look at how to develop objectives before we examine the general guidelines for filling out the Project Planner.

Objectives

This book's companion, *The Teacher's Guide to Winning Grants*, devotes an entire chapter to developing measurable project objectives. The principal needs to remind the proposal developer of the importance of objectives that demonstrate the type of changes that the grantor values. Proposed plans must meet or exceed the educational change defined in their objectives. My rule: no objectives, no need for a plan; no plan, no need to bother grantors.

A good objective tells the funder what will change and how much if funds are granted. Graduate training may have given you experience in setting affective, cognitive, psychomotor, and behavioral objectives, but many grantseekers do not understand the difference between an objective and a method. Some actually write objectives that focus on approaches or methods that will be used to bring about change. This confuses *what* will be accomplished with *how* it will be accomplished. Objectives deal with what will change; activities and methods tell how it will be brought about.

Make sure your grantseekers develop a well-constructed objective. Determine if there is more than one way to achieve it. If not—if there is only one possible approach—then you are dealing with a solution, not an objective. A well-developed objective focuses on an outcome, implying that there is more than one strategy that could reach it. If your grantseekers are confused about the differences between objectives and methods, ask them why they are performing a particular activity. The reply may give a clear sense of what will be measured as they close the gap in the area of need.

An objective provides a way to see how much change should occur by the project's end. A method tells how it will be accomplished. Objectives say what you want to accomplish, methods say how. Being aware of this distinction can dramatically strengthen a proposal.

Developing objectives may appear tedious, especially when your grantseekers are eager to move on to proposed solutions and proposals. But keep in mind that well-written objectives that focus on measurable change do the following:

- Make the proposal more interesting and compelling to the funder
- Enable grantseekers to measure the changes the proposal suggests
- Increase your school's reputation as a source of excellent proposals

More detailed guidelines for developing objectives are provided in *The Teacher's Guide to Winning Grants,* but, in general, a well-written objective includes an action verb and statement, measurement indicator, performance standard, deadline, and cost frame.

Action Verb and Statement

The direction of change to be accomplished is based on the information provided on the Needs Worksheet (Exhibit 3.2) and Goals Worksheet (Exhibit 3.4). Remember, you and your grantseekers are not suggesting or promising that a goal will be met or a gap between today and the ideal will be entirely eliminated by the funding of your proposal. You are suggesting that a measurable part of the gap will be closed by means of its prescribed actions, methods, and activities. You are not certain that your proposed approach will be entirely successful, but you are proposing that it will benefit education by at least partially closing the gap and expanding knowledge of what works.

For instance, any single project aiming to promote educationally responsible behavior by parents, teachers, and students is unlikely to do the job completely. Thus a grant proposal should suggest that the project will lessen, not eradicate, irresponsible behavior by parents, teachers, and students.

If you ask your grantseekers what will change as a result of a project, often some answers will have to do with knowledge and others with values and feelings. In the example just cited, some might specify outcomes in the area of cognition or knowledge, others in the area of attitudes and feelings. Because issues such as this are complex, your grantseekers may want to ask for help from the college or university faculty members on your grants advisory committee when constructing objectives.

Measurement Indicators

Just as there are many ways to accomplish objectives, there are several ways to measure change of need. Your grantseekers should begin by asking what students will do differently after experiencing the methods aimed at solving the problem and how that change can be measured. Are there standardized tests or evaluation instruments for this purpose? If not, can a way of measuring the desired change be developed?

In the sample project to increase educationally responsible behavior in parents, teachers, and students, the reduction in the gap between what exists now and what ought to be can be measured in a variety of ways. For instance, we could look for behavior that indicates a developing sense of responsibility: improved grades, less absenteeism, higher percentage of students successfully completing their grade, more time spent on homework, more teacher-parent contacts, more parent-child talks about education, and less time spent watching television. We might even develop an Educational Responsibility Scale that contains questions aimed at surveying many of these points.

Performance Standards

A grantor will look at the objectives, note the size of the grant requested, examine the measurement indicators, and compare the amount of the request with the expected amount of change.

For a multiyear project, your grantseekers may want to create objectives stating a one-year goal for change and increase the amount of expected change over subsequent years. For example, in the educationally responsible behavior project, the objective could be to achieve a 25 percent increase in one year and a 40 percent increase by the end of year two.

Deadline

Most government grants are for one year because of the way the federal budget appropriation cycle currently operates. However, there is a movement in Washington to allow multiyear awards because it is difficult to demonstrate behavioral change in just twelve months. It often takes a good part of a year just to develop and conduct pretests that provide the baseline data for posttests.

Thus far in our discussion, the objective of our sample project might be expressed like this:

> *To increase educationally responsible behavior in parents, students, and teachers in the XYZ Elementary School [action verb and statement] by 25 percent [performance standard] at the end of year one [deadline] and by 40 percent [performance standard] at the end of year two [deadline], as measured by the Responsible Education Scale [measurement indicator].*

Cost Frame

Include the cost of accomplishing the change in the body of the objective. This demonstrates that you have total command of your proposal. You know *what* you will measure, *how* you will measure it, *when* it will be accomplished, and *how much* it will cost. This provides a stark reminder of how much it costs to accomplish educational change. The one catch is that your grantseekers cannot know the cost until they have completed their project planner.

Completing a Project Planner

The following general guidelines follow the format of the planner sample shown in Exhibit 7.1.

Objectives and Methods

In the column labeled A/B, list your project objectives and label each—for example, Objective A, Objective B, Objective C, and so on. Under each, list the methods you will use to accomplish each of the objectives. Think of the methods as the tasks or activities you will use to meet the need. Label each of the methods under its appropriate objective. For example, A–1, B–1, C–1, and so on.

Month

In column C/D, record the month you will begin each activity or task and the month you will end each. Writing 1/4, for example, means you intend to begin the first month after you receive funding and carry out the activities over four months (sixteen weeks). If you know the expected start-up month, note it here.

Time

In column E, record the number of person hours, weeks, or months needed to accomplish each task listed in Column A/B.

Project Personnel

In column F, list the names of key personnel who will spend a measurable or significant amount of time on each task or activity listed and on each objective. (You have already recorded the amount of time in Column E.)

Personnel Costs

In the next three columns, list the salaries and wages (column G), fringe benefits (column H), and total compensation (column I) for each of the key personnel listed in column F.

Doing this may take some work. Start by coming up with a rough job description by listing the activities each person will be responsible for and the minimum qualifications you require. Determine whether each will be full- or part-time by looking at the number of hours, weeks, or months they will be needed. Once you have developed a rough job description, you can call a placement agency to get an estimate of the salary needed to fill the position.

Be sure to include services from your organization that will be donated. Put an asterisk next to all donated personnel and remember that their fringes as well as their wages will be donated. Identifying donated personnel is crucial when matching or in-kind contributions are required, and may be advantageous even if not; matching contributions show good faith and make you seem a better investment. Indeed, put an asterisk by *anything* donated (such as supplies, equipment, and materials) as you complete the remaining columns.

Consultants and Contract Services

In the next three columns, list the time (column J), cost per week (column K), and total cost (column L) of assistance to be provided by consultants and other contractors. These are individuals not in your normal employ who provide services not normally provided by someone in your organization. (Note: no fringe benefits are paid to these.)

Nonpersonnel Resources Needed: Supplies, Equipment, Materials

Use the next four columns to list the supplies, equipment, and materials needed to complete each activity and itemize the associated costs. In column M, list the items; in column N, list the cost per item; in column O list the quantity of each item; and in column P list the total cost.

Do not underestimate the resources needed to achieve your objectives. Ask yourself and your key personnel what is needed to complete each activity. Again, designate donated items with an asterisk.

Subtotal Cost for Activity

Add columns I, L, and P—the totals of personnel costs, consultants and contract services, and nonpersonnel resources—and note the sum in column Q. You can do this either for each activity or for each objective. If you do it by objective, you will have to add the subtotals for all the activities that fall under the objective.

Milestones and Progress Indicators

In column R, list what you will show the funding source to tell them how you are working toward accomplishing your objectives (such as a quarterly report). Think of these as milestones or progress indicators. In column S, record the dates by which the funding source will receive the listed milestones or progress indicators.

Involving Corporate Volunteers

Corporate volunteers can be extremely helpful in preparing the Project Planner. They may have access to computer software that can develop a spreadsheet and a forecast of cash flow for your project. However, as your school's representative to the corporate world, you must be aware of the problems in communication that can occur when you involve corporate people in developing educational programs.

Many corporate staff have been exposed to business seminars on management theories such as management by objectives, matrix management, total quality management, and the learning organization, to name a few. The management theory vocabulary, and that of the corporate world in general, is much different from that of the field of education. Hence, confusion can result when an educator and a corporate individual work together to develop goals or objectives. For example, in education, goals are long-range desires. They are normally part of a "guiding statement" and are therefore nonmeasurable and usually nonobtainable. In the corporate world, goals are daily steps taken to accomplish objectives—what an educator would call methods or activities. To make matters even more confusing, objectives in the corporate world are long-range and normally part of a guiding statement; in education they are what we want to accomplish and are measurable.

It is easy to imagine how this difference in understanding could extend to a proposal submitted for corporate funding. It would therefore be wise to ask one of your corporate volunteers to review the proposal prior to submission to ensure that the vocabulary is appropriate for a corporate funding source.

Project Planner Example

One way to complete a project planner is shown in Exhibit 7.2. In this example, the project director's salary is being requested of the funder, as are the salaries of two graduate students who will assist the director. The services of the project director and the graduate students are being contracted from West State University. Therefore, their time commitments and costs fall in columns J, K, and L on the Project Planner.

The project director, Dr. Smith, will ask West State University's Human Subject Institutional Review Board to examine the procedures involved in getting the students, parents, and teachers to agree to write contracts for change. It is anticipated that she will work half-time on the project for twelve weeks during months one through six and full-time for twenty-four weeks during months seven through twelve.

This case shows considerable matching and in-kind contributions, as noted by the asterisks. For example, the school district is donating the salary and fringe benefits of the project secretary. In addition, a significant portion of matching and in-kind contributions is coming from the Jones Corporation, which is donating the use of its corporate video production facility.

Although these contributions demonstrate frugality, commitment, and hard work, "overmatching" can become an issue. When a proposal has a huge matching component and requires only a small amount of grant funds, a prospective grantor may conclude that the *entire* proposal should be funded through matching and in-kind contributions. Still, most matching components are viewed favorably by grantors.

Using the Project Planner for Budgeting

It is best that you, the school administrator, review the Project Planner with the proposal creators to ensure that they have included all the elements necessary for the development of a realistic budget and the success of the plan. With this in mind, several key areas need emphasis.

Exhibit 7.2

SAMPLE PROJECT PLANNER

Proposal Developed for: _____

Project Director: _____   Proposed Start Date: _____   Proposal Year: _____

PROJECT PLANNER

PROJECT TITLE: A Contract for Educational Change – Parents, Students, and Teachers Charting a Course of Responsibility

A. List project objectives or outcomes A. B. B. List methods to accomplish each objective as A-1, A-2, ... B-1, B-2 ...	MONTH Begin/End	TIME	PROJECT PERSONNEL	Salaries & Wages	Fringe Benefits	Total	CONSULTANTS Time	Cost/Week	Total	Item (Supplies-Equipment-Materials)	Cost/Item	Quantity	Tot cost	SUB-TOTAL Total I,L,P	MILESTONES Item	Date
	C/D	E	F	G	H	I	J	K	L	M	N	O	P	Q	R	S
Objective A: Increase educational cooperation of teachers, parents, and students by 25% as measured on the Responsible Educational Practices (REP) survey in 12 months at a cost of $	1/12															
A-1 Administer the survey on sample	1/3															
Project Dir (PD) & 2 graduate assistants		4w	PD	West State U			4w	1000	4000	REP Surveys	2.00	500	1000	5350		
(Grad) administer survey, analyze,		3w	2 Grad				3w	1000	3000	Mail Surveys	.50	500	250			
and input results										Phone Follow Up	1.00*	200	200*			
A-2 Develop and teach curriculum.	3/6															
a. Instruct parents, students, and teachers		3w	3 Trainer	9000*		9000*	6w	1000	6000	Mail Invites	.50	1200	600			
on responsible use of time, homework,		6w	PD													
responsibility, and contracts for change																
b. Teach all parties how the homework		3w	2 Grad				6w	500	3000	Refreshments	250		250			
responsibility system will work and how																
the homework hot line can be accessed																
and used.																
A-3 Set up computer system to handle	1/3															
homework assignments and hot line.																
a. Purchase system hardware and software		2w	Tech	2000*	500*	2500*				Hardware	8000	1	8000			
upgrades.			Coord							Software	2000	1	2000			
b. Install phone lines to handle system.		1w	Phone Co							Install Lines	2000*		2000*			
A-4 Implement the program.	6/12															
a. Set up K-12 instructional program on		10w	PD				10w	1000	10000	Access System	1000	6	6000			
system.		5w	1 Grad				5w	500	2500	for 6 Months						
A-5 Evaluate effectiveness of project.	12/12															
a. Posttest with Responsible		2w	PD				2w	1000	2000	REP Survey	2.00	500	1000			
Educational Practices survey.		1w	1 Grad				1w	500	500							
b. Report log of usage		2w	PD				2w	1000	2000	Mail	.50	500	250			
on hot line.		1w	1 Grad				1w	500	500							
c. Survey teachers and students on impact of		2w	PD				2w	1000	2000	Phone Follow	1.00*	200	200*			
grades and test scores.		1w	1 Grad				1w	500	500							

	Total	Total	Tot cost	Total I,L,P	% of Total
Total Direct Costs or Costs Requested From Funder	0	36000	19350	55350	80%
Matching Funds, In-Kind Contributions, or Donated Costs	11500*	0	2400	13900	20%
Total Costs	11500	36000	21750	69250	100%

©David G. Bauer Associates, Inc.
(800) 836-0732

Budget Negotiation

The budget, in whatever form it is requested, should reflect the Project Planner totals for personnel costs (column I), consultants and contract services (column L), and nonpersonnel resources such as supplies, equipment, and materials (column P). By pointing out the importance of subtotaling the costs for each activity in column Q of the Project Planner, you will be ready to help your grantseekers negotiate a grant award. Beginning to discuss the strategy for negotiating the budget while finishing the plan will enable you to set the stage for an accountable and defensible budget.

The negotiation itself, however, should not be based on the budget categories (personnel, consultants, supplies, and so on). Rather, it should be based on the methods or activities that make up the budget totals.

Review with your grantseekers the effect of reducing funds for each activity. What impact would it have on attaining the change indicated in the objective? You may be able to reduce the size of your request by eliminating an activity or two without having much effect on the project; however, if you eliminate too many activities you will probably not be able to accomplish your project as outlined. Instead, it may be preferable to modify the objective and reduce the amount of expected change or the number of students or participants the project will reach.

Matching and In-Kind Contributions

As one signer of the proposal, the school administrator will be required to document any and all costs that have been designated as matching or in-kind contributions.

More and more grantors are requiring that a school or community demonstrate commitment to the project through a system of contributions. As funding becomes more limited and competition increases, this practice will become even more common.

How does a school that needs funding demonstrate that it has resources to donate to a grant? It might seem paradoxical, but try to look at it from the funders' point of view: they want to see commitment!

First, consider the time your advisory group members have volunteered to the project. Can this be considered an in-kind contribution?

Second, review your Project Planner. Are there any personnel costs or nonpersonnel resources that could be donated instead of requested from the funder?

Finally, are there any hidden costs in your school that could qualify as matching contributions? For example, I once worked on a grant proposal that called for developing an in-service course for teachers as a way of effecting change in the classroom. In seeking to meet the funding source's matching funds requirement, a school administrator revealed that under the teachers' contract the district was required to pay each educator a salary increase after completion of the course. We calculated the average age of the participating teachers and the total number of years that the increase would be paid out to all teachers, multiplied this figure by the salary increase, and were allowed to claim the resulting figure as a match.

I cannot guarantee what a grantor will accept as a matching or in-kind contribution, but be creative. Review your project and look for every possible matching contribution. If you have a grants advisory committee, the members may volunteer some of the match by lending the use of facilities and donating equipment, printing, travel, and so on.

Cash Flow

As principal, you may or may not be praised for helping to develop the proposal, but you will surely be blamed if problems with cash flow arise. You can avoid trouble with cash flow by doing the following:

- Having a project plan that forecasts your cash requirements properly
- Making your school district aware of the cash forecast
- Having the appropriate administrator sign a proposal that includes the projected cash need of the project

By reviewing your Project Planner you will have the information necessary to determine your cash flow needs. Column C/D of the Planner designates the beginning and end of each activity, and column Q tells how much money will be required to accomplish each. Transfer this information to the Grants Office Time Line (Exhibit 7.3) and you will have a fairly accurate estimate of your cash flow needs.

Grants Office Time Line

The Grants Office Time Line is a visual representation of your time frame. It also shows an estimate of the cash you will require to stay on schedule.

From the Project Planner, transfer your activity number to column 1 of the Time Line. Then draw a line from the activity's projected start date to its completion date. For example, if the activity is to begin in the second month of the project and end in the fourth month, draw a line from 2 to 4.

On the far right of the line, write the total cost of the activity from column Q of the Project Planner.

Federal and many state funders require a quarterly cash forecast. In these cases, place the estimated cash forecast in the appropriate quarterly

Exhibit 7.3

GRANTS OFFICE TIME LINE

ACTIVITY NO.	1	2	3	4	5	6	7	8	9	10	11	12	TOTAL COST FOR ACTIVITY
	1st QUARTER			2nd QUARTER			3rd QUARTER			4th QUARTER			TOTAL

QUARTERLY FORECAST OF EXPENDITURES ▲

column at the bottom of the Time Line. Estimate the total cash needed for those activities that take place over several quarters or that require advance expenditure, such as equipment purchase.

The subsequent chapters help you move from the Project Planner spreadsheet to the written proposal.

CHAPTER 7 CHECKLIST

Planning and Evaluation Worksheet

1. **Do you currently use a spreadsheet or planning document in the preparation of proposals?**

   _____ yes   _____ no

   If yes, does it provide your grantseeker with:

   - job descriptions for staff & consultants   _____ yes   _____ no
   - percentage of time allocated to task   _____ yes   _____ no
   - itemized equipment list   _____ yes   _____ no
   - cost summary for each objective   _____ yes   _____ no
   - cash flow or projected cash needs   _____ yes   _____ no
   - matching or in-kind contributions   _____ yes   _____ no

2. **Can you use corporate volunteers to help with:**
   - proposal editing   _____ yes   _____ no
   - budget assistance   _____ yes   _____ no
   - developing computer spreadsheets   _____ yes   _____ no

3. **Do you have a system for helping staff develop behavioral objectives?**

   _____ yes   _____ no

Chapter 8

Preparing Federal Grant Proposals for Your School

MANY PRINCIPALS PREPARE their school's federal proposals virtually by themselves. This chapter provides principals with useful guidelines and techniques for writing grants, but its main purpose is to help them develop a grants system that involves others in writing federal proposals.

Let us assume that one of your grantseekers is looking for federal grant funds to support a project. He or she has completed a proposal sign-on form (see Chapter Six) to ensure your support and your district central office's approval, and, with your guidance, has made preproposal contact and procured the information needed to develop a funding strategy and a project planner.

The Federal Grantseekers' Proposal Checklist (Exhibit 8.1) ensures that your proposal developers have collected all the information and items necessary to successfully compete for federal funding. Your office should disseminate the checklist and maintain a grants resource file that contains examples of each of the items on the checklist, including sample proposals.

Most schools, even district grants offices, do not have a *system* that enables their grantseekers to examine a proposal (with reviewers' comments) submitted by their district to the federal agency they are approaching or to review a funded proposal submitted by another school district. This is senseless, because studying such a proposal could have a real impact on a prospective proposal writer.

Several education associations, such as Capitol Publications (see bibliography), and private companies compile the items on the Federal Grantseekers' Proposal Checklist and sell the package. Although the information your grantseekers need to help them write a quality federal proposal can be obtained at no cost under the Freedom of Information Act, they would have to travel to Washington, D.C., to gather it. Of course, if they did so they would have the opportunity for face-to-face contact with the funding source.

Exhibit 8.1

FEDERAL GRANTSEEKERS' PROPOSAL CHECKLIST

Put a checkmark next to those items that you have a copy of:

_____ School Grantseekers' Preproposal Endorsement Worksheet

_____ *Catalogue of Federal Domestic Assistance*—Program Description

_____ *Federal Register*—Rules and Regulations

_____ *Federal Register*—Announcement of Proposal Submission Deadline

_____ Past Grantees for Program

_____ List of Last Year's Reviewers or Profile of Reviewers

_____ Sample Funded Proposal

_____ Sample of Past School District Proposal with Reviewers' Comments

_____ Grantor Strategy Worksheet

_____ Federal Research Worksheet

_____ Federal Funding Staff History

_____ Scoring System to Be Used in Review

Your school's success rate in the federal grants marketplace depends on how well your grantseekers do their homework and follow the stringent rules for completing a federal grant application. For example, applying for funds from CFDA 84.201 (School Dropout Demonstration Assistance Program) requires a proposal of no more than thirty double-spaced pages, typed in a font allowing at least twelve characters per inch. Thus the proposal *cannot* be thirty-one pages or single-spaced. It is important to remind your grantseekers to express their creativity by developing innovative solutions to the problem, not innovative ways of completing the application.

The basic parts of a federal proposal are usually similar for all applications. Differences between agencies occur in the preferred ordering of the parts of the proposal, the terminology, and the points allocated to each part. The basic parts of a federal proposal for an education project are these:

A. Proposal abstract or summary

B. Needs statement

C. Plan of operation for addressing the need

D. Key personnel who will operate the program

E. Budget and cost-effectiveness

F. How the effectiveness of the project will be evaluated

G. Adequacy of resources

H. Assurances

I. Attachments

In addition, federal agencies that fund research in education require a section on the project's hypothesis, specific aims, and research design.

It is most important that the federal proposal be constructed in a manner that the reviewer will understand. The reviewer must be able to read through the proposal rapidly. The salient parts must be evident and well documented so that the reviewer can ascribe a point value to each section. The points assigned to each area and the distribution of any additional points are outlined in each agency's specific proposal guidelines.

Proposal Abstract or Summary

Most proposals require one of these. The abstract may have to fit into a designated space or number of lines. Photoreduction is not allowed. Federal agencies normally state the specific font required so that the proposal can be read without magnification.

There is some disagreement over when in the proposal development process the abstract or summary should be written. Most experts believe it should be written last, as the grant writer reflects on the completed proposal and summarizes each section; others contend that writing the abstract first helps the grantee focus on the ideas the proposal will describe. One must allow for grantseekers' individual differences, but preparing a detailed outline, then writing the proposal, and finally writing an abstract that summarizes the proposal works efficiently for most people.

Whether the abstract is written first or last, make certain that it has the required format and follows all the rules. It should provide a short, concise, and easy-to-read description of the need for the project, the objectives, the solution, and the evaluation. Before writing the abstract, your proposal developers should review the required sections of the proposal and the point system that the reviewers will use to evaluate and rank it. Suggest that they highlight those sections worth the most points and refer to them in the same terms as the federal agency.

To convey as much information as possible in a limited amount of space, some grant writers push the abstract to the margins and cram in as many words as possible. This usually is confusing and difficult to read. The federal response has been to specify font size as well as number of lines. Especially considering that the reviewer may have already read several proposals, a "crammed" abstract could set a negative tone for the entire proposal and lead to a low score.

Use this exercise with your grantseekers to help them prepare to write their abstract. Review the following abstract:

This project will identify those students at risk for dropping out, will intervene and provide the motivation and tools necessary to complete their high school education, and will encourage postsecondary education and/or training. Over a three-year period, this project will extend services to 450 students including 5 elementary programs that feed into 3 middle schools, which, in turn, feed into 2 high school programs. Activities in this project will increase coping and daily living skills through classroom instruction, utilize community volunteers to tutor students and act as role models, increase awareness and incentive through two field trips, as well as track school attendance and classroom progress acting as a mediator between teachers, parents, and students to resolve problems as they arise.

Now consider whether this abstract does the following:

- Shows that the grantseeker has a command of the need

- Indicates that the project has measurable objectives

- Provides a synopsis of the methods

- Presents the proposal's main points in an interesting manner

The abstract indicates that services will be extended to 450 students, five elementary programs, and three middle schools. It also provides a rough idea of the types of activities prescribed to retain students. And it does this in one sentence of 57 words! However, the abstract does not even hint at the need or give any measurement indicators or criteria for success. Also, based on the abstract, the project appears to be geared to high schools, which raises the issue of why elementary and middle schools will be involved. But before we get too critical, we should note that the project summarized in this abstract was funded for approximately $97,000!

The Needs Statement

This section may also be referred to as the "Search of Relevant Literature," the "Extent of the Need," or the "Problem." One federal program refers to the needs statement as the "Criterion: Extent to which the project meets specific needs recognized in the statute that authorized the program, including consideration of the needs addressed by the project; how the needs were identified; how the needs will be met; and the benefits to be gained by meeting the needs." One successful grantee responded to this criterion with a description of the extent of the need that included descriptions of the following:

1. *Target Area:* Where the applicant was located and data that identified a significant needs population in the student body

2. *Needs for Services:* What school programs were available, and the void between what is and what should be

3. *How the Needs Will Be Met:* A general description of what was to be done

4. *Benefits to Be Gained:* The anticipated positive outcomes of the project

When developing the needs section, your proposal developers should take into consideration the type of reviewer that will be reading the proposal application and try to determine what the reviewer will find motivating and compelling. The needs section must show that your applicant has a command of the current literature in the field so as to demonstrate his or her credibility. Many excellent proposals lose critical points because the grantee fails to command the respect of the reviewer by overlooking the needs section and placing the emphasis on the project description and plan of operation.

The following "extent of the need" has been taken from a grant funded by the Department of Education for dropout prevention.[1]

The target population to be served by the project has experienced low academic achievement, high public assistance rates, high dropout rates, linguistic and cultural differences, geographic isolation, and inaccessibility to existing career and training information. These conditions have combined to create high unemployment, underemployment, poor self-image, and a resultant low standard of living among these people. Astin's study of college attrition clearly identifies family income as a significant factor which negatively impacts student success in postsecondary education and contributes to high dropout rates. Astin does note, however, that this correlation is influenced by such other "mediation" factors as ability, motivation, financial concerns, and parental education.[2]

. . . The target population occupies a rural mountainous and desert region covering over 8,000 square miles which is larger than the combined area of Delaware, Rhode Island, and Connecticut.

1. Proposal: Four Corners School, College and University Partnership Program, Submitted to U.S. Department of Education, Division of Student Services, CDFA 84-204, by San Juan School District College of Eastern Utah-San Juan Campus, Utah Navajo Development Council, July 9, 1988.

2. Alexander W. Astin, *Preventing Students from Dropping Out,* San Francisco: Jossey-Bass, 1977.

. . . It is pertinent to note that 79.3% of the active job applicants are ethnic minority and that 63.5% had less than a high school diploma.

Facts such as those presented in this excerpt convince the reviewer and the federal staff that the writer is knowledgeable about the subject of the proposal. Statistics in the needs section of a proposal show a command of the situation and make a positive impression, unlike "grant-loser statements" such as:

- Everyone knows the need for . . .
- Current statistics show . . .
- It is a shame our students do not have . . .
- You can't believe the number of times . . .
- Several (many, an increasing number of) students . . .

When reviewers read a needs section containing such weak, banal statements they vent their frustration on the scoring sheet, and the grantseeker loses valuable points. A strong needs statement must cite facts, studies, and references and must reflect the commitment and hard work that went in to gathering them.

Plan of Operation

The federal application may refer to this section as the "Plan of Operation," "Objectives and Methods," or "Project Methodology." The purpose of this section is to describe an organized solution to the need and problem you have identified; it should thus include your proposal's objectives, methods, and activities. Study a funded proposal to see how successful grantees have organized this section.

Review the section in Chapter Seven on constructing behavioral and measurable objectives and then review the following sample objectives from a proposal for an early intervention dropout program. Keep in mind that the proposal was funded for $750,000!

1. *1,500 kindergarten through sixth-grade at-risk students will benefit from the District's effort to institutionalize instructional improvement and variation by comprehensively upgrading all instructional and support services. This will include: attendance monitoring and immediate follow-up on absences; ombudsmen and advocates for students; junior high at-risk student tutoring of early grade at-risk students; extended school day programs; and off-site activities.*

2. *Seventy-five kindergarten through sixth-grade teachers and two paraprofessionals will receive training on topics such as:*

implementation of effective school postulates, individualizing instruction, thematic instruction, ombudsmen and advocates for students, the city as a resource, training parents, managing at-risk student programs, and understanding the needs of ethnic minority (especially Hispanic-American) and low income students.

3. *Approximately 500 parents of at-risk students will attend 30 to 40 hours of project-sponsored activities focusing on issues such as: basic literacy, parenting, how to help your child with homework, English as a second language, and social issues information about: drugs and alcohol abuse, AIDS, teenage pregnancy, and suicide.*

4. *The results of this program will be publicized and disseminated. Strategies will include: a recruitment video, a video that showcases the progress and achievements of students, a program brochure, TV spot announcements, and presentations at community events.*

Do these objectives describe what will be accomplished or how the project will be done? The latter, but for three-quarters of a million dollars, we should be told what area we can expect to see change in, and how much.

Some of your grantseekers may be misled by objectives that contain numbers. Numbers alone do not mean that an objective is well constructed or even measurable. For example, the aforementioned objectives tell us the number of parents to be trained but not what they will do differently as a result or what impact it will have on students.

The following objective is from another proposal funded by the Department of Education under a different program. It demonstrates the measurable component of an objective much more effectively.

By June 1, 1997, at least 65 percent of all students enrolled in the academic year program will improve at least 1.5 grade levels in mathematics, language mechanics, language expression, and reading ability as documented by pre-post Comprehensive Tests of Basic Skills scores.

Review Chapter Seven on developing a project planner. The project planner provides an organized approach for developing the proposed plan. Whether or not you or your grantseekers use such a planner, your school's proposal will be evaluated on the thoroughness and clarity of the methods you prescribe to meet the objectives and address the need. Studying a previously funded proposal will provide insight on how successful grantees have organized this section of their proposal.

There are many ways to present the methods or activities. In the following example, the successful grantseeker first presents a main objective, then a subobjective or process objective, and finally the methodologies.

OBJECTIVE 3. UPGRADE BASIC SKILLS

PROCESS OBJECTIVE 3.1: Students will be counseled and tutored during the academic year program to meet their individual academic needs and overcome areas of deficiency.

Methodologies:

    a)   Deficiencies of participants will be documented through use of CTBS scores, transcripts, and interviews with teachers, parents, students, and counselors. Through this process, an individual education plan will be prepared based on areas of strengths, but particularly on areas of weakness in which the student needs help. This will be in the form of a contract which the student and counselor will sign to agree to work together to strengthen the academic skills which need improvement.

    b)   The counselor will schedule bi-weekly, after-school tutoring, and counseling sessions to provide academic assistance as well as emotional support.

Personnel Responsible: *Project counselors, tutors, and teachers from each high school.*

Resources: *Textbooks, testing and teaching materials, media centers of each high school.*

Key Personnel

This section provides the reviewer with an indication of your project staff's ability to implement the methods aimed at meeting the objectives and closing the gap between what is and what ought to be.

One dilemma that proposal developers face is that key personnel often have not been hired at the time a proposal is submitted. In that case, the proposal should clearly show that capable staff can be hired or that your school can reallocate individuals who have the necessary skills. Remember, reviewers who otherwise favor a proposal will be put off if they are not convinced that individuals qualified to implement the project are readily available.

Review the following section on key personnel from a funded Department of Education proposal.

Criterion: *The quality of the key personnel the applicant plans to use in the project.*

Staff will consist of a full-time project director, a full-time assistant project director, four part-time regular school year counselors, four full-time summer counselors, eight college and peer tutors, 12 part-time instructors, and a full-time secretary. Inasmuch as project staff have not been identified at this time, resumes are not included. The partnership would like to affirm that no problems are anticipated in acquiring qualified, experienced, highly competent personnel. At least one week will be scheduled at the beginning of the project for the orientation of staff to the goals, objectives, plan of operation, and so on.

Do you feel confident that this applicant has the expertise necessary to conduct this project? Does the statement that "no problems are anticipated in acquiring qualified . . . personnel" make you feel comfortable? This is like asking someone to bet on an unknown horse simply because you believe it will be a winner. Every grantor wants to know what horses a prospective grantee has in its stable!

In this example, the applicant could have stated that the project director would be reporting to Dr. Smith, who is currently responsible for managing X million dollars or completing Y projects. Note, however, that the prospective grantee did at least follow the key personnel criterion with a detailed description of the major positions mentioned in the body of the proposal.

Keep in mind that many government grantors look at the *appropriate* use of personnel as well as their quality. If you are thinking about minimally involving one outstanding person in many grants, you should be aware that some funders will ask for an outline of the time each staff member will commit to the project and may require that the project director or principal investigator commit a significant percentage of her or his time. In other words, do not have one outstanding and well-known individual spend 2 percent of his or her time on fifty different projects!

Budget and Cost-Effectiveness

Federal program proposal requirements differ, but all require a budget. Your proposal's budget and the items that comprise it may be viewed in relationship to how they affect your students, teachers, or parents. The amount you request may be divided by the number of beneficiaries so that the federal program officer and reviewer can arrive at the cost per person served by the proposal. One of the primary concerns of a reviewer is that the budget request be reasonable and based on the cost of the activities or methods outlined in the proposal. For example, if a project is supposed to provide a model for other schools, it must be affordable enough to be replicated by schools and districts that may not receive grants.

The following sample is from a federally funded proposal. Note that in the actual proposal, references to the cost per student were removed by federal agency staff. This may have been to prevent readers from calculating a formula for what they believed to be the program or agency's "preferred" cost figure.

REASONABLENESS OF BUDGET

Criterion: *Costs are reasonable in relation to the objective of the project.*

Salaries and benefits are based upon institutional schedules and policies. Supplies have been computed on the basis of local vendor prices. Travel and communication costs in such a geographically isolated location may appear to be rather extensive. These have been kept to a minimum with rates on institutional policies.

The overall cost per participant from federal funds amounts to $_____$ the first year, decreasing to $\$_____$ the second year and $\$_____$ the third year. The budget is reasonable and cost-effective, particularly considering the geographic isolation of the target area.

The federal funding agency may also require a budget narrative, which is an explanation of how the salaries, consultant services, equipment, and materials are related to the completion of each method or activity.

The Department of Education's most common budget information form for nonconstruction projects is ED Form No. 524. A sample is shown in Exhibit 8.2. The instructions for completing this form are shown in Exhibit 8.3. If you have completed a project planner (see Chapter Seven), you already have all the information you need to complete ED Form No. 524.

Evaluation

Objectives developed according to the methods suggested in Chapter Seven contain the basic steps for evaluation. Most projects demand some sort of preassessment survey so that baseline data can be gathered. Once the intervention steps or model project has been employed, the original baseline data can be compared with posttest evaluation data to demonstrate change in the target population or reduction of the problem.

Using outside consultants to evaluate the project is preferred by many reviewers in the hope that it may encourage an unbiased, independent evaluation. By discussing the evaluation section with the prospective grantor before submitting the proposal, your grantseekers should be able to determine the funding source's preferences.

Exhibit 8.2

ED FORM NO. 524

Budget Categories	Project Year 1 (a)	Project Year 2 (b)	Project Year 3 (c)	Project Year 4 (d)	Project Year 5 (e)	Total (f)
1. Personnel						
2. Fringe Benefits						
3. Travel						
4. Equipment						
5. Supplies						
6. Contractual						
7. Construction						
8. Other						
9. Total Direct Costs (lines 1-8)						
10. Indirect Costs						
11. Training Stipends						
12. Total Costs (lines 9-11)						

U.S. DEPARTMENT OF EDUCATION

BUDGET INFORMATION

NON-CONSTRUCTION PROGRAMS

OMB Control No. 1875-0102

Expiration Date: 9/30/98

Name of Institution/Organization

Applicants requesting funding for only one year should complete the column under "Project Year 1." Applicants requesting funding for multi-year grants should complete all applicable columns. Please read all instructions before completing form.

SECTION A - BUDGET SUMMARY
U.S. DEPARTMENT OF EDUCATION FUNDS

ED FORM NO. 524

Exhibit 8.2 (continued)

Name of Institution/Organization

Applicants requesting funding for only one year should complete the column under "Project Year 1." Applicants requesting funding for multi-year grants should complete all applicable columns. Please read all instructions before completing form.

SECTION B - BUDGET SUMMARY
NON-FEDERAL FUNDS

Budget Categories	Project Year 1 (a)	Project Year 2 (b)	Project Year 3 (c)	Project Year 4 (d)	Project Year 5 (e)	Total (f)
1. Personnel						
2. Fringe Benefits						
3. Travel						
4. Equipment						
5. Supplies						
6. Contractual						
7. Construction						
8. Other						
9. Total Direct Costs (lines 1-8)						
10. Indirect Costs						
11. Training Stipends						
12. Total Costs (lines 9-11)						

SECTION C - OTHER BUDGET INFORMATION   (see instructions)

ED FORM NO. 524

Exhibit 8.3

INSTRUCTIONS FOR ED FORM NO. 524

Public reporting burden for this collection of information is estimated to vary from 13 to 22 hours per response, with an average of 17.5 hours, including the time for reviewing instructions, searching existing data sources, gathering and maintaining the data needed, and completing and reviewing the collection of information, including suggestions for reducing this burden, to the U.S. Department of Education, Information Management and Compliance Division, Washington, D.C. 20202–4651; and the Office of Management and Budget, Paper Reduction Project 1875–0102, Washington, D.C. 20503.

General Instructions

This form is used to apply to individual U.S. Department of Education discretionary grant programs. Unless directed otherwise, provide the same budget information for each year of the multi-year funding request. Pay attention to applicable program specific instructions, if attached.

Section A—Budget Summary
U.S. Department of Education Funds

All applicants must complete Section A and provide a breakdown by the applicable budget categories shown in lines 1–11.

Lines 1–11, columns (a)–(e): For each project year for which funding is requested, show the total amount requested for each applicable budget category.

Lines 1–11, column (f): Show the multi-year total for each budget category. If funding is requested for only one project year, leave this column blank.

Line 12, columns (a)–(e): Show the total budget request for each project year for which funding is requested.

Line 12, column (f): Show the total amount requested for all project years. If funding is requested for only one year, leave this space blank.

Section B—Budget Summary
Non-Federal Funds

If you are required to provide or volunteer to provide matching funds or other non-Federal resources to the project, these should be shown for each applicable budget category on lines 1–11 of Section B.

Lines 1–11, columns (a)–(e): For each project year for which matching funds or other contributions are provided, show the total contribution for each applicable budget category.

Lines 1–11, column (f): Show the multi-year total for each budget category. If non-Federal contributions are provided for only one year, leave this column blank.

Line 12, columns (a)–(e): Show the total matching or other contribution for each project year.
Line 12, column (f): Show the total amount to be contributed for all years of the multi-year project. If non-Federal contributions are provided for only one year, leave this space blank.

Section C—Other Budget Information

Pay attention to applicable program specific instructions, if attached.

1. Provide an itemized budget breakdown, by project year, for each budget category listed in Sections A and B.

2. If applicable to this program, enter the type of indirect rate (provisional, predetermined, final or fixed) that will be in effect during the funding period. In addition, enter the estimated amount of the base to which the rate is applied, and the total indirect expense.

3. If applicable to this program, provide the rate and base on which fringe benefits are calculated.

4. Provide other explanations or comments you deem necessary.

The evaluation section of your school's proposal must clearly delineate the following:

- What will be evaluated

- When the pre- and postevaluations will occur

- How much change is predicted

- Who will perform the evaluation

- How much the evaluation component will cost

In the example provided on the Sample Project Planner (see Exhibit 7.2), West State University was named as the evaluator; thus the grantee would not be evaluating the effects of its own program. By including a few West State University professors in the proposal, the grantee built credibility and demonstrated the efficient use of local resources. Using West State University's computer resources and graduate students in the evaluation process also demonstrated the cost-effectiveness of the grantee's proposal.

Adequacy of Resources

Every proposal should include this information whether or not the funding source requests it because it lets the funder know why your school rather than another should receive a grant. You can play a particularly useful role in gathering this information by having the individuals and groups involved in grantseeking brainstorm a list of reasons why your school deserves a grant. The key is to focus on the resources or unique aspects of your school and its personnel that would appeal to the reviewer.

Complete the School Resources Worksheet (Exhibit 8.4) well in advance of your proposal's due date.

Completing the worksheet can be enjoyable and more worthwhile than it might appear at first glance. First, it encourages you to focus on the positive aspects of your school, and by brainstorming the positive, you actually combat the negative. Remember, funding sources are not interested in what is wrong with your school and how bad things are. They want to know what forces are at work to ensure success.

Second, the list of your school's positive attributes will empower your grantseekers as they begin to search for external funds. When a potential grantor asks them why their school should be chosen for a grant, they will be able to cite not one but several reasons.

Update your School Resources Worksheet annually and be sure to list all of your school's positive areas, including staff, advisory committees, and so on. The areas that most influence federal grantors and reviewers include the following:

Exhibit 8.4

SCHOOL RESOURCES WORKSHEET

When considering a grant to our school, the funding source will want to be assured that we have the resources to carry out the proposed project. The prospective funding source will want to know what we are good at. Please take a few minutes to help your school put its best foot forward. Prepare a list of possible answers to the grantor's question of why our school should be awarded a grant.

Resources We Can Offer:

- Buildings, Facilities, Space
- Equipment—Computers, etc.
- Supplies/Materials
- Unique Arrangements with Other Organizations
- Our Geographic Location
- Student Composition/Makeup
- Uniqueness of Faculty, Staff
- Awards, Honors, or Other Recognition We Have Received
- Other Unique, Interesting Credibility Builders

- *Equipment:* Demonstrate that you have enough standard office equipment (desks, chairs, and so on) to support the additional staff called for in your proposal. If your proposal calls for nonstandard equipment such as modems and VCRs and you are not requesting funds from the grantor to purchase them, make it clear that they are being donated by you, the grantee, to the project. Your assurance demonstrates that you have adequate resources.

- *Supplies and Materials:* Any supplies or materials that you will be making available should also be noted. This will strengthen your case.

- *Facilities:* Describe the facilities that will be used to support the project, especially unique or different types such as computer labs, swimming pools, and so on. If another organization will be involved in the project, your proposal should show how facilities will be jointly used or shared to ensure the success of the project.

Assurances

District officials will be required to provide signed assurances that the project will abide by a myriad of federal rules and regulations. Assurances deal with a wide range of issues such as drug-free workplaces and political lobbying. No doubt your district's central office has signed assurances in the past and will be able to help you in this process. For your general information, the *Catalog of Federal Domestic Assistance* (CFDA) outlines required federal assurances.

One area of assurances that many school districts overlook is human subjects review. It is not necessary for your school district to organize an Institutional Review Board (IRB) to examine every federal proposal to assure that the human subjects involved are treated humanely; however, as a grantee you should develop a relationship with your local college or university so that you can arrange to have its IRB review and approve your federal proposals.

Attachments

As we have seen, reactive grantseeking limits the time to write a proposal. Because of this, the applications of reactive grantseekers often have to be submitted without letters of support and agreement from cooperating organizations and community groups. This is a red flag to reviewers. It often diminishes potential grantees' credibility and results in the loss of valuable points. Be sure to take the time to gather your letters of support and agreement in advance.

It is a good idea to include your Project Planner as an attachment. Other attachments may include maps, pictures, a layout of your school's building, support data for the statement of need, surveys, and questionnaires.

Reviewers find it helpful when you reference the attachments in the body of your proposal and include a separate table of contents for the attachment section.

CHAPTER 8 CHECKLIST

Evaluation and Planning Worksheet

Which of the following checklists, files, and/or worksheets are already a part of your grants system? Which would you like to add or incorporate into your system?

1. **The Federal Grantseekers' Proposal Checklist**
   _____ Already part of grants system
   _____ Add to grants system

2. **Federal Grants File containing samples of the materials listed on the Federal Grantseekers' Proposal Checklist**
   _____ Already part of grants system
   _____ Add to grants system

3. **School Resource Worksheets compiled into one comprehensive list of your school's positive attributes**
   _____ Already part of grants system
   _____ Add to grants system

Chapter 9

Improving and Submitting Your School's Federal Grant Proposal

THE MAIN PURPOSES of this chapter are to outline a method for you to improve the proposals your school submits to federal agencies and to review basic information on submission, application transmittal, signature requirements, and the intergovernmental review of federal proposals.

The quality of the proposal your grantseekers submit to the federal funding source influences how peer reviewers and agency staff will view your school and grantseekers for many years to come. Just as teachers do not easily forget a bad impression made by a student, reviewers and government staff members do not easily forget the negative impression created by a poorly constructed proposal.

Thus it should be reviewed prior to submittal in order to guarantee that you are sending the federal grantor a proposal you can be proud of and that is your school's best effort. Even if your proposal is not selected for funding, putting it through a presubmittal review will assure you that it was the high level of competition rather than careless mistakes that accounted for its rejection.

By this time most grantseekers are tired. They want to submit their proposal and get it out of their lives. But you cannot allow them to jeopardize all their hard work by submitting a proposal that has not passed the last test: the mock review. The principal's role in quality control cannot be overemphasized. By instituting and supporting the mock-review process, you give your school's grantseeking effort the attention and credibility that will result in more submissions and greater success.

The more you know about the review system used by the prospective federal grantor, the more closely you can simulate the mock review and the greater the benefits. Through preproposal contact, your grantseekers should have developed some insights into how the granting agency selects reviewers, the reviewers' backgrounds, and what type of scoring system they follow. This type of information will help you carry out a mock review that closely resembles the official review.

Your grantseekers must be ahead of the submission deadline by at least several days in order to perform a mock review. One way to ensure that there is time is to state on your School Grantseekers' Preproposal Endorsement Worksheet (Exhibit 6.1) that your office *requires* a mock review before it will sign the final proposal and submit it to the district central office. To assure that compliance, instruct your grantseekers to turn the proposal over to you several days before the deadline. This will let them know well beforehand what is expected of them.

The term *quality circle* best describes the mock review process. Invite a few volunteers who are dedicated to improving education and who share a concern for your school's image and reputation to participate in the circle. They need not be experts in the grants field or in your proposal's particular subject area. Although you want the circle members to resemble the levels of expertise of the reviewers on the federal review committee, you should also invite several individuals with a "clean" perspective to participate. For example, ask a business leader from your grants advisory committee, a college student, a secretary, or an accountant. These many different perspectives will help expose your proposal's weaknesses and strengths.

Your help in organizing the mock review will impress on the volunteers the importance of the process. You can either telephone candidates or ask them in writing or in person to participate in the mock-review process. Let them know that your proposal's chance of success will be greatly improved through this presubmission review and that you are asking them to participate because you need their fresh perspective. Brief them on the general approach you would like them to take. It is important to tell them that although you would like the mock review to be as rigorous as possible, this does not mean that they must spend vast amounts of time reading the proposal, only as much time as the actual reviewers do—and some of them read proposals pretty quickly! Tell them you will send a package that includes a description of the background and types of reviewers, the time allotted to read each proposal, and the scoring system that the reviewers will use. Make sure they know that they do not have to be experts in the subject but that they should make every attempt to read the proposal from the real reviewers' points of view. The sample letter in Exhibit 9.1 can be used to invite individuals to participate in your quality circle.

Each federal agency that makes grants follows a different system for reviewing proposals. For instance, the National Science Foundation's

---

Exhibit 9.1

SAMPLE LETTER INVITING INDIVIDUAL TO PARTICIPATE IN FEDERAL PROPOSAL QUALITY CIRCLE

Date

Name
Address

Dear _____:

I would like to take this opportunity to follow up on our conversation to secure your input in helping our school district submit the very best grant proposal possible. We are asking that you review the enclosed proposal from the point of view of a federal reviewer. The attached materials will help you role-play the actual manner in which this proposal will be evaluated.

Please read the information on the reviewers' backgrounds and the scoring system and limit the time you spend reading the proposal to the time constraints that the real reviewers will observe. A Quality Circle Scoring Worksheet has been provided to assist you in recording your scores and comments.

A meeting of all the mock reviewers comprising our quality circle has been scheduled for [date]. Please bring this worksheet with you to the meeting. The meeting will last less than one hour. Its purpose is to analyze the scores and brainstorm suggestions to improve the proposal.

Sincerely,
[Name]
[Phone Number]

---

system is very different from the system used by the National Endowment for the Humanities, and that one is much different from that of the Department of Education. These differences emphasize the need for pre-proposal contact with the funder and early data gathering about the review process.

Have your grantseekers try to obtain the following information from the granting agency:

- *Where and How the Review Occurs:* Are the reviewers mailed a package of proposals and asked to review them at home? Do the reviewers meet at one place to review the proposals? If so, for how long? Provide this information to your volunteers and replicate the situation.

- *Average Time Spent Reading Each Proposal:* Most reviewers are very busy people, and the time they spend reading proposals varies greatly.

- *Number of Proposals Each Reviewer Evaluates:* A key element in your role playing is to ask your volunteers to think of your proposal as the last one in a pile. If reviewers each read ten proposals, your school's should be thought of as the tenth.

At the very least, you *must* give the members of your quality circle the point system, rules, and time constraints they should abide by. Volunteer mock reviewers often want to do such a good job that they spend more time reviewing the proposal than the real reviewers will! Make sure your mock reviewers understand that spending an inordinate amount of time reviewing the proposal will be counterproductive to what you are trying to accomplish through role playing. Make sure they understand that spending too much time will be counterproductive.

In general, the Education Department uses a review system known as the Education Department General Administrative Regulation (EDGAR). However, not every agency in the Education Department follows EDGAR. Some have their own published regulations with a specific set of criteria for evaluating and judging applications. If the agency you are approaching does not have a set of published guidelines, it probably follows EDGAR, but always double-check through preproposal contact.

EDGAR's main areas of evaluation include these:

1. How the proposed project meets the purposes of the authorizing statute

2. The extent of the need for the project

3. How the plan of operation meets the need

4. The availability of qualified key personnel to implement the plan

5. Whether the budget is cost-effective and relative to the plan

6. How the plan's progress in meeting the objectives will be evaluated

7. Whether the applicant has sufficient resources to house the project and support the plan

To help your volunteers review and evaluate your school's proposal from the proper perspective, provide them with the Selection Criteria Overview (Exhibit 9.2) and the Scoring Distribution Worksheet (Exhibit 9.3).

It is important that your grantseekers verify that the point values suggested in parentheses on the Selection Criteria Overview are accurate for each grant program they plan to approach. This verification should be done in preproposal contact with the funding source. In some cases, federal officials may make changes in the point values to reflect a shift in emphasis or to allow grantees with special circumstances to score higher in the review process.

Review with your quality circle the Selection Criteria Overview and the points assigned to each section. Refer them to the Scoring Distribution Worksheet for help in allocating points. The purpose of the Scoring Distribution Worksheet is to promote consistency in scoring within the

Exhibit 9.2

SELECTION CRITERIA OVERVIEW

Meeting the Purposes of the Authorizing Statute   **(5 pts)**

1.   What are the purposes of the authorizing statute?

2.   What are the objectives of this project?

3.   How will these objectives further the purposes of the authorizing statute?

Extent of Need for the Project   **(25 pts)**

1.   What needs are outlined by the authorizing statute?

2.   What needs does the applicant identify?

3.   How did the applicant identify those needs? That is, what specific documentation or evidence does the application offer to support the applicant's assessment of need?

4.   Are the needs identified by the applicant consistent with the purposes of the authorizing statute?

5.   Does the applicant identify too many or too few needs for the proposed time frame and resources of the project?

6.   Are the outlined needs well defined so that the project can be focused on them, or are they generic?

Plan of Operation   **(20 pts)**

1.   Do the project objectives serve the purposes of the authorizing statute?

2.   How well is the project designed? Are project objectives consistent with stated needs? Are project activities consistent with project objectives? Are project objectives measurable?

3.   How will the applicant use its resources and personnel to achieve each objective?

4.   Has the applicant developed an effective management plan that will ensure proper and efficient administration of the project?

5.   Do project milestones represent a logical progression of times and tasks?

6.   Does the applicant propose a realistic time schedule for accomplishing objectives?

7.   Will the proposed activities accomplish the project's objectives successfully?

8.   Are the planned educational approaches based on sound research that indicates they will be successful for the population to be served?

9.   Does the project have clearly developed provisions for providing equal access to eligible participants who are members of traditionally underrepresented groups (racial or ethnic minorities, women, handicapped persons, elderly persons)?

Quality of Key Personnel   **(15 pts)**

1.   Do the job descriptions adequately reflect skills needed to make the project work?

2.   Are the duties of personnel clearly defined?

3.   What relevant qualifications do the proposed personnel possess, especially the project director? (Focus on their experience and training in fields related to the objectives of the project, though other information may be considered.)

(continued)

Exhibit 9.2 (continued)

4. Will proposed personnel need to be trained for the project?

5. How much time will the proposed personnel actually devote to the project?

6. To what extent does the applicant encourage employment applications from members of tradition-ally underrepresented groups (ethnic or racial minorities, women, handicapped persons, elderly persons)?

Budget and Cost Effectiveness   (10 pts)

1. Is the budget adequate to support the project's proposed activities?

2. Are overall project costs reasonable in relation to project objectives?

3. How much of the project's total cost is devoted to administrative costs?

4. Are budget items sufficiently justified?

5. Is the budget padded?

Evaluation Plan   (15 pts)

1. Are the proposed methods of evaluation appropriate to the project?

2. Will the proposed evaluation be objective?

3. Will the proposed evaluation methods measure the effectiveness of project activities in meeting project objectives?

4. Will the evaluation plan produce valid and reliable data concerning the accomplishment of project objectives?

5. Does the evaluation plan measure the project's effect on the project audience?

Adequacy of Resources   (10 pts)

1. Are the proposed facilities adequate for project purposes?

2. Is the proposed equipment adequate for project purposes?

3. Does the applicant have access to special sources of experience or expertise?

---

range of points allowed for each section. Emphasize the need for a candid evaluation and ask the mock reviewers to avoid inflating a positive score or comment in one section to make up for a low score or comment in another.

Each mock reviewer should be given a Technical Review Package (Exhibit 9.4). The worksheets in this are very similar to those used by the federal reviewers, which makes the mock review resemble the real review as much as possible. In addition, getting acquainted with these worksheets gives the mock reviewers experience that will prove valuable should they ever get the opportunity to really review federal grant applications and proposals.

The principal's office (or the grants office) can reproduce the worksheets in the Technical Review Package. Providing them to your mock reviewers

Exhibit 9.3

SCORING DISTRIBUTION WORKSHEET

The numerical scores you assign to an application's response to the selection criteria must be consistent with the comments you write. Comments and scores should reflect the same overall assessment. You should never attempt to mitigate a negative comment with a positive score, or vice versa.

Comments indicate whether the application's response to the selection criteria is poor, adequate, or good; scores indicate how poor, adequate, or good. If 10 points are possible, 0–2 is poor, 3–4 is weak, 5–7 is adequate, 8–9 is superior, and 10 is outstanding. Four points means the response is merely weak, whereas 8 indicates it is above average or superior. Whatever total points are possible, use the midpoint as adequate and choose your scores accordingly. Do not hesitate to use the full range of points. It is perfectly acceptable to assign a score of 10 or 0, for example. Your guiding rule should be consistency.

Always go back and check your scores to make sure that you have written them correctly and used the appropriate point scale. You should also double-check the scores on the summary page of the Technical Review Form to make sure that they match the scores listed under each selection criterion and that the final total has been computed without error.

You may want to use the following table as a guide when assigning points:

Total	Poor	Weak	Adequate	Superior	Outstanding
25	0–8	9–12	13–19	20–23	24–25
20	0–6	7–9	10–15	16–18	19–20
15	0–4	5–7	8–11	12–13	14–15
10	0–2	3–4	5–7	8–9	10
5	0–1	2	3	4	5

in the form of a package will keep the committee focused on each section of the proposal and on the important areas each section contains.

The major difference between your worksheets and those used by actual reviewers is that yours request suggestions for improvement. As the mock reviewers identify weaknesses in the proposal, ask them to list any suggestions they have to reduce or eliminate the weaknesses. Stress that the proposal developers still have a few days to incorporate their suggestions into the proposal.

Your volunteers can review the proposal at home or work, or they may prefer to meet to score the proposal and discuss its positive and negative points. The arrangement you decide on should be based on how the federal reviewers do it. Performing the mock review in a group enables the principal to be facilitator—a key role. It is best if the proposal writers are not at this meeting so that the group members will be as candid as possible.

Ask the volunteers to read the proposal and to evaluate and score each section before moving on to the next. Have them put a plus sign (+) beside

Exhibit 9.4

TECHNICAL REVIEW PACKAGE

Technical Review Form

School Application No. _____

CFDA No. _____

Federal Program: _____

Applicant Organization: _____

Selection Criteria	Maximum Points	Assigned Points
Meeting Purposes of Statute	_____	_____
Need for Project	_____	_____
Plan of Operation	_____	_____
Quality of Key Personnel	_____	_____
Budget Cost Effectiveness	_____	_____
Evaluation Plan	_____	_____
Adequacy of Resources	_____	_____
Total Points	_____	_____

SUMMARY COMMENTS

Strengths: _____
_____

Weaknesses: _____
_____

Suggestions for Improvement: _____
_____

Meeting the Purposes of the Authorizing Statute

Maximum Points _____   Awarded _____

1. What are the purposes of the authorizing statute?
2. What are the objectives of this project?
3. How will these objectives further the purposes of the authorizing statute?

Strengths: _____
_____

Weaknesses and Suggestions for Improvement: _____
_____

Extent of the Need for the Project

Maximum Points _____   Awarded _____

1. What needs are outlined by the authorizing statute?
2. What needs does the applicant identify?
3. How did the applicant identify those needs; that is, what specific documentation or evidence does the application offer to support the applicant's assessment of need?

(continued)

Exhibit 9.4 (continued)

4. Are the needs identified by the applicant consistent with the purposes of the authorizing statute?
5. Does the applicant identify too many or too few needs for the proposed time frame and resources of the project?
6. Are the outlined needs well defined so that the project can be focused on them, or are they generic?

Strengths: _____

_____

Weaknesses and Suggestions for Improvement: _____

_____

Plan of Operation

Maximum Points _____   Awarded _____

1. Do the project objectives serve the purposes of the authorizing statute?
2. How well is the project designed?

    • Are project objectives consistent with stated needs?
    • Are project activities consistent with project objectives?
    • Are project objectives measurable?

3. How will the applicant use its resources and personnel to achieve each objective?
4. Has the applicant developed an effective management plan that will ensure proper and efficient administration of the project?
5. Do project milestones represent a logical progression of times and tasks?
6. Does the applicant propose a realistic time schedule for accomplishing objectives?
7. Will the proposed activities accomplish the project's objectives successfully?
8. Are the educational approaches planned based on sound research that indicates they will be successful for the population to be served?
9. Does the project have clearly developed plans for providing equal access to eligible participants who are members of traditionally underrepresented groups (racial or ethnic minorities, women, handicapped persons, elderly persons)?

Strengths: _____

_____

Weaknesses and Suggestions for Improvement: _____

_____

Quality of Key Personnel

Maximum Points _____   Awarded _____

1. Do the job descriptions adequately reflect skills needed to make the project work?
2. Are the duties of personnel clearly defined?
3. What relevant qualifications do the proposed personnel possess, especially the project director? (Focus on their experience and training in fields related to the objectives of the project, though other information may be considered.)
4. Will proposed personnel need to be trained for the project?
5. How much time will the proposed personnel actually devote to the project?

Exhibit 9.4 (continued)

6. To what extent does the applicant encourage employment applications from members of traditionally underrepresented groups (ethnic or racial minorities, women, handicapped persons, elderly persons)?

Strengths: _____

_____

Weaknesses and Suggestions for Improvement: _____

_____

Budget and Cost Effectiveness

Maximum Points _____   Awarded _____

1. Is the budget adequate to support the project's proposed activities?
2. Are overall project costs reasonable in relation to project objectives?
3. How much of the project's total cost is devoted to administrative costs?
4. Are budget items sufficiently justified?
5. Is the budget padded?

Strengths: _____

_____

Weaknesses and Suggestions for Improvement: _____

_____

Evaluation Plan

Maximum Points _____   Awarded _____

1. Are the proposed methods of evaluation appropriate to the project?
2. Is the proposed evaluation objective?
3. Will the proposed evaluation methods measure the effectiveness of project activities in meeting project objectives?
4. Will the evaluation plan produce valid and reliable data concerning the accomplishment of project objectives?
5. Does the evaluation plan measure the project's effect on the project audience?

Strengths: _____

_____

Weaknesses and Suggestions for Improvement: _____

_____

Adequacy of Resources

Maximum Points _____   Awarded _____

1. Are the proposed facilities adequate for project purposes?
2. Will the proposed equipment be adequate for project purposes?
3. Does the applicant have access to special sources of experience or expertise?

Strengths: _____

_____

Weaknesses and Suggestions for Improvement: _____

_____

those areas they think the reviewer will consider positive and a minus sign (–) beside those areas they think will be viewed negatively. Stress that identifying both the positive *and* negative aspects of each section will help the proposal developers understand the mock reviewers' scores and enable them to improve the negative areas of their proposal without changing the positive aspects.

Send or give your volunteer reviewers the Quality Circle Information Worksheet (Exhibit 9.5) and any additional information you and your grantseekers have gathered that might help them. For example, information on last year's grantees may be useful, especially if the mix of grantees is likely to remain the same.

Review with your proposal developers the score each section of the proposal received from the volunteer reviewers. Pay particular attention to the positive points. Then have them focus on how to improve areas that did not score well. Although your proposal writers will be able to explain most of the problem areas to you verbally, remind them that they will not get this opportunity in the real review. By coordinating the mock review process but not participating in the actual critique, you are in a perfect position to summarize the volunteers' scores and comments and to review them in a nonthreatening manner with the grantseekers.

When rewriting and retyping of the proposal are required, it is especially important for you to volunteer any support services your office can offer. Remember, your grant writers are probably beginning to get tired at this point. Think of them as racehorses in the home stretch; they may need a little prodding to get to the finish line, but don't push them too hard. This is exactly the time when a true leader will display his or her skills at getting volunteers and staff to put in the extra effort that translates into grants success. For example, making your secretary available for editing will go a long way in ensuring that the mock reviewers' suggestions are incorporated into an improved proposal. Once all the necessary revisions have been made, your school's proposal will finally be ready for submittal.

Submittal

In most cases, Standard Form (SF) 424 (see Exhibit 9.6) must be attached as a facesheet to grant applications or proposals being submitted to a federal agency. Instructions for completing this form are shown in Exhibit 9.7.

The proposal should not be bound or stapled together unless the funder gives permission to do so. Usually federal funders prefer that proposals be clipped with pressure tension clips so that they can remove or add forms as needed.

Exhibit 9.5

QUALITY CIRCLE INFORMATION WORKSHEET

The following information is being provided to assist you in reviewing the attached federal grant application/proposal.

The Setting—The proposals are read at:

_____ The reviewer's location
_____ The federal agency's location
_____ Another site selected by the federal agency

The Time Factor

Number of proposals the reviewer evaluates: _____
Amount of time the reviewer spends evaluating each proposal: _____

Background of Reviewers

Age range: _____
Educational background: _____
_____
Known viewpoints or biases:_____
_____

List of last year's reviewers available?   _____ yes _____ no
(If yes, please attach) _____

Other Information

Applications/proposals received by the agency last year: # _____
Grants awarded by the agency last year: # _____
$ range for proposals from schools such as ours: $ _____

Application Transmittal

The federal application package will contain specific directions on how to transmit your school's proposal by mail or hand delivery. The instructions shown in Exhibit 9.8 have been taken from the Department of Education's federal guidelines. However, note that the various federal granting agencies have different rules regarding transmittal.

There are two key elements in submitting federal proposals and transmitting applications: first, the submittal and transmittal processes outlined by the funding agency should be strictly adhered to, and second, the proposal should be submitted *early*, not merely on time. Submitting a week early demonstrates to the granting agency that your school is well organized. In addition, federal bureaucrats may correlate the timely submittal of your proposal with the timely submittal of the reports required after funding, which favorably impresses officials who have to oversee and administer many grants.

Exhibit 9.6

STANDARD FORM (SF) 424

OMB Approval No. 0348-004

APPLICATION FOR FEDERAL ASSISTANCE	2. DATE SUBMITTED	Applicant Identifier
1. TYPE OF SUBMISSION Application Preapplication ☐ Construction ☐ Construction ☒ Non-Construction ☐ Non-Construction	3. DATE RECEIVED BY STATE	State Application Identifier
	4. DATE RECEIVED BY FEDERAL AGENCY	Federal Identifier

5. APPLICANT INFORMATION

Legal Name:	Organizational Unit:
Address (give city, county, state and zip code):	Name and telephone number of the person to be contacted on matters involving this application (give area code):

6. EMPLOYER IDENTIFICATION NUMBER (EIN): ☐☐ ☐☐☐☐☐☐☐	7. TYPE OF APPLICANT: (enter appropriate letter in box) ☐

7. TYPE OF APPLICANT:
A. State H. Independent School District
B. County I. State Controlled Institution of Higher Learning
C. Municipal J. Private University
D. Township K. Indian Tribe
E. Interstate L. Individual
F. Intermunicipal M. Profit Organization
G. Special District N. Other (Specify):

8. TYPE OF APPLICATION
☐ New ☐ Continuation ☐ Revision

If Revision, enter appropriate letter(s) in box(es): ☐ ☐
A. Increase Award B. Decrease Award C. Increase Duration
D. Decrease Duration Other (specify):

9. NAME OF FEDERAL AGENCY

10. CATALOG OF FEDERAL DOMESTIC ASSISTANCE NUMBER 8 4 ☐☐☐ TITLE:	11. DESCRIPTIVE TITLE OF APPLICANT'S PROJECT:

12. AREA AFFECTED BY PROJECT (cities, counties, states, etc.):

13. PROPOSED PROJECT: **14. CONGRESSIONAL DISTRICTS OF:**

Start Date	Ending Date	a. Applicant	b. Project

15. ESTIMATED FUNDING:

		16. IS APPLICATION SUBJECT TO REVIEW BY STATE EXECUTIVE ORDER 12372 PROCESS?
a. Federal	$ .00	a. YES THIS PREAPPLICATION/APPLICATION WAS MADE AVAILABLE TO THE STATE EXECUTIVE ORDER 12372 PROCESS FOR REVIEW ON:
b. Applicant	$ .00	
c. State	$ .00	DATE: _____
d. Local	$ .00	b. NO ☐ PROGRAM IS NOT COVERED BY E.O. 12372
e. Other	$ .00	☐ OR PROGRAM HAS NOT BEEN SELECTED BY STATE FOR REVIEW
f. Program Income	$ .00	**17. IS THE APPLICANT DELINQUENT ON ANY FEDERAL DEBT?**
g. Total	$ .00	☐ Yes If "Yes" attach an explanation ☐ No

18. TO THE BEST OF MY KNOWLEDGE AND BELIEF, ALL DATA IN THIS APPLICATION / PREAPPLICATION ARE TRUE AND CORRECT. THE DOCUMENT HAS BEEN DULY AUTHORIZED BY THE GOVERNING BODY OF THE APPLICANT AND THE APPLICANT WILL COMPLY WITH THE ATTACHED ASSURANCES IF THE ASSISTANCE IS AWARDED.

a. Typed Name of Authorized Representative	b. Title	c. Telephone Number
d. Signature of Authorized Representative		e. Date Signed

Previous Editions Not Usable

Authorized for Local Reproduction

Standard Form 424 (Rev 4-88)
Prescribed by OMB Circular A-102

Exhibit 9.7

INSTRUCTIONS FOR THE SF 424

This is a standard form used by applicants as a required facesheet for preapplications and applications submitted for Federal assistance. It will be used by Federal agencies to obtain applicant certification that States which have established a review and comment procedure in response to Executive Order 12372 and have selected the program to be included in their process, have been given an opportunity to review the applicant's submission.

1. Self-explanatory.

2. Date application submitted to Federal agency (or State if applicable) & applicant's control number (if applicable).

3. State use only (if applicable).

4. If this application is to continue or revise an existing award, enter present Federal identifier number. If for a new project, leave blank.

5. Legal name of applicant, name of primary organizational unit which will undertake the assistance activity, complete address of the applicant, and name and telephone number of the person to contact on matters related to this application.

6. Enter Employer Identification Number (EIN) as assigned by the Internal Revenue Service.

7. Enter the appropriate letter in the space provided.

8. Check appropriate box and enter appropriate letter(s) in the space(s) provided:

    —"New" means a new assistance award.

    —"Continuation" means an extension for an additional funding/budget period for a project with a projected completion date.

    —"Revision" means any change in the Federal Government's financial obligation or contingent liability from an existing obligation.

9. Name of Federal agency from which assistance is being requested with this application.

10. Use the Catalog of Federal Domestic Assistance number and title of the program under which assistance is requested.

11. Enter a brief descriptive title of the project. If more than one program is involved, you should append an explanation on a separate sheet. If appropriate (e.g., construction or real property projects), attach a map showing project location. For preapplications, use a separate sheet to provide a summary description of this project.

12. List only the largest political entities affected (e.g., State, counties, cities).

13. Self-explanatory.

14. List the applicant's Congressional District and any District(s) affected by the program or project.

15. Amount requested or to be contributed during the first funding/budget period by each contributor. Value of in-kind contributions should be included on appropriate lines as applicable. If the action will result in a dollar change to an existing award, indicate *only* the amount of the change. For decreases, enclose the amounts in parentheses. If both basic and supplemental amounts are included, show breakdown on an attached sheet. For multiple program funding, use totals and show breakdown using same categories as item 15.

16. Applicants should contact the State Single Point of Contact (SPOC) for Federal Executive Order 12372 to determine whether the application is subject to the State intergovernmental review process.

17. This question applies to the applicant organization, not the person who signs as the authorized representative. Categories of debt include delinquent audit disallowances, loans and taxes.

18. To be signed by the authorized representative of the applicant. A copy of the governing body's authorization for you to sign this application as official representative must be on file in the applicant's office. (Certain Federal agencies may require that this authorization be submitted as part of the application.)

Exhibit 9.8

APPLICATION TRANSMITTAL INSTRUCTIONS

An application for an award must be mailed or hand delivered by the closing date.

Applications Delivered by Mail

An application sent by mail must be addressed to the U.S. Department of Education, Application Control Center, Attention: CFDA Number _____, 400 Maryland Avenue SW, Washington, D.C. 20202-4725. An application must show proof of mailing consisting of one of the following:

- A legibly dated U.S. Postal Service postmark.
- A legible mail receipt with the date of mailing stamped by the U.S. Postal Service.
- A dated shipping label, invoice, or receipt from a commercial carrier.
- Any other proof of mailing acceptable to the U.S. Secretary of Education.

If an application is sent through the U.S. Postal Service, the Secretary does not accept either of the following as proof of mailing:

- A private metered postmark, or
- A mail receipt that is not dated by the U.S. Postal Service.

An applicant should note that the U.S. Postal Service does not uniformly provide a dated postmark. Before relying on this method, an applicant should check with the local post office.

An applicant is encouraged to use registered or at least first-class mail.

Late applicants will be notified that their applications will not be considered.

Applications Delivered by Hand/Courier Service

An application that is hand delivered must be taken to the U.S. Department of Education, Application Control Center, Room 3633, General Services Administration National Capital Region, 7th and D Streets SW., Washington, D.C. 20202-4725.

The Application Control Center will accept deliveries between 8:00 a.m. and 4:30 P.M. (Washington, D.C.) daily, except Saturdays, Sundays, and federal holidays.

Individuals delivering applications must use the D Street entrance. Proper identification is necessary to enter the building.

In order for an application sent through a courier service to be considered timely, the courier service must be in receipt of the application on or before the closing date.

Necessary Signatures and Other Requirements

Your school's federal grant application cover letter and assurances must be signed by your authorized district representative. Your district grants office may help you procure the necessary signatures and meet all of the requirements. These may include signed and dated school board resolutions that endorse the grant application and any matching or in-kind contributions associated with the grant.

Intergovernmental Review

The purpose of intergovernmental proposal review is to provide a mechanism for coordinating federally funded projects with state plans. This reduces the chances of the federal government supporting a program that a state has decided should not be part of its plan or that does not take the direction that the state wishes. Not all federal programs require an intergovernmental review, and not all states have the same review requirements. However, if an intergovernmental review is required, and your district has a grants office or a formal grants procedure, the district will most likely handle the review.

If you, the principal, must process the review, find your state's single point of contact in Exhibit 9.9 beginning on page 170 and call to ensure that you comply with your state's requirements.

CHAPTER 9 CHECKLIST

Evaluation and Planning Worksheet

The following items are essential to a successful grants system. Designate which ones are already part of your system and which ones you would like to add.

1. **Quality circle mock review committee or other proposal improvement committee with same function**
   _____ Already part of grants system
   _____ Add to grants system

2. **District submittal and sign-off procedures**
   _____ Already part of grants system
   _____ Add to grants system

3. **School sign-off and principal's signature system**
   _____ Already part of grants system
   _____ Add to grants System

4. **Federal Grants Submission Checklist ensuring applicant compliance in following areas:**
   • Necessary signatures
   • Inclusion of board resolutions
   • Inclusion of consortium agreements
   • Accuracy of budget figures
   • Number of copies of proposal submitted
   • Binding regulations
   • Transmittal procedures
   • Acknowledgment of proposal receipt
   _____ Already part of grants system
   _____ Add to grants system

Exhibit 9.9

EXECUTIVE ORDER-INTERGOVERNMENTAL REVIEW

The Education Department General Administrative Regulations (EDGAR), 34 CFR 79, pertaining to intergovernmental review of Federal programs, apply to the program included in this application package.

Immediately upon receipt of this notice, all applicants, other than federally recognized Indian Tribal Governments, must contact the appropriate State Point of Contact to find out about, and to comply with the State's process under Executive Order 12372. Applicants proposing to perform in more than one State should contact, immediately upon receipt of this notice, the Single Points of Contact for each State and follow the procedures established in those States under the Executive Order. A list containing the Single Point of Contact for each State is included in the application package for this program.

In States that have not established a process or chosen a program for review, State, area wide, regional, and local entities may submit comments directly to the Department.

Any State Process Recommendation and other comments by a State Point of Contact and any comments from State, area wide, regional, and local entities must be mailed or hand-delivered by the date in the Program announcement for Intergovernmental Review to the following address:

> The Secretary
> E.O. 12372-CFDA # 84.200
> U.S. Department of Education, FB-10, Room 6213
> 600 Independence Avenue, SW
> Washington, DC 20202

In those States that require review for this program, applications are to be submitted simultaneously to the State Review Process and the U.S. Department of Education.

Proof of mailing will be determined on the same basis as applications.

Please note that the above address is not the same address as the one to which the applicant submits its completed application.

DO NOT SEND APPLICATIONS TO THE ABOVE ADDRESS.

State Single Points of Contact

In accordance with Executive Order #12372, "Intergovernmental Review Process," this listing represents the designated State Single Points of Contact. Upon request, a background document explaining the Executive Order is available. The Office of Management and Budget point of contact for updating this listing is: Donna Rivelli (202) 395-5090. The States not listed no longer participate in the process. These include: Alabama; Alaska; Kansas; Hawaii; Idaho; Louisiana; Minnesota; Montana; Nebraska; Oklahoma; Oregon; Pennsylvania; Virginia; and Washington. This list is based on the most current information provided by the States. Information on any changes or apparent errors should be provided to the Office of Management and Budget and the State in question. Changes to the list will be made only upon formal notification by the State.

ARIZONA
Ms. Janice Dunn
Arizona State Clearinghouse
3800 North Central Avenue
Fourteenth Floor
Phoenix, Arizona 85012
Telephone: (602) 280-1315

ARKANSAS
Ms. Tracie L. Copeland
Manager, State Clearinghouse
Office of Intergovernmental Service
Department of Finance
  and Administration
P.O. Box 3278
Little Rock, Arkansas 72203
Telephone: (501) 371-1074

CALIFORNIA
Mr. Glenn Staber
Grants Coordinator
Office of Planning & Research
1400 Tenth Street
Sacramento, California 95814
Telephone: (916) 323-7480

Exhibit 9.9 (continued)

COLORADO

State Single Point of Contact
State Clearinghouse
Division of Local Government
1313 Sherman Street, Room 520
Denver, Colorado 80203
Telephone: (303) 866-2156

CONNECTICUT

Mr. William T. Quigg
Intergovernmental Review
    Coordinator
State Single Point of Contact
Office of Policy and Management
Intergovernmental Policy Division
80 Washington Street
Hartford, Connecticut 06106-4459
Telephone: (203) 566-3410

DELAWARE

Ms. Francine Booth
State Single Point of Contact
Executive Department
Thomas Collins Building
Dover, Delaware 19903
Telephone: (302) 736-3326

DISTRICT OF COLUMBIA

Mr. Rodney T. Hallman
State Single Point of Contact
Office of Grants Management &
    Development
717 14th St. N.W., Suite 500
Washington, DC 20005
Telephone: (202) 727-6551

FLORIDA

Florida State Clearinghouse
Intergovernmental Affairs Policy
    Unit
Executive Office of the Governor
Office of Planning & Budgeting
The Capitol
Tallahassee, Florida 32399-0001
Telephone: (904) 488-8114

GEORGIA

Charles H. Badger, Administrator
Georgia State Clearinghouse
270 Washington Street, S.W.
Room 534A
Atlanta, Georgia 30334
Telephone: (404) 656-3855

ILLINOIS

Mr. Steve Klokkenga
State Single Point of Contact
Office of the Governor
State of Illinois
107 Stratton Building
Springfield, Illinois 62706
Telephone: (217) 782-1671

INDIANA

Ms. Jean S. Blackwell
Budget Director
State Budget Agency
212 State House
Indianapolis, Indiana 46204
Telephone: (317) 232-5610

IOWA

Mr. Steven R. McCann
Division for Community Progress
Iowa Department of Economic
    Development
200 East Grand Avenue
Des Moines, Iowa 50309
Telephone: (515) 281-3725

KENTUCKY

Mr. Ronald W. Cook
Office of the Governor
Department of Local Government
1024 Capitol Center Drive
Frankfort, Kentucky 40601
Telephone: (502) 564-2382

MAINE

State Single Point of Contact
Attn: Joyce Benson
State Planning Office
State House Station #38
Augusta, Maine 04333
Telephone: (207) 289-3261

MARYLAND

Mary Abrams, Chief
Maryland State Clearinghouse
Department of State Planning
301 West Preston Street
Baltimore, Maryland 21201
Telephone: (301) 225-4490

MASSACHUSETTS

Ms. Karen Arone
State Clearinghouse
Executive Office of Communities
    and Development
100 Cambridge Street, Room 1803
Boston, Massachusetts 02202
Telephone: (617) 727-7001

MICHIGAN

Richard S. Pastula
Director
Michigan Department of Commerce
Office of Federal Grants
P.O. Box 30225
Lansing, Michigan 48909
Telephone: (517) 373-7356

MISSISSIPPI

Ms. Cathy Mallette
Clearinghouse Officer
Office of Federal Grant Management
    and Reporting
Dept. of Finance and Administration
301 West Pearl Street
Jackson, Mississippi 39203
Telephone: (601) 949-2174

MISSOURI

Ms. Lois Pohl
Federal Assistance Clearinghouse
Office of Administration
P.O. Box 809
Room 430, Truman Building
Jefferson City, Missouri 65102
Telephone: (314) 751-4834

NEVADA

Department of Administration
State Clearinghouse
Capitol Complex
Carson City, Nevada 89710
Attn: Ron Sparks
Clearinghouse Coordinator
Telephone: (702) 687-4065

NEW HAMPSHIRE

Mr. Jeffrey H. Taylor, Director
New Hampshire Office of State
    Planning
Attn: Intergovernmental Review
    Process/James E. Bieber
2 1/2 Beacon Street
Concord, New Hampshire 03301
Telephone: (603) 271-2155

NEW JERSEY

Gregory W. Adkins, Acting Director
Division of Community Resources
NJ Dept. of Community Affairs
Direct correspondence to:
Andrew Jaskolka
State Review Process
Division of Community Resources
CN 814, Room 609
Trenton, New Jersey 08625-0814
Telephone: (609) 292-9025

(continued)

Exhibit 9.9 (continued)

NEW MEXICO

Mr. George Elliott
Deputy Director
State Budget Division
Rm 190, Bataan Memorial Building
Santa Fe, New Mexico 87503
Telephone: (505) 827-3640

NEW YORK

New York State Clearinghouse
Division of the Budget
State Capitol
Albany, New York 12224
Telephone: (518) 474-1605

NORTH CAROLINA

Mrs. Chrys Baggett, Director
Office of the Secretary of Admin.
N.C. State Clearinghouse
116 West Jones Street
Raleigh, N. Carolina 27603-8003
Telephone: (919) 733-7232

NORTH DAKOTA

North Dakota State Single Point of
   Contact
Office of Intergovernmental
   Assistance
Office of Management & Budget
600 East Boulevard Avenue
Bismarck, N. Dakota 58505-0170
Telephone: (701) 224-2094

OHIO

Mr. Larry Weaver
State Single Point of Contact
State/Federal Funds Coordinator
State Clearinghouse
Office of Budget & Management
30 East Broad Street, 34th Floor
Columbus, Ohio 43266-0411
Telephone: (614) 466-0698

RHODE ISLAND

Mr. Daniel W. Varin
Associate Director
Statewide Planning Program
Department of Administration
Division of Planning
265 Melrose Street
Providence, Rhode Island 02907
Telephone: (401) 277-2656
Please direct correspondence and
   questions to:
Review Coordinator
Office of Strategic Planning

SOUTH CAROLINA

Ms. Omeagia Burgess
State Single Point of Contact
Grant Services
Office of the Governor, Room 477
1205 Pendleton Street
Columbia, South Carolina 29201
Telephone: (803) 734-0493

SOUTH DAKOTA

Ms. Susan Comer
State Clearinghouse Coordinator
Office of the Governor
500 East Capitol
Pierre, South Dakota 57501
Telephone: (605) 733-3212

TENNESSEE

Mr. Charles Brown
State Single Point of Contact
State Planning Office
500 Charlotte Avenue
309 John Sevier Building
Nashville, Tennessee 37219
Telephone: (615) 741-1676

TEXAS

Mr. Tom Adams
Governor's Office of Budget and
   Planning
P.O. Box 12428
Austin, Texas 78711
Telephone: (512) 463-1778

UTAH

Utah State Clearinghouse
Office of Planning and Budget
Attn: Ms. Carolyn Wright
Room 116, State Capitol
Salt Lake City, Utah 84114
Telephone: (801) 538-1535

VERMONT

Mr. Bernard D. Johnson
Assistant Director
Office of Policy Research & Coord.
Pavilion Office Building
109 State Street
Montpelier, Vermont 05602
Telephone: (802) 828-3326

WEST VIRGINIA

Mr. Fred Cutlip
Director
Community Development Division
West Virginia Development Office
Building #6, Room 553
Charleston, West Virginia 25305
Telephone: (304) 348-4010

WISCONSIN

Mr. William C. Carey, Section Chief
Federal/State Relations Office
Wisconsin Department of
   Administration
101 South Webster Street
P.O. Box 7864
Madison, Wisconsin 53707
Telephone: (608) 266-0267

WYOMING

Ms. Sheryl Jeffries
State Single Point of Contact
Herschler Building
4th Floor, East Wing
Cheyenne, Wyoming 82002
Telephone: (307) 777-7574

TERRITORIES

GUAM

Mr. Michael J. Reidy, Director
Bureau of Budget and Management
   Research
Office of the Governor
P.O. Box 2950
Agana, Guam 96910
Telephone: (671) 472-2285

NORTHERN MARIANA ISLANDS

State Single Point of Contact
Planning and Budget Office
Office of the Governor
Saipan, CM
Northern Mariana Islands 96950

PUERTO RICO

Norma Burgos/Jose E. Caro
Chairman/Director
Puerto Rico Planning Board
Minillas Government Center
P.O. Box 41119
San Juan, Puerto Rico 00940-9985
Telephone: (809) 727-4444

VIRGIN ISLANDS

Mr. Jose George, Director
Office of Management & Budget
#41 Norregade Emancipation
   Garden Station, 2nd Floor
St. Thomas, Virgin Islands 00802
Please direct correspondence to:
Linda Clarke
Telephone: (809) 774-0750

Chapter 10

Developing Foundation and Corporate Grants Support for Your School

FEDERAL GRANTSEEKING is characterized by an abundance of rules, regulations, and forms, whereas foundation and corporate grantseeking are typified by a distinct lack of guidelines. Even the terms used by foundation and corporate grantors are not standard. For example, most foundations and corporations prohibit personal contact and request that prospective grantees make their request for a grant in writing. Some refer to this written request as a letter proposal; others call it a letter of inquiry, concept paper, or simply letter. Fewer than 10 percent announce that guidelines are available, but many state that they are not required and will accept a proposal even if the prospective grantee does not request or follow guidelines.

Even if the grantors state that they will accept a letter, grantseekers should develop a distinctly different proposal for each foundation and corporation they approach. Only a few large private funders have strict application requirements. They usually prefer to see a concept paper before even giving an application form to a prospective grantee. If they do have guidelines, it is imperative that prospective grantees follow them. For example, restrictions on the number of pages and attachments must be strictly adhered to.

The foundation and corporate grants marketplace is very different from the federal grants arena in other ways as well. As you may recall from Chapter Four, private grantors have few office workers, staff, or paid reviewers and lack well-developed proposal review procedures or predetermined scoring systems for proposal evaluation. Only a very few larger foundation and corporate grantors have a specified proposal format and use experts in the subject area to review proposals. In general, proposals submitted to them are read by board members or trustees, who have a limited amount of time to review the hundreds they receive. Nor are these decision makers usually experts in the fields of interest funded by the organization; few are professional reviewers. But they know what their foundation or corporation is looking for and answer only to their fellow trustees, board members, or stockholders. They prefer short proposals that can be read rapidly. This means your school's proposal must stimulate a prospective funding source's interest right from the beginning and be able to maintain it. The best way for your grantseekers to win the reader's respect is to demonstrate that they have purposefully singled out that particular grantor and have especially tailored their approach to the grantor's needs.

Grantors can sense immediately when one proposal has been "shotgunned" to a list of prospective funders. They know that they were lumped together with others and that their individual values and needs were ignored for the convenience of the grant writer. Considering the forethought and effort you and your grantseekers have invested in the proactive grants process, you definitely do not want your school to be guilty of this.

Remember that you are striving for a 50 percent success rate from your grants system. Foundation or corporate proposals must not, therefore, be direct-mail fund-raising pieces; the return on these is typically less than 1 percent. Foundations and corporations are one of your school's most prestigious groups of potential supporters. You must be sure that the proposal they see reflects your school's best effort rather than the most convenient or easiest solution for the grant writers.

The Letter Proposal

The most common type of proposal to a foundation or corporation takes the form of a letter on the prospective grantee's letterhead. Most private funders limit the length of letter proposals to two or three pages and do not allow attachments. These are the main components of a letter proposal:

1. An introductory paragraph stating the reason for writing
2. Paragraph explaining why the grantor was selected
3. Needs paragraph
4. Solution paragraph
5. Request-for-funds paragraph
6. Uniqueness paragraph
7. Closing paragraph
8. Signatures
9. Attachments (if allowed)

Have your proposal writers draft a letter proposal for your school's project. Encourage them to include all these components and to use data from their research and Project Planner. Remind them that their letter proposal should be tailored to the grantor's point of view and reflect any information they have on the funding source's preferred format. It is also important to remind your proposal developers that the proposal reader probably will not have a degree in education and therefore might not know or understand as much about the proposed project as they do.

Introduction

Mention in the introduction any linkages or contacts your school may have with the foundation or corporation. These include any of your school's key volunteers who have name recognition with the foundation or corporation or who are on the board of the funding source. Any contacts who have already talked to the foundation or corporation's board members or trustees on behalf of your school district should also be mentioned. But keep the focus on the grantor. Under no circumstances should your letter proposal begin with "We are writing to you because we need . . ." What you need is not the primary concern of grantors; they are concerned about what they value and need. Therefore, place the emphasis on them: "John Smith suggested I contact the Jones Foundation with an exciting project that deals with _____, an area about which our school and your board share a deep concern."

If your school does not have an established linkage or contact with the foundation or corporation, the proposal should start by explaining why your grantseekers selected that particular foundation or corporation to approach or how they knew it would be interested in the educational need addressed in your proposal.

Why the Grantor Was Selected

Your proposal developers should show that they have done their homework by demonstrating their knowledge of the grantor. For foundations, they should invest a few minutes reviewing the organization's IRS 990 PF tax return and analyzing and synthesizing the information. By compiling the statistics on past grants made to the field of education, they might discover an interesting fact or statistic that does not appear in any foundation resource publication. They could also cite a program previously funded by the foundation to demonstrate their familiarity with the foundation's granting pattern and history. For instance, if a foundation's tax return indicates that approximately 25 percent of its grants are related to children, your proposal developers could combine two years of data and say something like this:

My research indicates that in a recent two-year period, the Smith Foundation made _____ grants totaling over _____ dollars for projects focusing on children and their ability to successfully compete in our society. Your granting pattern has prompted us to submit to you this proposal for improving our students' competitive edge by enhancing our faculty's ability to involve parents in the education of children attending Neighborville Middle School.

Corporate grants are more difficult to research than foundation grants because they are not recorded on publicly available records like the 990 IRS PF tax return. Information on corporate grantors will have to be gathered through linkages, preproposal contact, or company workers who have volunteered to assist your school. As competition for corporate grants increases, companies are focusing their support on those nonprofit organizations to which their workers donate their time and money. Corporate volunteer programs and programs such as "Dollars for Donors" try to increase contact with workers and to get them involved in volunteerism. Your grant developers may therefore want to mention volunteerism in the second paragraph: "Harry Higgs, chairperson of our volunteer group and a Jones Corporation employee, has stated that the Jones corporation places a high value on quality education for young people."

Whether you are approaching a foundation or a corporation, this section of your letter proposal should do the following:

- Inform the funder if its employees donate time to your school

- Show that your grantseekers did their homework and are aware of the funding source's giving patterns and priorities

- State your conviction that the grantor is special and has unique needs and interests

- Inspire the grantor to read on because your school has a special request that fits these needs and interests

Although the request for funds usually appears in a later part of the letter (usually along with the budget information), your proposal developers can mention it in this section if they choose. Placing it here avoids the problem of getting a grantor interested in your project only to disappoint them later if it turns out that the amount you request is too much for its grants budget. If your proposal developers decide to put your school's grant request in this section they should compare the amount you are asking for with one of the foundation's or corporation's past grants or with their average grant amount for that area of interest. For example: "It is because of your concern for _____ that we encourage you to consider a grant for $25,000."

The Need for Your Project

The need referred to here is not the proposal developers' need to get the project funded but rather the documented need that your program aims to reduce. However, your proposal developers should not describe your school's project in this section. Unfortunately, overzealous grantseekers have a tendency to jump right into a description of what they want to do. The project and solution should be presented after the funding source understands what the problem is and that it *must* be addressed irrespective of the specific project or grantee. Again, research on the grantor will help your proposal developers tailor the description of the need to them. Your proposal should seek to demonstrate that there is a gap between what exists and what ought to be for your school, community, students, and so on. The more your grantseekers know about the funder's values and perspectives, the better they will be able to document the need. The needs section must do the following:

- Be motivating and compelling so that it captures and maintains the funder's interest

- Demonstrate that your grantseekers have a command of the literature and are aware of the pertinent studies concerning the problem

- Appeal to the perspective and interests of the grantor

Have your proposal developers review their research concerning the granting pattern of the foundation or corporation. Being aware of the types of projects the grantor has funded in the past and where the projects were implemented provides valuable insight and enables your grantseekers to tailor the data presented in the needs section. Federal and state grantors and their paid staff and reviewers expect such material as statistics, literature searches, research references, and quotes, but foundation and corporate readers may be more motivated by the human element, although they too will expect the proposal to reflect a command of the facts. The best avenue to take with a foundation or corporation may be to present a fact-filled story or case study to help them see the problem. The following is an example:

> *National studies have demonstrated that children watch television an average of _____ hours per day. A survey of the fourth graders at ABC Elementary School showed that their television viewing surpassed the national average by 20 percent. One possible cause of this disparity could be that the children from ABC Elementary School spend more time alone than many children. One fourth grader surveyed said, "I ride a bus for one hour to get home after school. I'm lonely and tired and my mom doesn't get home until late, so TV is my friend—and a lot*

better friend than my brother! People who say TV is violent have never lived with my brother."

It is important that your proposal developers determine what type of needs documentation best motivates the prospective grantor. Does the funding source's distribution of past grants demonstrate any specific geographic preferences? What types of grantees have been supported in the past? Can this information help your proposal developers select the right data, studies, or examples to document the need?

When approaching corporate funders, have your proposal developers focus on the corporation's areas of concern and on the locations of company plants or centers of operation. How can the problem addressed in your school's proposal affect the corporation's marketplace and products? You will find that corporations are normally concerned with the education of their future employees, who may well be their employees' children.

Solution

This section of the letter proposal is often difficult to construct because of the limited space available. The previous paragraphs focus on the grantor. If your grantseekers were fortunate enough to make preproposal contact with the funding source to discuss two or three possible solutions to the problem, you can be more confident in choosing one specific approach. But even when your proposal developers have limited insight into which solution the grantor might favor, they still must choose one approach and present it in this paragraph.

Naturally, your grant writers have much more information on the proposed solution than they can fit into a few short paragraphs. The challenge is to decide what information to include and what to exclude. Typically, proposal writers describe the solution in such great detail that they confuse rather than enlighten. This is another area where the principal can step in. By playing a supportive role, the principal can help the proposal writers maintain the proper perspective and recognize when they are providing too many details as well as when the proposal's conceptual framework is weak.

The object of this section is to give the prospective grantor a basic understanding of the solution your grant writers have chosen to meet the needs they have outlined. To do this, your proposal developers should try to think like the grantor. Ask them to keep in mind the qualities they would want to see in the solution if they were on the foundation or corporate board.

The Project Planner (see Chapter Seven) can help your grant writers keep the project summary short. If possible, include the Project Planner they have developed as an attachment. If attachments are not allowed, include the Project Planner as page two of a three-page letter proposal. It will clearly demonstrate to the funder the relationship between your project's activities or methods and its success. The Project Planner is also an excellent basis for the budget section or paragraph, particularly when you consider that it can summarize five or more pages of narrative on one spreadsheet! If your grant writers do not want to develop a project planner, remind them that a spreadsheet will be viewed very positively by the businessperson reading the proposal.

Whether or not a project planner is included, the plan or solution must appear interesting, plausible, affordable, and well organized. The objectives should be summarized in such a manner that the funder can envision how funding your school's proposal will shrink the gap between what is and what ought to be.

The letter proposal must focus on one solution—the one that has the greatest chance of matching the values of the prospective grantor. If your grant writers have done their homework, they know what the grantor values and will have described a need that the grantor will agree is important. By this point in the proposal the prospective grantor should believe that it is essential that the gap be closed (indicating commitment) and closed now (indicating urgency) and that to put off funding the proposal will only result in a larger gap later. Readers should feel that they cannot put your school's proposal down until they have read your suggested solution.

The grantor will likely agree that the need your grant writers have described exists, but may disagree with the solution. Even if your grantseekers did their homework, funding sources may have values, feelings, or prejudices that remain hidden. Thus prospective grantors could say any or all of the following:

- That they do not think your solution will work
- That they have already funded a grant that tried the same solution
- That other applicants have better or more interesting solutions

Assuming that by this point the grantor is still interested in the potential benefits of your solution, he or she will move on to the next item in your letter proposal.

Request for Funds

Grantors have limited funds and can finance only a fraction of the proposals they receive. Estimates are that private funders grant only 10 percent of the requests made to them. Ultimately they must judge which proposals produce what benefits for how many in the population or field they are concerned about.

Your school's letter proposal should clearly state the amount of grant funds being requested. If appropriate, have your proposal writers divide the cost of the project by the number of individuals it will serve. This will provide an estimate of the cost per person served. Remember that your school's project will have a "roll-out" or future benefit because each student served will go through life with more skills, better job opportunities, and so on. If your school's proposal deals with parent or teacher training, have your proposal writers roll out the project's benefits to the number of individuals these trained people will come in contact with. When they are describing facilities, have them identify how many students will use the facility over its lifetime. For example: "X number of families will utilize the Middlesex Recreational Facility for Y hours over a ten-year period."

When requesting equipment or technology, divide the cost by individuals served and what the skills they learn are worth over an entire lifetime. Depending on your situation, the cost per person served could be only pennies per hour.

Multiple Funders

If the project requires funding from more than one source, the letter proposal must state the amount requested from each prospective grantor. Thus the request-for-funds section should inform the grantor that your school will be seeking additional grant funds from other corporations or foundations. Your proposal writers should avoid saying, for example, that they *hope* to get funded by the Smith Corporation, the Jones Foundation, and so on. Instead, they should state the exact number of other grantors being approached, the grantors who have agreed to fund the project, the total amount already granted, and the amount outstanding.

For jointly funded projects it is crucial that the grantor know that your school's proposal is being tailored to each prospective funding source and that your grantseekers have done their homework. Some grantors may be justifiably concerned that their part of the project will be overshadowed by the other grantors or that they will not receive appropriate credit. To ensure that the grantors realize how critical their roles are, a colored highlighter can be used to visually separate each grantor's part of the total project on the Project Planner. By referring to this spreadsheet each grantor will see how integral its contribution is to the success of the whole plan.

Matching Costs and In-Kind Contributions

Required matching costs and in-kind contributions are usually associated with federal grantors, but some foundation and corporate grantors also require that a portion of a project's costs be borne by the grantee.

Providing a voluntary match will look good to any funder. The principal's handling of how matching or in-kind contributions will be secured and documented is particularly important. Even if a matching or in-kind contribution is not required, you, as the principal, may still want to include a documented contribution to demonstrate both your and your school's dedication to the project, because private grantors want to be sure that the organizations they fund are committed to supporting their projects after grant funds are depleted. By demonstrating your school's commitment in advance through a matching or in-kind contribution, you show that you have not applied for the grantor's money without carefully analyzing your own commitment. Matching and in-kind contributions should be designated on your Project Planner with an asterisk. The total should be placed at the bottom of the Project Planner in the column headed "Matching Funds, In-Kind Contributions, or Donated Costs."

What to Do if the Grantor Requests a Budget

Perhaps 75 percent of foundations do not require submission of a detailed, formal budget with the letter proposal. Only a few hundred will request that a specific budget format be used.

If your proposal writers have developed a project planner, preparing the budget will be a simple task. For a letter proposal budget, they should provide a summary of the major line items on the Project Planner and inform the grantor that more detailed budget information is available upon request.

If no budget format is specified, your proposal developers should present the budget in a paragraph or block form, using a minimum of space and short columns rather than long ones. Here is an example:

We are requesting a grant of $20,000 from the Smith Foundation. To demonstrate our school's support of this important project we will provide $8,000 in matching support. A detailed budget is available upon request.

	Request	*Match*	*Total*
Salaries & Wages	$10,000		$10,000
Stipends/Teachers In-Service		7,000	7,000
Consultants/Evaluation	3,000		3,000
Computer Equipment/Software	7,000		7,000
Printing/Materials		1,000	1,000
TOTAL	$20,000	$8,000	$28,000

Uniqueness

Why should your school, classroom, or consortium get this grant? Because funding sources will debate this issue anyway, why not address the subject first? Couldn't another school successfully initiate the methods and carry out the proposed project? Your proposal writers need a person with a broader perspective to help them develop the answers to these questions. They need you, the principal, to play the role of school cheerleader.

First, your school developed the project idea. Second, your proposal writers documented the school's need. In other words, the opportunity to act is where you are. And third, your project idea was developed with the help of experts in curriculum development, evaluation, and so on. You arranged for their input, gathered them together, and worked with them. In short, your school has already invested many, many hours developing a project that will be a successful model.

But in addition to these strong and valid reasons, you still need to examine more closely why your school deserves the funds necessary to implement the proposed solution. Brainstorm with your proposal writers the qualities that can convince the grantor that your school is indeed the best school to fund. For instance, in addition to superior facilities, you may also have unique individuals whose commitment and expertise make your school the funding source's most logical choice. It is extremely helpful when the school's administrator singles out the commitment of the project director or other key personnel in the body of the proposal. For example, "Jane Doe is slated to direct the project. Ms. Doe has been recognized as an outstanding educator by the State Department of Education and has over twelve years of experience in classroom teaching." As your signature should appear on the proposal, you are the best person to highlight the exemplary qualifications of the project personnel.

The uniqueness paragraph can also outline the ways that your district's structure will help implement the proposal and, equally important, how the relationship between your school and the district will work to ensure continuation of the project after the grant ends. With the changes in site-based management, more grantors are becoming aware of the emerging role of the building or community-school principal. In addition, grantors are interested in the unique relationship between schools and their districts and in how communities are involved in setting their schools' goals and objectives. The uniqueness paragraph or section provides the opportunity to explain these functions.

Closing Paragraph

In the closing paragraph your proposal writers should reaffirm your school's commitment to the project and invite the funder to work with your school to achieve the project's goals. They should also reaffirm your willingness to provide the funding source with any additional materials necessary to make the grant decision. The grantor should be invited to visit your school to observe both the need and the unique qualities that your staff and volunteers bring to the project. In addition, the name and phone number of your project director should be included in the closing paragraph, especially when the proposal is printed on your school stationery or the superintendent's. The final paragraph might include something like this: "Please contact myself or Jane Doe, the project director, at 555-358-4501 with questions about this proposal." If you do not feel comfortable with a grantor asking you detailed questions, it is best to admit up front that neither you nor the superintendent created the proposal. This can be accomplished by offering to arrange a conference call between the grantor and the project director or by suggesting that the grantor speak with the project director or your district grants office staff.

Signatures

Taking the grantor's point of view into consideration, whose signature from your district will have the strongest impact on the funding decision? The general rule is that the letter proposal should be signed by the highest-ranking individual in the school system. In most cases, your school's letter proposal will be signed by your superintendent or you, the principal. Some schools require the signature of an assistant superintendent for instruction, a business officer, or a curriculum specialist. Some proposals are submitted with two signatures, those of the president of the school board and of a top-ranking school administrator. It may be appropriate to have two signatures for proposals that require special cooperation, collaboration, or coordination. For example, a consortium proposal may have the signatures of all the cooperating parties to demonstrate that the collaboration is real.

Unlike foundation and corporate proposals, a federal application may call for a school board resolution that is documented by the inclusion of a signed copy of the board minutes. Even though private grantors do not require this documentation, they may nevertheless respond favorably to a statement confirming that the school, community, and district have passed a resolution to apply to their foundation or corporation and to complete the project.

Attachments

Most foundations and corporations do not allow or encourage attachments. Attachments may help answer questions that arise during the reading of a proposal, but the problems they create for understaffed foundations and corporations often preclude their inclusion.

What about pictures, videotapes, audiotapes, and slides? It seems that in this age of electronics, these components would be not only allowed but encouraged. During preproposal contact, electronic tools may be highly effective in helping the grantor see the problem. However, it may be inappropriate to include them with the proposal. Remember, not all reviewers have access to playback equipment. The bottom line is to find out what is allowed before submitting the proposal. You can include your school's website address to increase their knowledge about your school, or your e-mail address for questions.

What's in Store for the Future?

Foundations in some states are joining together to support a common format for applications for grants. New Jersey has moved ahead on this idea, but it is unlikely to catch on rapidly. If your grantseekers follow the guidelines found in the various resource books, make preproposal contact when allowed, and expand your school's informal linkage with funding sources, you can be fairly certain that your proposal's format will be acceptable to your prospective grantor.

Two sample letter proposals (Exhibits 10.1 and 10.2), one to a foundation and one to a corporation, follow for your review.

CHAPTER 10 CHECKLIST

Evaluation and Planning Worksheet

1. Does your school have a format that helps foundation and corporate grantseekers prepare letter proposals?

   _____ yes   _____ no

2. Are there unwritten rules regarding contact with grantors?

   _____ yes   _____ no

3. Is there a file containing samples of funded foundation and corporate proposals that your grantseekers can examine?

   _____ yes   _____ no

Exhibit 10.1

SAMPLE LETTER PROPOSAL TO A FOUNDATION

January 6, 1998

Ms. Elaine Finsterwald, Trustee
Smith Foundation
123 Money Place
Clotin, NC 28699

Dear Ms. Finsterwald:

The Smith Foundation is synonymous with the word *education*. Since 1927, your grants have provided creative solutions to the educational needs of young people in Jonesboro and our state. Your recent annual report highlights your commitment to increase family involvement and responsibility in education. The $1.5 million in grants you have awarded over the past three years to strengthen families clearly demonstrates your dedication and concern.

[If applicable, mention previous support to your school district or the number of children who have been touched by any past support. For example, "Your grant to renovate an elementary classroom into the Smith Computer Lab has directly touched the lives of over 5,000 students in four years. Scores on standardized tests have improved 40 percent." If the Smith Foundation has not funded education directly, show how their support for your school-based project relates to their interest in programs related to the welfare of children, improving family life, parental responsibility and involvement, and so on.]

Previous generations have progressed through our schools with the involvement and encouragement of teachers and parents. Today, classroom leaders lack much of the support they were accustomed to getting from parents. Today's educator must deal with parents working several jobs and must compete with television and video games for a child's time and attention.

How much time do children spend watching television versus doing homework? A study of 25,000 middle school children conducted by the Department of Education reported 21.4 hours per week of television versus 5.6 hours of homework (*Wall Street Journal,* March 1992). When asked if parents placed limits on television, two-thirds of the parents surveyed said yes, while two-thirds of the children said no. These results suggest that some parents may have a problem setting priorities for their children.

Other results of the study point to the deterioration of parental responsibility and involvement in educational activities. For instance, four out of five parents surveyed reported that they regularly discuss schoolwork with their children, while two out of three children said parents rarely or never discuss schoolwork with them. Apparently the breakdown in communication between parents and children is at crisis proportions.

The need exists to develop and implement programs that encourage parents to become involved in their children's education. This means more than just visiting the school. For example, the Department of Education study also showed that 50 percent of parents had visited their child's school for meetings, but only 33 percent had visited their child's classroom.

What happens when parents take responsibility for working with their children and their children's school?

- Students whose parents discuss schoolwork with them get higher grades.
- Restrictions on television viewing tend to boost grades.

(continued)

Exhibit 10.1 (continued)

While some adults may think that the way to improve education is to increase funding for schools, taxpayers in Harrison, Arkansas, do not. While national test scores for students in Harrison rank in the top 10 percent of the country, Harrison ranks 272d out of Arkansas's 327 school districts in education taxes (*USA Today,* November 18, 1991). The key is parental involvement. Parents volunteer for one hour a week at each of the town's elementary schools, and parents and teachers meet each year to establish education goals for the next year.

What can we do in Clotin to promote the sharing of education among schools, parents, and children? We propose to utilize technology and old-fashioned responsibility. For only $2 per student we will ask parents to sign on to involvement through a contract for support. Each month a contract will be completed by the teacher, parent, and student. The contract will be done on three-part carbonless paper and will outline what can be expected from each to encourage better use of both in-school and out-of-school time—use that reinforces the student's education. From homework to more educational choices in family entertainment, all those involved will seek to make sure that the student gets the most out of his or her time.

To help parents maintain better access to their child's teacher(s) and to reinforce the completion of homework, we will install a computer-based program in our schools that lists each child's homework assignments. In addition, parents and students can help themselves through use of a computer-based "homework help line." Even if parents do not have access to computers, the contract for education will provide a communication vehicle for them. The added benefit of technology will provide a whole new way for the three partners in education—parent, child, and teacher—to communicate and increase learning.

The attached Project Planner outlines each objective and the activities that will foster the changes we desire. From increasing test scores to promoting public and volunteer service, Clotin schools will provide the catalyst for the education and involvement of parents in their children's responsible use of out-of-school time.

We request a grant from the Smith Foundation of $20,000 to initiate this project. Based upon our preliminary work with the teachers and Parent Advisory Committee of Clotin Schools, we anticipate the involvement of 1,600 students, 460 parents, and 60 teachers. Your grant funds will represent an investment of $20 per person served for the first year of the project. We are also in the process of securing funds from the ABC Foundation, the DEF Telephone Company, and the XYZ Power Company. These groups have already committed to granting $40,000 for this project. Our school district will provide $6,000 of in-kind contributions to support the project.

The Clotin Elementary School is fortunate to have Renee Weathers as the project director. Ms. Weathers was named 1997 Outstanding Teacher of the Year by the State Education Department. She will be assisted by the Parents Advisory Committee, chaired by Sam Price. The Committee is supported by a group of 140 parents, who have already volunteered 200 hours to develop the program and this proposal.

Clotin schools' tax exempt status is _____, and our tax exempt number is _____. Renee Weathers is available at 200-861-4000 to answer your questions and to provide additional information that will help you arrive at your funding decision.

Sincerely,

Attachment

Exhibit 10.2

SAMPLE LETTER PROPOSAL TO A CORPORATION

January 12, 1998

Clyde L. Baker
Contributions Officer
Widget Corporation
4321 Commercial Park
Rocker, NY 14570

Dear Mr. Baker:

John Allen, your marketing manager, advised me to contact you for consideration of a grant from Widget Corporation. John, who has volunteered over 100 hours to our Parents Advisory Committee, has told us of your company's interest in and efforts to promote responsible behavior in your employees and their families. It is with this common interest in mind that Casper Schools request a grant of $20,000 from the Widget Corporation for the Responsibility in Education through Academic Partners Program (REAP).

John Allen has been instrumental in guiding our schools' curriculum group toward understanding the changes technological advances have brought to Widget Corporation and how these changes influence what types of employees and skills your corporation will require in the future.

Technological advances have also brought changes to the family. Everything from health to educational achievement to parent/child communication has been affected by television, videos, and computer games.

We have learned in education that what children devote their time to determines the skills they develop. Unfortunately, our children are devoting an inordinate amount of time to television and computer games. A study of 25,000 middle school children conducted by the Department of Education revealed that the children surveyed spent an average of 5.6 hours per week on homework and 21.4 hours per week watching television. In addition, when asked if parents placed limits on television, two-thirds of the parents surveyed said yes, while two-thirds of the children said no.

We are not suggesting that television viewing is inherently bad. However, the amount of television children watch is one possible indication of the responsibility parents take for their children's "out-of-school" time and ultimately for their education.

A parent's responsible involvement in his or her child's education can also be evaluated by the time spent discussing schoolwork within the family and the type or quality of parental contact with the child's school. The Department of Education's study revealed some disturbing facts in these areas as well.

• Four out of five parents surveyed reported that they regularly discussed schoolwork with their children, while two out of three children said they rarely or never discussed schoolwork with their parents.

• Fifty percent of the parents surveyed reported visiting their child's school for meetings, while only 33 percent had visited their child's classroom.

When you compare what can result from parental involvement and responsibility in education with what can result from a lack of parental involvement and responsibility in education, the problem is clear and the goal evident. Students whose parents discuss schoolwork with them get higher grades, and restrictions on television viewing tend to boost grades.

What can be done? This is the question that brought John Allen and over 100 other parents together to prepare a plan for action. The program they developed is entitled Responsibility in Education through Academic Partners (REAP).

(continued)

Exhibit 10.2 (continued)

REAP proposes to use technology and old-fashioned responsibility to promote the sharing of education among schools, parents, and children. For only $2 per student we will ask parents to sign on to involvement through a contract for support. Each month a contract will be completed by the teacher, parent, and student. The contract will be done on three-part carbonless paper and will outline what can be expected from each to encourage better use of both in-school and out-of-school time—use that reinforces the student's education. From homework to more educational choices in family entertainment, all those involved will seek to make sure that the student gets the most out of his or her time.

To help parents maintain better access to their child's teacher(s) and to reinforce the completion of homework, we will install a computer-based program in our schools that lists each child's homework assignments. In addition, parents and students can help themselves through use of a computer-based "homework help line." Even if parents do not have access to computers, the contract for education will provide a communication vehicle for them. The added benefit of technology will provide a whole new way for the three partners in education—parent, child, and teacher—to communicate and increase learning. The objectives of our project and the activities aimed at bringing about the desired changes are summarized on the enclosed Project Planner spreadsheet.

The Widget Corporation's support will be recognized in the REAP program's informational brochure, and space will be set aside on the brochure's inside cover for a statement from Widget Corporation.

Alice Jones has been selected as the project director. She is eminently qualified and has worked with parents in this region for over twenty-five years. As a sign of commitment, the school district has agreed to provide support services valued at $6,000.

The volunteers have done all they can do. The time is right. Please join with us in sowing the seeds for responsible, parental involvement in education.

Money alone does not ensure a great education. Responsible commitment does. In Harrison, Arkansas, national test scores ranked among the top 10 percent in the country, while education taxes rank 272nd out of Arkansas's 327 school districts. What's the key? Parental involvement. Approximately 100 parents volunteer one hour per week at each of the town's elementary schools, and parents and teachers work together each year to determine the following year's educational goals.

This project is truly an investment in our community. Alice Jones is ready to provide any additional information you may need to make your funding decision. Please call her at 321-987-0645. Our schools' tax exempt status is _____ and our tax exempt number is _____.

Sincerely,

Chapter 11

Improving and Submitting Your School's Foundation/ Corporate Proposal

THE RESEARCH YOUR GRANTSEEKERS have gathered on the prospective funding source provides them with the deadlines for proposal submission. If possible, validate deadlines through preproposal contact with the grantor. Many foundations and corporations state that proposals are read periodically or as needed. Remind your proposal writers that "as needed" does not mean when they need the money or want to start the project. Foundations and corporations do not respond to the constraints of their grantees; they expect grantees to respond to theirs. One foundation, typical of many, makes its grants decisions in the summer for the next calendar year. So plan ahead!

If there is a deadline, your school's proposal should be submitted slightly in advance of it. This eliminates the need for special delivery or express mail service. Still, special delivery is relatively inexpensive; your grant writers may want to send their proposal this way so that they can obtain a signed assurance that the proposal was safely delivered. Also, your grantseekers should review the exact wording of the funding source's instructions for submitting proposals. Does the grantor want to receive the proposal by a certain date, or must it be simply mailed by that date? Many private grantors request receipts.

As the principal, you should initiate an early discussion of deadlines to encourage your proposal writers to aim for early submission. This allows time for mock review, which will increase the proposal's chance of being funded. By emphasizing the importance of the mock review and early submission as your group initiates grantseeking, you dramatically increase the likelihood that they will be done. Naturally, it is to everyone's benefit to submit a proposal that reflects your proposal writers' best efforts and that is a credit to your school.

Organizing a Proposal Improvement Group

Invite four or five individuals to form a group that aims to help improve your school's proposals by performing mock reviews. This group should follow the basic concepts of quality circles and total quality management, by which employees volunteer to commit personal time to improving company products and services. Encourage your school and community's most talented individuals to get involved in the mock review, including parents, students, educators, foundation or corporate board members, or anyone else you would like to involve. (A foundation or corporate board member can provide particularly valuable insight into the private grants-review and decision-making process.) By inviting them to take part voluntarily, you facilitate a positive grant atmosphere that reinforces the commitment your grant developers have demonstrated. Once volunteers realize how easy it is to develop a quality proposal, they will become valuable resources for your school's grants program and take responsibility for developing their own proposals.

It is much easier (and possibly more enjoyable) to perform a mock review for foundation and corporate proposals than for the government variety described in Chapter Nine. It can be fun to pretend to be a wealthy foundation or corporate board member. (Only community foundations actively recruit board members who reflect the economic and racial diversity of the geographic area they fund.) Also, it takes less time to read and comment on foundation and corporate proposals because they are usually far shorter than government proposals.

Use the sample letter in Exhibit 11.1 as the basis for your invitation to participate in a proposal improvement group. Basically, you ask individuals to take part in the mock review of a proposal. The volunteers will play the roles of actual funders and carry out the real review process as closely as possible. They may be relieved to learn that the purpose of the exercise is not to get their opinions of the proposal but rather to get their impressions of how the proposal will look to the funder.

In most cases, the group will spend only five or ten minutes reviewing the proposal. The entire evaluation process should be completed in less than an hour. If the proposal is being submitted to one of the few large foundations that use a longer format and have experts review proposals, you may ask your volunteers to review, comment on, and score the proposal before they meet as a group. Even most large foundations want a concept paper or outline similar to the letter proposal described in Chapter Ten. Whether the foundation allows five pages or ten, the best way to get information on the actual review process is to request it during preproposal contact.

Exhibit 11.1

INVITATION TO PARTICIPATE IN FOUNDATION/CORPORATE PROPOSAL IMPROVEMENT GROUP

Date

Name

Address

Dear _____:

Thank you for speaking with me on [date] about the possibility of getting your input to assist our school district in submitting the very best grant proposal possible. Could you now review the enclosed proposal from the point of view of a reviewer? The attached materials have been designed to assist you in playing the role of actual reviewers who may evaluate our proposal.

Please read the information on the reviewers' backgrounds and the scoring system, and limit the time you spend reading the proposal to the time real reviewers will spend. A Quality Circle Scoring Worksheet has been provided to help you record your scores and comments.

A meeting of all mock reviewers in our quality circle has been scheduled for [date]. Please bring this worksheet with you to the meeting, which will last less than an hour. The meeting's purpose is to analyze the scores and brainstorm suggestions to improve the proposal.

Sincerely,

[Name]

[Phone Number]

The Proposal Improvement Scoring Sheet

Complete the first half of this worksheet (Exhibit 11.2) before your group meeting. Give a copy of the worksheet to each member of the group. The principal or other individual selected to represent your administration should provide the worksheets, set up the meeting, and facilitate the mock review process.

The worksheet you distribute to group members should contain the following information:

- Who at the foundation or corporation reads proposals
- Their backgrounds
- How much time they devote to reviewing each proposal
- What scoring system or criteria they use for evaluation
- The funder's past granting history

Unfortunately, in most cases you will not have much to record. Private grant funds are not public money, so private grantors are not required to provide information on their review process. In addition, most private grantors do not employ an elaborate scoring or evaluation system; they simply read proposals quickly and ask their fellow board members what looks good.

Exhibit 11.2

FOUNDATION/CORPORATE PROPOSAL IMPROVEMENT SCORING WORKSHEET

The following information is being provided to help you review the attached foundation/corporate grant application/proposal.

The Proposal Will Be Read by:

_____ funding official   _____ board members

_____ funding staff   _____ other _____

_____ review committee

Amount of Time Spent Reviewing Each Proposal:

_____

_____

_____

Background of Reviewer(s):

College degrees (majors)_____

Socioeconomic background—upper class, middle class, etc. _____

_____

Known Viewpoints and Past Granting History:

Who has been funded for what types of projects and for what amounts of money? _____

_____

_____

_____

Positive Points   Rank Order

Negative Points   Rank Order

Other Comments/Suggestions for Improvement:

How can you help your grantseekers obtain background on private funding officials? Much valuable information can be found in resource books such as *Who's Who* and *Standard and Poor's Register of Directors and Executives*. Also, regional and even local editions of some books describe wealthy and influential individuals. The printed rosters of many membership groups and service clubs may include valuable background information that can give your grantseekers insight. Provide your group with brief biographies of the funder's board members, or at least basic information such as age and educational background. As your school's proposal will be based on educational principles, information on the reviewers' background will help your mock reviewers evaluate the vocabulary in the proposal.

Also give the volunteers a description of the funding source and any information you have on the types of proposals they funded in the past, the number of projects they have funded, and the amount of each grant. If the grantor is a foundation, a copy of its tax return will be helpful. At the beginning of the meeting, review the information about the grantor to be sure your group members develop an appropriate impression of the funding source's point of view.

If you are unable to find out how much time the grantor is likely to spend on each proposal, limit the group's time to five minutes.

Instruct your volunteers to read the proposal quickly and to make believe that they have read many such proposals and have a large stack to review. Ask them to designate any areas they think would appeal to the grantor with a plus sign, and areas that need improvement with a minus sign.

At the conclusion of the time allowed, you can be very useful as the group facilitator and recorder—if you believe your volunteers will speak openly in front of you. If you are in doubt about that, ask a volunteer to fill the role.

Instruct the recorder to print, not write, the positive points on the worksheet. There is no need for consensus; the participants then hold a brief discussion about the positive points, after which they rank them—according to the grantor's perspective, not that of the mock reviewers. The mock reviewers should repeat this procedure for the negative areas. Then they should suggest improvements for any area they think may be viewed negatively by the grantor.

If an area of the proposal is unclear, it should be listed as a problem area to be improved. Do not allow proposal developers to take part in the mock review; they may be allowed to observe, but not to defend their proposal. After all, they will not be present to answer questions or offer explanations for the real reviewers. If you feel their presence may prevent reviewers from offering a frank evaluation of the proposal, ban them entirely.

The group recorder will provide you with the rank orders of positive and negative areas so that you will know how strongly the mock reviewers felt about specific parts of the proposal. This, plus the group's list of suggestions for improvement, will help the proposal developers rewrite portions of the proposal and put the finishing touches on the final version.

Review the rewritten proposal to be certain that the proposal developers have not overreacted to the criticisms at the expense of the positive areas. Many are so sensitive to criticism that in their zeal to fix the proposal they place all their energy in the areas to improve. In general, proposal developers cut positive areas so they have more space to improve the negative ones. This may not be best. The principal can assist by keeping the proposal developers focused on the values and perspectives of the funder and by promoting a balance between maintaining the strengths of a proposal while improving the weaknesses.

CHAPTER 11 CHECKLIST

Evaluation and Planning Worksheet

1. **Do you have a system of presubmission review for foundation and corporate proposals to ensure quality?**

   _____ yes   _____ no

2. **Do you use a mock review process to educate and encourage others to become involved in proposal preparation?**

   _____ yes   _____ no

3. **Who from your school could play a positive, voluntary role in the preproposal review process?**

   _____

   _____

   _____

   _____

4. **List any community members who could provide insight into the preproposal review system and whose involvement in the mock review process would provide a communications link to the community.**

   _____

   _____

   _____

   _____

Chapter 12

The Decision: Contacting Grantors and Dealing with Success/Rejection

AS THE PRINCIPAL, you will be asked by your anxious proposal developers to check on the status of their submitted proposal. To help handle this and avoid action that would jeopardize your school's grant at this critical time, consider the following suggestions.

Postproposal Federal Grantor Contact

Once your school's proposal has been logged by a federal grantor, it is considered to be in submission. During this time it will be assigned to a review panel and spend several months in the review process.

To put it bluntly, a federal agency will consider contact by you or your grantseekers during this time as an attempt to unfairly influence the review and outcome. So contact with the funder should be made only on the rare occasion when further information would impact its decision, as when one of the following is the case:

- A new advance in education allows you to drastically cut the grant amount requested (because of new equipment, software, assessment tools, or the like)

- Another grantor has agreed to partially fund the project, so you need less money

- You need to pull your school's proposal from submission and the review process because another funding source has decided to fund it totally.

Short of these or other dramatic reasons, instruct your grantseekers to avoid contact with the grantor while their proposal is being reviewed, including contact by elected officials or other advocates.

Postproposal Foundation or Corporate Grantor Contact

Contact with federal bureaucrats may be a legal issue during this period; with corporate and foundation grantors it may be an ethical issue. Considering how few grant-related employees most private grantors have, contacting them may also be difficult.

In general, contact corporations or foundations after the proposal has been made for the same reasons you would contact federal grantors. In writing, forward to them only significant changes in the amount of funding requested, along with a brief but thorough explanation of what has occurred and how it will modify your school's proposal.

Such changes should be relatively rare. If one occurs, you might consider asking one of your links to the funder to ask how (and if) you should correspond with it.

The Decision

A key ingredient in an efficient grants program is knowing how to creatively handle your staff's excitement at being notified of a grant award or their disappointment at being turned down. In addition to helping your rejected grantseekers reassess their proposal, you must help successful grantseekers avoid the pitfalls of overexuberance. Grantseekers have put their egos and hard work on the line and deserve special consideration at this critical juncture. There are a few techniques you can apply that will make a big difference in their attitude and involvement in future grantseeking. The techniques vary according to the type of grantor and the grantseeking outcome.

Federal Granting Agencies

Handling Rejection

When individuals have expended hard work and energy in applying for a federal grant, the rejection notice hits them very hard. The principal can help prepare the grantseekers in advance of the notification by sending them a note or phoning to thank them again for their hard work, and to remind them that notification will be made soon and that even a 50 percent success rate means failure half the time. Remind them that all is not lost if the proposal gets turned down on the first attempt and that the process of preparing a proposal is a learning and growing experience. Talking with your grantseekers prior to notification is particularly useful because most rejected grantseekers go into a denial and withdrawal phase after they receive the dreaded response.

The principal is in a unique position to support the disappointed grantseeker. Many disgruntled grantseekers feel a need to protest the negative decision and appeal the rejection. Remind them that few appeals ever win anything but enemies. Further, because your grantseekers may have to interface with the same program officers again, it is best not to irritate them. Appeals can also hold up the entire award process. For all these reasons they should be avoided in all but the most extreme circumstances. Recognize the grantseekers' disappointment and offer your assistance in writing a thank-you letter (instead of a complaint) to the federal agency.

The purpose of this letter is to thank the officials for their time and help, to let them know you understand their limitations and funding constraints, and to request the reviewers' comments. The letter is an opportunity to demonstrate a positive grantseeking attitude and to show your sincere concern for the funders and the difficulty of their job.

In your request for the reviewers' comments, advise the agency that you will use these comments to prepare another proposal. Ask for a list of recipients of this year's grant awards and for any other information they feel would help your grantseekers. Include a self-addressed label for their convenience in returning the information you request.

Explain that your research indicated that this particular grants program presented a great opportunity for funding because of its concern for your school's and grantseekers' area of interest. Inform them that you or your grant writer will be contacting them in the near future concerning their next submission date and grants cycle. You may also ask if they anticipate the availability of any unsolicited funds (funds that are granted at the discretion of the program administrator) or if there is any chance that one of the successful applicants may not expend all of their grant award in the prescribed time. (You could use any unexpended funds or unsolicited funding to do a portion of your school's project, enabling your school to be a more attractive applicant in the future.)

You might receive a letter that gives you a priority score and explains that while you are not yet rejected, the score is not adequate to attract funding. In this case, encourage your grantseekers to react in a constructive, positive way and not to burn any bridges or alienate future funding opportunities.

One pitfall that many temporarily unsuccessful grantseekers fall into is avoidance of the grantor. Help your grantseekers keep in contact with the funding source. Encourage them to anticipate the next deadline and be sure they realize that their chances for a grant award may actually be greater *after* their rejection because they will have access to the reviewers' comments and a list of recipients.

The principal's encouragement and assistance are key to the resubmittal of a proposal. If resubmitted, the proposal should be judged by a new panel of reviewers, which gives it a new chance of being funded. But try to be objective about the likelihood of the project being funded upon resubmittal. If the original proposal got a very low score, ask the federal grantor whether it would be better to develop a whole new approach or solution instead of resubmitting a reworked proposal.

Finally, initiate the process of preproposal contact all over again. Review the list of this year's grantees. Do you know any whom you could contact? What was the average grant size? Where are the grantees located?

Handling an Award

Many federal program officers who grant millions of dollars each year never receive thank-you letters or requests for reviewers' comments from successful (that is, funded) grantees. In many cases, applicants do not realize that they will not receive reviewers' comments unless they request this valuable feedback in writing. To make your school stand out as an institution that is dedicated to learning and improving, *be different.* Send a thank-you letter and include a request for reviewers' comments and a self-addressed label. Remember, your grantseekers need to know what they did correctly so they can repeat the techniques that resulted in success. In addition, reviewers' comments can provide the basis for your legitimate praise of your grant writers. Invite the federal granting officials to visit your school. Of course, once you accept federal funds, they have the legal authority to come for a site visit, but it looks better if you invite them.

Negotiating the Final Award

One key problem in dealing with federal funds is the art of negotiating the final budget. Remember that reviewers are instructed to look for padding in budgets and therefore may offer you less than you requested. It is not uncommon for overexuberant grantseekers to agree to a budget that is significantly reduced from the grant figure submitted in the proposal. The principal can play a critical role in the negotiation process needed to arrive at a figure that both the grantor and the grantee believe will allow the proposal to be successfully carried out. As the grantseekers have invested hours of work in developing the project, their ability to remain objective in reducing budget items is questionable, and they may jeopardize their future relationship with the funder by being either too flexible or too rigid in arriving at the final figures.

The principal can play the role of negotiator and buffer between the two sides. Your goal is to arrive at a budget that is realistic and fair to your school, the granting agency, and your grantseekers. If your grantseekers have developed a project planner you will find that this document is invaluable in helping you set up a realistic basis for negotiating the grant award. If you do not have a project planner to negotiate from, it is never too late. Ask the government granting official to allow you a few days to complete a detailed task analysis and spreadsheet that will document each expenditure proposed in the project. Propose that you send the spreadsheet to him or her so that together you can analyze how any suggested budget adjustments will have an impact on your program's methods and the accomplishment of its objectives.

Try to remain flexible. Look at the process of negotiating a final award as a team effort aimed at eliminating waste and inefficiency while ensuring that the program will attain its objectives at the levels specified in the proposal. If the negotiations seriously threaten your program's ability to have an impact on the problem, you should request a reduction in the degree of change (progress) called for in the objectives. Changing the number of students, clients, or individuals served by the project can also bring the costs down. Unfortunately, some grantseekers make up their budget requests out of rough estimates, which often causes the government grantor to view the negotiation process as a search for the "fluff." By referring to your Project Planner, the funding official will be able to relate each expenditure to the successful completion of the project. This will enhance the funder's image of you, your school, and your grants team as knowledgeable, honest, and worthy of trust.

The negotiation is further complicated when the federal agency uses a grants or contracts officer to negotiate the budget and a program officer to discuss the project. Fiscal people have difficulty relating the degree of change and the attainment of objectives to money. To deal with this situation, request a conference call between the program and fiscal officers and always defer to the program officer when changing the objectives and scope of the project.

In many ways, the principal has as much of a vested interest in the successful negotiation of the grant as the government officials. All sides want to be certain that the plan proposed by your grantseekers is well designed and that the project will be a credit to the government sponsor and to your school. The Project Planner will provide a way to see what happens to the proposed activities and methods when categories of budgets are altered. For example, if the amount proposed for personnel is cut, whose time on the project will be reduced and what will be the effect on the activities and objectives? When the amount specified for consultants is reduced, what activities will this affect? If the proposal evaluation was to be conducted by consultants, how will the project now be evaluated? Who will collect the data? If the amount for equipment is eliminated or reduced, what will be affected?

In arriving at the final budget, the cash flow, and the reimbursement system, remember that your district's central office, business administrator, or district grants person should be part of the negotiation and final agreement. It is also essential that your central office not agree to budget amounts without agreement from you and your grantseekers.

By involving your district office staff in the negotiations and utilizing a spreadsheet such as the Project Planner, you will have a sound basis for moving into the implementation stage of the project. Most of the problems associated with administering and carrying out grants can be traced to the improper negotiation of the budget and to the lack of agreement of project staff on the appropriate expenditure of funds called for in the proposal.

Foundation and Corporate Grantors

Handling Rejection

The principal can provide a valuable service to the school and the rejected grantseekers by encouraging a thoughtful response to the foundation or corporation's grant denial. Unlike the federal grantor, the private grantor normally does not have the personnel resources or independent review system necessary to provide your grant writers with reviewers' comments and scores. Because private grant funds do not come from tax dollars, there is no Freedom of Information Act to invoke, and you have no legal right to know the basis for the private grantor's decision. What is important here is to maintain your contact with the grantor and to make sure your volunteers' efforts to secure the grant do not go for naught. If you have used a personal link to make preproposal contact, you have a responsibility to that person to keep his or her relationship with the foundation or corporation on good terms. Send a letter apprising the person of the rejection and thanking him or her for helping.

Send the foundation or corporation a thank-you letter. As the principal or the district office may exercise some control over contacts with prospective grantors, you may want to send the letter from your office. In your letter, inform the funding source that your grantseekers will reapply for a grant unless the funder advises you that they should not. Even if the grantor's board members meet only once per year, when they meet next year they will find your thank-you letter from last year along with your school's *new* grant request. In your letter, acknowledge that you understand that they have limited staff so that they can use their resources to make grants instead of payroll. You will not lose anything by sincerely thanking them for the time they invested in reading your proposal and for the opportunity to compete for their funds. You might even invite them to attend a school or community meeting or to visit your school before the next round of grants to see your school's unique qualifications firsthand.

To keep your grantseekers' motivation up, you must play the role of both realist and cheerleader. You must help your grantseekers understand that some proposals will be rejected and that they must make the best of the situation and get ready to resubmit! For obvious reasons, initiating grantor-grantee correspondence is best not left to the disappointed grantseeker.

Handling an Award

You, the principal, must keep your grantseekers from making image-damaging mistakes with funding sources even when their proposals are funded. You might receive a phone call or a letter from your district office or from the grantor informing you of your school's good fortune. Immediately send a thank-you letter to all of your volunteers and linkages who helped with preproposal contact or proposal preparation. Send the foundation or corporate grantor a thank-you letter. Invite the grantor to visit your school and ask if he or she would like to view a presentation by your students, teachers, or parents. You could also ask if a short video on your project to show at a future board meeting would be useful. Be sure to request any comments that can be provided on your school's proposal, including negative as well as positive feedback. Mention that as the school's educational leader you are always ready to learn, as are your grantseekers.

Some foundations meet so infrequently and have such limited staff that a check for the entire grant amount is sent with the notification of the award. If a check from the grantor is not included in the acceptance letter, request information on the payment procedure in your thank-you letter.

Service Clubs and Organizations

Handling Rejection

When your school's request for a grant is denied by a local service club, civic group, or fraternal organization, the need to send a thank-you letter is even greater than with federal, foundation, and corporate grantors because you are likely to see these grantors in your school and community again and again. In your thank-you letter, request suggestions for improvement and directions for resubmittal. Let the club, group, or organization know that the problem your proposal described is not going to go away and that you will be back to seek their support. These funders interpret persistence as commitment. As a committed educational leader and community member, it is your duty to bring to the community's attention the positive aspects of the educational system and to remind these groups of the opportunities they have to help improve it.

Handling an Award

Voluntary organizations, service clubs, and fraternal groups like to have their members and donors see and hear about educational changes they have supported. Send them a thank-you letter immediately upon receiving word of your grant award and volunteer to make a presentation at one of their future meetings or conferences. If you can, include your students, teachers, and parents in the presentation.

CHAPTER 12 CHECKLIST

Evaluation and Planning Worksheet

Review the following suggested techniques for dealing with grantseeking outcomes and indicate which ones are currently being employed at your school.

1. **Thank-you letter sent to government officials when proposal is rejected**
    _____ yes _____ no

2. **Thank-you letter sent to foundations and corporations when proposal is rejected**
    _____ yes _____ no

3. **Reviewers' comments automatically and routinely requested**
    Rejected proposal: _____ yes _____ no
    Funded proposal: _____ yes _____ no

4. **Involved in the final budget negotiation**
    School principal: _____ yes _____ no
    Grantseeker: _____ yes _____ no
    Business office: _____ yes _____ no
    Grants office: _____ yes _____ no

5. **Grantseekers' use of a spreadsheet to justify the budget**
    _____ yes _____ no

Chapter 13

The Principal's Role in Administering Grant Funds

THE POLICIES AND PROCEDURES of a school district's grants system have historically been aimed at expending funds and operating programs that are extensions of the central office's federal and state grants programs, particularly federal entitlement programs. Many school districts employ a grants system that mirrors the one used by the majority of public and private institutions of higher education. Colleges and universities have developed extensive centralized grants systems for both securing and administering outside grant funds. (They often refer to these as sponsored projects.) However, the challenge of developing resources in the 1990s has demonstrated the weaknesses and limitations of the centralized system. It has become evident that centralized grants offices may not be the best vehicle for encouraging grantseeking or for ensuring high-quality proposals from the elementary to postsecondary levels. In fact, decentralized grants programs generate higher levels of interest and enthusiasm on the local level, and that translates into grants success! But questions arise regarding the role of decentralized grantseeking versus that of decentralized grants administration.

As site-based management and school-community empowerment have proliferated across the United States, the role of the principal has expanded to include the seeking of alternative sources of funding and increased responsibility for how those outside funds are administered. This has created quite a dilemma in districts that have encouraged their schools to seek alternative sources of support while trying to retain control of the disbursement and administration of those funds. As one entrepreneurial principal of a junior high remarked, "The easiest part of grantseeking is the actual soliciting of the outside funding. The hardest part is getting the awarded grant funds from the district central office to my school."

Principals now find themselves in the unique position of being given more autonomy and responsibility for marshaling community support and involvement in meeting the challenge of educating our nation's youth. This same movement toward local decision making and responsibility is taking place in colleges and universities. Many institutions of higher education are now adopting the methods that primary and secondary education have initiated to promote change at the local level through grant funding. Many colleges are pursuing a decentralized, departmentally based proposal development system. Some of these revolve around part-time (or released-time) grant specialists, whose job is to encourage professors to become more interested, involved, and successful in attracting grant funds from outside the university. Interesting and confusing issues and problems in the development and operation of these emerging systems have arisen throughout all levels of education, primary through graduate school.

Empowering local support through the methods suggested in the preceding chapters will evoke strong motivation, exceptional efforts, and successful grantseeking. Some of the controversial issues in grantseeking begin to appear when multiple approaches are made to the same grantors and school districts begin to lose their credibility. For example, when six of a district's elementary schools deluge one corporation with requests, the company may feel that the school district should have decided which one project meets its need most closely. They may object to having to assume the responsibility of deciding which of the six to fund and the accompanying risk of offending the rejected ones.

The complexities of grantseeking and site-based management become increasingly apparent when the administration of grant funds is added to the issues of grantseeking. The grantor gets even more confused over whom to send the grant money to—the district or the school. Our educational resource development systems are in a state of flux, and you must be aware of the potential problems of acting independently, of the benefits of coordinating your actions with those of your district grants office, and of the possibility of developing a new grants system.

The perfect grants system has not yet been developed, and the temptation to copy another district's system should be avoided. The ultimate goal is to capture the energy, creativity, and involvement of your school and community by encouraging them to use the potential of grantseeking to reach their educational goals and objectives.

The remainder of this chapter presents important issues in the effective administration of your school's grant funds. This information is provided to stimulate your thinking, increase your knowledge base, and help you avoid some of the pitfalls involved in accepting outside funding. This list of considerations is by no means exhaustive; the sources in the bibliography provide a more detailed analysis of each area.

Fund-Raising Versus Grantseeking

What can you do when your school cannot get a grant to deal with an area of concern? When the grants mechanism is inappropriate or unsuccessful, many schools consider using alternative fund-raising strategies.

Grantseeking is only one strategy for developing financial resources outside your usual tax-based or tuition system. Grantseeking targets government, corporate, and foundation funds. However, grantseeking does not target the over $120 billion donated per year by individuals, who give this money away through means other than grants. Although 46 percent of individual donations goes to religious organizations, the sizable amount of $60 billion plus is distributed to nonprofit groups through other nongrant fund-raising strategies. Many school districts and public and private schools are realizing that money can be made through special events (raffles, pancake breakfasts), direct mail (soliciting donations through the mail), bequests (being willed a donation), and a host of other fund-raising techniques.

You will find that the more you empower and involve your community in seeking grants to deal with their school's problems and opportunities, the more they will want to find *other* ways to get the money your school needs. Indeed, some schools are so successful at fund-raising that they develop a separate foundation to solicit and administer the funds raised. There are a variety of ways that a school district can use a separate, local educational foundation, the IRS-designated charitable organization known as a 501(c)(3), independent from the school district. Of crucial importance is the role a school foundation plays in grantseeking and grant administration.

When submitted through a school foundation, your proposal's chances of being funded by a private grantor may be enhanced. Administering the foundation or corporate grant submitted through a school foundation may also be easier. However, you should always act in agreement with your district central office. Although it may seem simpler to go through your school's foundation, your district office's participation is crucial in the case of federal grants because you need its help in following the federal rules regarding compliances and assurances. Your district's personnel and business offices perform the many valuable functions that support a superior grants program.

Check out Bauer Associates' newest publication, "How to Start a School Foundation," available spring 1999.

Fiscal Agent

All grantors want to be assured that the school they fund has the fiscal capability to disburse and account for the expended grant funds. Some grantors will request audited budget statements as evidence of fiscal accountability. The district central office is the likely agent to handle the account for a school's grants, although in some school districts the fiscal agent is the business office, the treasurer, or one of the assistant superintendents. The role of the fiscal agent is to monitor the expenditure of grant funds and to request the payment of federal grant funds by submitting an estimate of how the funds will be expended over the period of the grant. The Office of Management and Budget (OMB) has strict guidelines on how these funds are to be transferred and used. More sophisticated districts are connected by computers. Once the request is made via computer, the grant funds are deposited automatically in the district's designated bank. In less sophisticated districts, grant funds are expended by the school and then repaid by the federal government.

School principals need to have a basic knowledge of their district's system. Many principals complain bitterly about their inability to expend funds. Whether the problem is an outdated system that is slowed by red tape and the need for multiple signatures on request forms or fiscal information that is not timely or usable, your role as facilitator and troubleshooter is critical to grants success. Not providing your fiscal officer with an accurate forecast of expenditures may be the cause of the problem. Federal rules regulate the amount of money to be requested per quarter of the grant cycle and strictly limit the accumulation of unexpended funds. The development of a sound budget, Project Planner, and Grants Office Time Line will help you project an accurate cash forecast (see Chapter Seven). The school principal can avoid many problems by helping the fiscal agent document the cash needed.

Changing Budgets

You must anticipate changes in your budget because of the impact it will have on your cash requests. Government grant rules allow for small changes (perhaps 5 percent of the budget line), but even in these cases the changes must be documented. I always recommend notifying the grantor in writing of the changes. Do not let the rules scare your project director. The implementation of a proactive grants system and adequate planning provides the basis for documenting your expenditures, making cash requests, and changing the budget. The key to making a budget change is to back up the request with a rationale that is linked strongly to the project's activities or methods and how the change will help accomplish the predetermined objectives. The federal grants or contracts officer will prevent you from getting in trouble and tell you how to keep your grant transactions legal.

Equipment

Whether your grant is sponsored by the government, a foundation, or a corporation, you are ethically (and in some cases legally) responsible for maintaining an accurate record of all equipment purchased under your grant, including documentation that the equipment order was awarded to the lowest bidder. Grantors' rules may vary, and your business office may have regulations that are more stringent than the grantor's. You should help your grantees forecast the equipment needed to implement each of your school's proposals so that bids can be reviewed and the equipment purchased before the grant is completed.

It seems obvious that equipment should be ordered early in the grant cycle, but last-minute ordering does occur. Do not allow your project director to order equipment near the end of the grant award. This is a red flag to the funder, because it makes it appear that the equipment was not an integral part of the project. In fact, last-minute orders will probably not be delivered until after the completion of the grant period.

Inventorying Equipment

On a recent visit to evaluate a grants process of a major school district, I found several years' worth of equipment inventory identification stickers filed in a desk drawer. Funders deserve to know where the equipment they purchased for you is located. Do not rely on the district central office or your project director to take care of your equipment inventory. When a piece of equipment is missing or an insurance claim is made, it will be your responsibility to come up with the name of the manufacturer, make, serial number, year purchased, and purchase price. You should also know where each piece of equipment purchased by grant funds is and make sure that all equipment maintenance is up-to-date.

In evaluating one school district's grants system, I discovered that ten laptop computers were sent out to bid, ordered, inventoried (numbered), and then sent to ten different schools in the district. When I visited the schools, I could locate only five of them. I quickly pointed out to the assistant superintendent how upset grantors would be if they arrived for a visit and wanted to see children using the computers they had supplied, only to find half of the computers missing. The assistant superintendent immediately telephoned the school principals and began to ask questions. To make a long story short, if your school does not have a credible inventory system, develop one!

Personnel Policy and Procedures

The school principal needs the district office's assistance when hiring individuals to work on a funded project. This important information is often in a manual explaining how to expend grant funds in that district. The manual may describe the procedures for hiring, evaluating, and terminating grant-supported employees. You may want more control of your grant funds, but you still need your personnel office to provide the valuable functions that keep your grantees in compliance with the labor laws, including those covering the drug-free workplace and many, many other areas.

Indirect Costs

One of the least understood areas in the grants field is that of the recovery of costs associated with the acceptance of any grant award. The term *indirect costs* is usually identified with federal grants, whereas *administrative costs* or *overhead* is usually identified with foundation and corporate grants. The concept of indirect cost or administrative cost recovery is quite simple and sensible. However, it is hard to explain these costs to grantseekers who see a large piece of their grant going to the district's central office. Point out to your project director that direct costs such as those for project personnel, equipment, and consultants are requested in the budget and covered in the grant and explain that although indirect costs such as those for district personnel and business office staff are not requested in the budget, they too must be covered by the grant. The personnel costs for handling the grant, along with the costs related to supplying the building and office space in which the grant will be carried out, are indirect costs or administrative charges.

Recent newspaper articles on the excessive indirect costs charged by a few of the three thousand plus universities in the country have generated much negative opinion. Indirect costs are real! It costs your district money to accept and handle outside grant funds, and these costs should be legitimately passed on to the grantor when possible.

Many foundations and corporations have adopted a policy of no payment for indirect costs. However, they do understand that there are costs associated with your taking responsibility for their funds, and some may allow a small administrative cost of 8 percent of the total amount requested of the funder.

You should also be aware that the federal government usually does not repay all of the costs of operation. Different federal agencies and even different grant programs within an agency have different payment policies. For example, the federal government and school districts have a negotiated rate on special government programs involving food and milk. This usually very low (less than 5 percent) rate is referred to as your school's *restricted indirect cost rate.* If your grantseekers are creative they may be able to find funding from a government program that will pay your school's *unrestricted indirect cost rate.*

I once developed a school and community program for prevention education that was funded under a grant from the National Institute for Alcohol Abuse and Alcoholism (NIAAA). The program guidelines requested inclusion of an unrestricted indirect cost rate. My fiscal officer had never negotiated an unrestricted rate. Our school had a restricted rate of 2.5 percent. When he completed the forms necessary to develop our unrestricted rate (forms provided by the federal government's Regional Controller's Office), our rate was calculated at 27 percent of the total grant award, which turned out to be an additional $40,000! These funds were used to help the district offset the costs of implementing the project in our school facilities and for handling the personnel, payroll, and equipment transactions.

Many grantseekers are not concerned with recovering indirect costs because they do not see that the funds benefit them. But they may be wrong. By law, the funds recovered under indirect costs go into the district's general funds. Because they repay genuine costs of operation, they can be reallocated to anything the school district wants, including things that may directly benefit the classroom leader, grantseeker, and so on. In colleges and universities, these funds are used for a variety of purposes such as these:

- Support for a better grant-prospecting system

- Support for a central office grants program

- Returning a portion to the schools that have been successful

- Funding travel to meet with grantors

Evaluating Your School's Grants Effort

The desired result of your grants program is to use the grant-funding mechanism to meet your school's goals and objectives. This result can be achieved through an efficient system that encourages community and volunteer involvement while maximizing your existing resources.

Review the checklists at the end of each chapter and compile your suggestions for improvement. Note your suggestions on a spreadsheet or a project planner. Be realistic in determining what you can accomplish within the limitations of your setting; remember, you cannot change your school's grants program overnight.

To evaluate the success of your techniques, you need baseline data. Even if your current system allows you to identify the number of proposals submitted from your school and the number funded, there is much more information you need to collect to evaluate success. For example, by using a School Grantseekers' Preproposal Endorsement Worksheet (Exhibit 6.1) you can analyze the number of proposal ideas generated compared with the number that are submitted, pending, awarded, and rejected each year. By tracking your grant system to the initial proposal idea, you can find out why some proposals were never submitted. Logging or tracking proposals from the principal's office will allow you to give recognition and encouragement to members of your staff who are pursuing grant-funded opportunities.

Increasing Your School's Grants Productivity

In an effort to increase grant activity while decentralizing their district grants office, many schools have established the position of school-community grants coordinator. This position varies from school to school. In some it is a volunteer position; in others it is a paid part-time or full-time position. The focus of the job also varies. It can focus entirely on schools and education or it can focus on the community and encompass a variety of concerns, including health, education, job development, and the elderly.

The best approach for empowering your school and community through access to grantseeking is up to you to decide. You may choose to discuss the idea of a school-community grant coordinator position with your grants advisory committee and, in doing so, suggest that one way to fund the position would be through a grant from a corporation, foundation, or community group. A dedicated staff person can focus your school and community's grants effort and maximize your grants potential. Your school-community grants office should have a number of specific goals and responsibilities. Following are some suggestions.

Suggested Goals

- Increase the number and quality of proposals developed to meet the school's mission.

- Promote an acceptance rate of 50 percent in submitted proposals and consortium efforts.

- Promote involvement of community organizations in developing solutions to school and community problems.
- Provide a focal point for community efforts to find and attract grant funding opportunities.

Objectives

- The school-community grants coordinator will increase the quality of the school's proposals by _____ percent as measured by a pre- and postassessment in one year at a cost of $_____.
- The school-community grants coordinator will increase school-community consortium proposals by _____ percent in one year at a cost of $_____.

School-Community Grants Office Responsibilities

- Operate a grants resource center for the school and community
- Help the school-community develop ideas into fundable proposals
- Coordinate and act as a resource to grantseekers who are addressing similar needs or developing similar projects
- Serve as a resource for those with questions on grantseeking
- Organize a system to match community members' skills with proposal development needs
- Provide grantseekers with grants planning tools, videotapes, and other instructional aids
- Maintain files of grant activity, from idea generation to submittal to notices of award and rejection
- Collect examples and samples of funded projects
- Provide grantseekers with grant strategy and consulting
- Help proposal developers with proposal preparation, submittal, and notification of outcome
- Help successful grantees with implementation, grants management, and submittal of reports to grantors

Evaluation

Pre- and postassessment of the objectives specified

Budget

The cost will depend on the percentage of time allocated to the accomplishment of the objectives. You may decide to list in-kind contributions of secretarial or support staff. You may want to include a percentage of the released time for your coordinator.

Using the Project Planner

List on a project planner the duties your committee decides to include in the job description for your school-community grants coordinator position. Break the duties down into the steps that must be taken to support them and develop a cost analysis for each step listed on the planner.

The Sample Project Planner in Exhibit 13.1 will help you develop a plan tailored to meet your school's needs. Remember, you can apply for a grant to develop your school's grant potential. By submitting to a foundation or corporation a cost-effective plan to mobilize your community's involvement in creating and developing funds for change, you may be able to put your plan in place sooner than you think!

Exhibit 13.1 suggests some of the steps you may want to take to set up a school grants coordinator. Review with your school grants advisory committee the tasks that will be assigned to this office. Determine whether the office will serve the community and, if so, include those tasks. The committee can then determine the personnel needed to accomplish the tasks. By means of this spreadsheet, volunteers can immediately see how catalytic they are in the grants process and how their volunteerism has an impact on the cost of services.

Designate all donated and volunteer resources with an asterisk. List all supply, telephone, proposal production, and equipment needs. Do not forget that those items that your school will supply should be designated with an asterisk. Remember also that including college or university students in the project may lower the cost of collecting data, developing surveys, and evaluating results.

Using Consultants

Some schools hire consultants to write their proposals because they lack the funds to hire a permanent, on-staff grants person. As mentioned earlier, be wary of this. Many funding sources feel that if a grantee cannot write its own proposal, it may also have trouble implementing the proposed solution.

However, the use of a grants consultant may be appropriate if several of the past grantees funded by your prospective grantor used one. If you do use consultants, avoid those who want to work for a percentage of the funded proposal. Although this arrangement may seem safe and economical (you pay only when you get an award), it is illegal under federal guidelines because it represents a cost incurred before the award date. Federal grantors will pay only for what happens after the funding begins, not for locating and getting the grant.

Exhibit 13.1

SAMPLE PROJECT PLANNER

PROJECT PLANNER

PROJECT TITLE: School Grants Office/Coordinator

Proposal Developed for:

Project Director:

Proposed Start Date:

Proposal Year

Page 1 of 4

A. List project objectives or outcomes A. B. B. List methods to accomplish each objective as A-1, A-2, ... B-1, B-2 ...	MONTH Begin End	TIME	PROJECT PERSONNEL	PERSONNEL COSTS Salaries & Wages	Fringe Benefits	Total	CONSULTANTS CONTRACT SERVICES Time	Cost/Week	Total	NON-PERSONNEL RESOURCES NEEDED SUPPLIES - EQUIPMENT - MATERIALS Item	Cost/Item	Quantity	Tot cost	SUB-TOTAL ACTIVITY COST Total I, L, P	MILESTONES PROGRESS INDICATORS Item	Date
	C/D	E	F	G	H	I	J	K	L	M	N	O	P	Q	R	S

OBJECTIVES:

A. Increase the number and quality of proposals designed to meet the school's stated mission from __% to __% as measured by pre- and postassessment.

A-1 Review school records to determine grants activity (submission and acceptance) prior to grants office.
a) check with district office and develop grants history
b) input data in computer
c) produce report

A-2 Develop a School Grants Advisory Committee.
a) develop list of members and resources they can contribute
b) set up meeting to brainstorm grant area interest-set objectives
c) develop webbing and linkages program

A-3 Set up grant opportunity searching system
a) review computer-based system
b) order or locate printed material
c) develop audiovisual resources on grants

A-4 Develop a school grantseekers support system.
a) develop and print a guide for grantseeking for your school
b) promote brainstorming and grant ideas to solve problems
c) develop a reward and motivation system to provide encouragement to grantseekers

Total Direct Costs or Costs Requested From Funder
Matching Funds, In-Kind Contributions, or Donated Costs
Total Costs

100%   % of Total

©David G. Bauer Associates, Inc.
(800) 836-0732

Exhibit 13.1 (continued)

Page 2 of 4

PROJECT PLANNER

PROJECT TITLE: School Grants Office/Coordinator

Proposal Developed for: _____

Project Director: _____

Proposed Start Date _____

Proposal Year _____

A. List project objectives or outcomes A. B. B. List methods to accomplish each objective as A-1, A-2, ... B-1, B-2 ...	MONTH Begin C/D	End	TIME E	PROJECT PERSONNEL F	PERSONNEL COSTS Salaries & Wages G	Fringe Benefits H	Total I	CONSULTANTS CONTRACT SERVICES Time J	Cost/Week K	Total L	NON-PERSONNEL RESOURCES NEEDED SUPPLIES - EQUIPMENT - MATERIALS Item M	Cost/Item N	Quantity O	Tot cost P	SUB-TOTAL ACTIVITY COST Total I,L,P Q	MILESTONES PROGRESS INDICATORS Item R	Date S
B. Achieve an acceptance rate of 50% in submitted proposals.																	
B-1 Set up a preproposal contact system.																	
a) procure a long distance phone line from volunteer																	
b) develop budget for travel to D.C. and state capitol																	
B-2 Set up funder files.																	
a) copies of reports, guidelines, and tax returns																	
b) lists of grantees																	
c) lists of reviewers																	
d) records of contact with grantors																	
e) sample proposals and comments																	
B-3 Develop and implement a quality circle or mock proposal review program.																	
a) develop list of volunteers to serve from a variety of school and community backgrounds																	
b) set up procedures booklet to assist mock review by type of grantor:																	
• federal/state																	
• foundation																	
• corporate																	
Evaluation: A & B Compare number of proposals submitted and awarded between preassessment and postassessment.																	

Total Direct Costs or Costs Requested From Funder

Matching Funds, In-Kind Contributions, or Donated Costs

Total Costs

% of Total ... 100%

©David G. Bauer Associates, Inc.
(800) 836-0732

Consultants should charge you a fee based on the time they spend developing your proposals, and you should pay them regardless of whether you get funded. Remember, the ability to attract grant funds depends on your school's credibility, quality of ideas, and plan, not on the reputation of the consultant.

CHAPTER 13 CHECKLIST

Evaluation and Planning Worksheet

1. **Do you have current, published guidelines on how to administer:**
   - federal grant funds?   _____ yes   _____ no
   - private grant funds?   _____ yes   _____ no

2. **Does your district have guidelines or policies on grantseeking and fund-raising?**
   _____ yes   _____ no

3. **Does your district office provide you with the following fiscal support, guidelines, procedures, and so on?**
   - guidelines for handling personnel paid on grants   _____ yes   _____ no
   - purchasing assistance, inventory control   _____ yes   _____ no
   - procedures for easily accessing grant funding information (budget category expenditures, and so on)   _____ yes   _____ no
   - guidelines for changing budgets   _____ yes   _____ no

4. **Does your district have federally negotiated indirect cost rates for:**
   - unrestricted federal programs   _____ yes   _____ no
   - restricted federal programs   _____ yes   _____ no

5. **How are the funds recovered from your school's indirect cost reimbursement rate shared with your school and proposal developers?**
   _____
   _____

6. **Does your school's proposal development system allow you to evaluate its success?**
   _____ yes   _____ no

7. **Could your school benefit from a part- or full-time school grants coordinator?**
   _____ yes   _____ no

Bibliography

Government Grant Resources

Commerce Business Daily

The government's contracts publication, published five times a week, the *Daily* announces every government Request for Proposal (RFP) that exceeds $25,000 and upcoming sales of government surplus. **Price:** $275 annually for domestic, $324 for first class; $137 domestic for six months, $162 for first class. **Order from:** Superintendent of Documents, PO Box 371954, Pittsburgh, PA 15250-7954, 202-512-1800, fax 202-512-2250, website www.access.gpo.gov/su_docs/

Catalog of Federal Domestic Assistance (CFDA)

This is the government's most complete listing of federal domestic assistance programs with details on eligibility, application procedures, and deadlines, including the location of state plans. It is published at the beginning of each fiscal year with supplementary updates during the year. Indexes are by agency program, function, popular name, applicant eligibility, and subject. It comes in looseleaf form, punched for a three-ring binder. **Price:** $72 annual subscription. **Order from:** Superintendent of Documents, PO Box 371954, Pittsburgh, PA 15250-7954, 202-512-1800, fax 202-512-2250, website www.access.gpo.gov/su_docs/

The Federal Register

Published five times a week (Monday through Friday), the *Register* supplies up-to-date information on federal assistance and supplements the *Catalog of Federal Domestic Assistance (CFDA)*. It includes public regulations and legal notices issued by all federal agencies and presidential proclamations. Of particular importance are the proposed rules, final rules, and program deadlines. An index is published monthly. **Price:** $555 per year. **Order from:** Superintendent of Documents, PO Box 371954, Pittsburgh, PA 15250-7954, 202-512-1800, fax 202-512-2250, website www.access.gpo.gov/su_docs/

United States Government Manual

This paperback manual gives the names of key personnel, addresses, and telephone numbers for all agencies and departments that constitute the federal bureaucracy. **Price:** $40 per year. **Order from:** Superintendent of Documents, PO Box 371954, Pittsburgh, PA 15250-7954, 202-512-1800, fax 202-512-2250, website www.access.gpo.gov/su_docs/

Academic Research Information System, Inc. (ARIS)

ARIS provides timely information about grant and contract opportunities, including concise descriptions of guidelines and eligibility requirements, upcoming deadlines, identification of program resource persons, and new program policies for both government and nongovernment funding sources.

Biomedical Sciences Report $240

Social and Natural Science Report $240

Arts and Humanities Report $145

All three ARIS Reports and Supplements $575

Order from: Academic Research Information System, Inc., The Redstone Building, 2940 16th Street, Suite 314, San Francisco, CA 94103, 415-558-8133, fax 415-558-8135, e-mail arisnet@dnai.com, website www:arisnet.com

Federal Grants and Contracts Weekly

This weekly contains information on the latest Requests for Proposals (RFPs), contracting opportunities, and upcoming grants. Each ten-page issue includes details on RFPs, closing dates for grant programs, procurement-related news, and newly issued regulations. **Price:** $389 for 50 issues. **Order from:** Capitol Publications, Inc., 1101 King Street, PO Box 1453, Alexandria, VA 22313-2053, 800-655-5597, fax 703-739-6437, website www.grantscape.com

Health Grants and Contracts Weekly

Price: $379 for 50 issues. **Order from:** Capitol Publications, Inc., 1101 King Street, PO Box 1453, Alexandria, VA 22313-2053, 800-655-5597, fax 703-739-6437, website www.grantscape.com

Education Daily

Price: $598 for 250 issues. **Order from:** Capitol Publications, Inc., 1101 King Street, PO Box 1453, Alexandria, VA 22313-2053, 800-655-5597, fax 703-739-6437, website www.grantscape.com

Education Grants Alert

Price: $399 for 50 issues. **Order from:** Capitol Publications, Inc., 1101 King Street, PO Box 1453, Alexandria, VA 22313-2053, 800-655-5597, fax 703-739-6437, website www.educationdaily.com

Washington Information Directory, 1998/1999

This directory is divided into three categories: agencies of the executive branch, Congress, and private or "nongovernmental" organizations. Each entry includes the name, address, telephone number, and director of the organization and a short description of its work. **Price:** $110.00. **Order from:** Congressional Quarterly Books, 1414 22nd NW, Washington, DC 20037, 800-638-1710, fax 800-380-3810, e-mail bookhelp@cqualert.com

Foundation Grant Resources

Many of the following research aids can be found through the Foundation Center Cooperating Collections Network. If you wish to purchase any of the following Foundation Center publications, contact: The Foundation Center, 79 Fifth Avenue, Dept. VL, New York, NY 10003-3076, 800-424-9836. In NY State: 212-807-3690, fax 212-807-3677, website www.fdncenter.org

Corporate Foundation Profiles, 10th edition, 1998

This Foundation Center publication contains detailed analyses of 195 of the largest corporate foundations in the United States. An appendix lists financial data on 1,000 smaller corporate grantmakers. **Price:** $155. **Order from:** The Foundation Center

The Foundation 1,000, 1997/1998 Edition

This research aid profiles the 1,000 largest U.S. foundations by foundation name, subject field, type of support, and geographic location. There is also an index that allows you to target grantmakers by the names of officers, staff, and trustees. **Price:** $295. **Order from:** The Foundation Center

The Foundation Directory, 1998 Edition

This is the most important single reference work available on grantmaking foundations in the United States. It includes information on foundations having assets of at least $2 million or annual grants exceeding $200,000. Each entry includes a description of giving interests, along with address, telephone numbers, current financial data, names of donors and contact person, and IRS identification number. Includes six indexes: state and city, subject, foundation donors, trustees and administrators, and alphabetical foundation names. The trustees index is very valuable in developing linkages to decision makers. **Price:** $215 hardcover. $185 soft-cover. **Order from:** The Foundation Center

The Foundation Directory Supplement, 1998
The *Supplement* updates the *Directory* so that users will have the latest addresses, contacts, policy statements, application guidelines, and financial data. **Price:** $125. $320 hardcover: *Directory* and *Supplement*. $290 soft-cover: *Directory* and *Supplement*. **Order from:** The Foundation Center

The Foundation Directory Part 2, 1998 Edition
This *Directory* provides information on over 4,800 midsize foundations with grant programs between $50,000 and $200,000. Published biennially. **Price:** $185. $485 hardcover: *Directory, Supplement, Part 2*. $455 softcover: *Directory, Supplement, Part 2*. **Order from:** The Foundation Center

The Foundation Grants Index, 1998 Edition
This cumulative listing of over 73,000 grants of $10,000 or more made by over 1,000 major foundations is indexed by subject and geographic locations, by the names of recipient organizations, and by key words. **Price:** $165. **Order from:** The Foundation Center

Foundation Grants to Individuals, 10th Edition, 1997
Comprehensive listing of over 3,300 independent and corporate foundations that provide financial assistance to individuals. **Price:** $65. **Order from:** The Foundation Center

The National Guide to Funding for Elementary and Secondary Education, 4th Edition, 1997
Includes over 2,300 sources of funding for elementary and secondary education and over 6,300 grant descriptions listing the organizations that have successfully approached these funding sources. **Price:** $140. **Order from:** The Foundation Center

Education Grant Guides, 1997/1998 Editions
There are seven Grant Guides in the field of education, including: Elementary and Secondary Education, Higher Education, Libraries and Information Services, Literacy, Reading and Adult/Continuing Education, Scholarships, Student Aid and Loans, Science and Technology Programs, and Social and Political Science Programs. There are twenty-four other guides in areas other than education, such as children and youth, alcohol and drug abuse, minorities, and the like. Each guide has a customized list of hundreds of recently awarded grants of $10,000 or more. Sources of funding are indexed by type of organization, subject focus, and geographic funding area. **Price:** $75 each. **Order from:** The Foundation Center

The Taft Foundation Information System

Foundation Reporter: This annual directory of the largest private charitable foundations in the United States supplies descriptions and statistical analyses. $400

Foundation Giving Watch: This monthly publishes news and the "how-to's" of foundation giving, with a listing of recent grants. Yearly subscription $149. **Order from:** Taft Group, 835 Penobscot Building, Detroit, MI 48226, 800-877-8238, fax 800-414-5043, website www.gale.com

Foundation and Corporate Grants Alert

Price: $297 for 12 issues. **Order from:** Capitol Publications, Inc., 1101 King Street, PO Box 1453, Alexandria, VA 22313-2053, 800-655-5597, fax 703-739-6437, website www.grantscape.com

Private Foundation IRS Tax Returns

(Available from the IRS or free to use at Foundation Center)

The Internal Revenue Service requires private foundations to file income tax returns each year. Form 990-PF provides fiscal details on receipts and expenditures, compensation of officers, capital gains or losses, and other financial matters. Form 990-AR provides information on foundation managers, assets, and grants paid or committed for future payment. The IRS makes this information available on aperture cards that may be viewed at libraries operated by the Foundation Center or at its regional cooperating collections. You may also obtain this information by writing to the appropriate IRS office (see accompanying list). Enclose as much information about the foundation as possible, including its full name, street address with zip code, its employer identification number if available, and the year or years requested. It generally takes four to six weeks for the IRS to respond, and it will bill you for all charges, which vary depending on the office and number of pages involved.

INTERNATIONAL REVENUE SERVICE CENTER REGIONAL OFFICES

Central Region (Indiana, Kentucky, Michigan, Ohio, West Virginia)
Public Affairs Officer, Internal Revenue Service Center, PO Box 1699, Cincinnati, OH 45201

Mid-Atlantic Region (District of Columbia, Maryland, Virginia, Pennsylvania— Zip Codes 150–168 and 172)
Public Affairs Officer, Internal Revenue Service Center, 11601 Roosevelt Blvd., Philadelphia, PA 19154

Midwest Region (Illinois, Iowa, Minnesota, Missouri, Montana, Nebraska, North Dakota, Oregon, South Dakota, Wisconsin)

Public Affairs Officer, Internal Revenue Service Center, PO Box 24551, Kansas City, MO 64131

North Atlantic Region (Connecticut, Delaware, Maine, Massachusetts, New Hampshire, New York, New Jersey, Rhode Island, Vermont, Pennsylvania—Zip Codes 169–171 and 173–196)
Public Affairs Officer, Internal Revenue Service Center, PO Box 400, Brookhaven, NY 11742

Southeast Region (Alabama, Arkansas, Georgia, Florida, Louisiana, Mississippi, North Carolina, South Carolina, Tennessee)
Public Affairs Officer, Internal Revenue Service Center, PO Box 47-421, Doraville, GA 30362

Southwest Region (Arizona, Colorado, Kansas, New Mexico, Oklahoma, Texas, Utah, Wyoming)
Public Affairs Officer, Internal Revenue Service Center, PO Box 934, Austin, TX 78767

Western Region (Alaska, California, Hawaii, Idaho, Nevada, Washington)
Public Affairs Officer, Internal Revenue Service Center, PO Box 12866, Fresno, CA 93779

Corporate Grant Resources

Annual Survey of Corporate Contributions
This annual survey of corporate giving is sponsored by the Conference Board and the Council for Financial Aid to Education. It includes a detailed analysis of beneficiaries of corporate support but does not list individual firms and specific recipients. **Price:** $30 for Associates. $120 for Nonassociates. **Order from:** The Conference Board, 845 Third Avenue, New York, NY 10022, 212-759-0900, fax 212-980-7014, website www.conference-board.org

The National Directory of Corporate Giving, 5th Edition
This directory provides information on over 1,905 corporate foundations plus an additional 990 direct, corporate giving programs. It also has an extensive bibliography and six indexes to help you target funding prospects. **Price:** $225. **Order from:** The Foundation Center, 79 Fifth Avenue, Dept. VL, New York, NY 10003-3076, 800-424-9836. In NY State 212-807-3690

Directory of Corporate Affiliations
This directory lists divisions, subsidiaries, and affiliates of thousands of companies with addresses, telephone numbers, key persons, employees, etc. **Price:** $1029.95 plus handling and delivery. **Order from:** Reed Elsevier,

PO Box 31, New Providence, NJ 07974, 800-323-6772, fax 908-665-6688, website www.bowker.com

Dun and Bradsteet's Million Dollar Directory, 5 volumes
The five volumes list names, addresses, employees, sales volume, and other pertinent data for 160,000 of America's largest businesses. **Price:** $1,445 for 5 volumes. **Order from:** Dun and Bradstreet Information Services, 3 Sylvan Way, Parsippany, NJ 07054, 800-526-0651, fax 973-605-6911, website www.dnbmdd.com

Standard and Poor's Register of Corporations, Directors and Executives
This annual register provides up-to-date rosters of over 400,000 executives of the 77,000 nationally known corporations they represent, with their names, titles, and business affiliations. **Price:** $749 for one year, includes quarterly supplements. **Order from:** Standard and Poor's Corporation, 25 Broadway, 17th Floor, Attn: Sales, New York, NY 10004, 212-208-8000

Taft Corporate Giving Directory, 1998 Edition
This directory provides detailed entries on 1,000 corporate foundations. Included are nine indexes. **Price:** $425 plus postage and handling. **Order from:** Taft Group, 838 Penobscot Building, Detroit, MI 48226, 800-877-8238, fax 800-414-5043, website www.gale.com

Corporate Giving Watch
This monthly reports on corporate giving developments. **Price:** $149 a year. **Order from:** Taft Group, 838 Penobscot Building, Detroit, MI 48226, 800-877-8238, fax 800-414-5043, website www.gale.com

Computer Research Services

Congressional Information Service Index (CIS Index)
CIS covers congressional publications and legislation from 1970 to date. It covers hearings, committee prints, House and Senate reports and documents, special publications, Senate executive reports and documents, and public laws. It includes monthly abstracts and index volumes. Noncomputer grant-related materials are also available from CIS, including a CIS Federal Register Index, which covers announcements from the Federal Register on a weekly basis. **Price:** Sliding scale. Call for quote. **Order from:** Congressional Information Services, Inc., 4520 East-West Highway, Suite 800, Bethesda, MD 20814, 800-638-8380, fax 301-951-4660, website www.cispubs.com

DIALOG Information Services
3460 Hillview Avenue, Palo Alto, CA 94304, 800-334-2564. A commercial organization that provides access to hundreds of databases in a range of

subject areas. DIALOG has no start-up fees or monthly minimum charges, but there is an annual fee. Foundation Center files also have a cost per minute to search on-line. Each full record printed off-line or by DIALOG has an additional cost.

Federal Assistance Program Retrieval System (FAPRS)
The *FAPRS* lists more than 1,300 federal grant programs, including planning and technical assistance. There is a $53 hookup fee. All states have *FAPRS* services available through state, county, and local agencies as well as through federal extension services. For further information, call 202-708-5126 or write to:

1. Your congressperson's office; it can request a search for you, in some cases at no charge.

2. Federal Domestic Assistance Catalog Staff, GSA/IRMS/WKU, 300 7th Street SW, Reporters Building, Room 101, Washington, DC 20407, fax 202-401-8233, website www.gsa.gov/fdac

Foundation Center Databases
The Foundation Center maintains two databases on DIALOG, one on grantmakers and the other on the grants they distribute. For more information contact DIALOG at 800-334-2564 or the Foundation Center's DIALOG support staff at 212-807-3690.

The Sponsored Programs Information Network (SPIN)
This is a database of federal and private funding sources. **Price:** Call for quote or visit its website. **Order from:** InfoEd, 2301 Western Ave., Guilderland, NY 12084, 518-464-0691, fax 518-464-0695, website www.infoed.org

FC Search: The Foundation Center's Database on CD-ROM, Version 2.0
This fund-raising CD-ROM covers over 47,000 foundations and corporate givers, includes descriptions of nearly 200,000 associated grants, and lists approximately 200,000 trustees, officers, and donors. **Price:** Stand-alone (single user) version $1,195; Network (2–8 users at a single site) $1,795. Prices include one user manual. Additional copies of user manuals are $19.95 each. **Order from:** The Foundation Center, 79 Fifth Avenue, New York, NY 10003-3076, 800-424-9836. In NY State 212-807-3690.